WHO WON
THE
OIL WARS?

For Louise, my idea of beautiful energy

WHO WON
THE
OIL WARS?

ANDY STERN

COLLINS & BROWN

First published in 2005 by Collins & Brown
The Chrysalis Building
Bramley Road
London W10 6SP

An imprint of **Chrysalis** Books Group plc

Produced by Conspiracy Books
PO Box 51726, London NW1 9ZH

British Library Cataloguing-in-Publication Data:
A catalogue record for this book is available from the
British Library.

ISBN 1-84340-291-2

1 3 5 7 9 8 6 4 2

Printed and bound in Great Britain by
Creative Print & Design (Wales), Ebbw Vale

Contents

Acknowledgements

The author would like to thank the many people who have helped with this book, in one way or another, with their support, encouragement, ideas and inspiration, including:

Philippe Aerts, Clive Bates, Alison Birkett, Dominique Caby, William Cannell, Bryan Christie, Moray Coulter, Molly Frances, Sidney and Vera Gale, Alex Games, Ann Glasser, Melissa Hardinge, Jessica Jeavons, Gemma Jimenez, Andreas Kortenkamp, David Levey, Sue Mayer, George Metaxas, Alison and Eric Richmond, Heather Rigg, Esther Selsden, Leni and Luc Steels, Alex Stitt, David Thompson, Nigel Thornton, Laurent d'Ursel, Frans Van den Ouweland and Jackie Wullschlager.

Special thanks to Clare Nuttall for her invaluable help with research.

Thanks are also due to my editors Will Steeds and Mal Peachey for their guidance and optimism throughout the writing of this book.

I would also like to thank my parents, Monica and Paul, without whose support and unwavering encouragement to take up medicine or law I might never have become a writer.

Most of all, I would like to thank Louise Gale for her editorial and conceptual contribution, her love and constant encouragement.

Introduction

Since the birth of the modern oil industry in the middle of the 19th century, the pursuit of oil has brought out three characteristics in mankind: greed, corruption and belligerence.

The freewheeling goldrush years in the US soon gave way to the all-devouring empire created by John D. Rockefeller, whose fortune was built on sharp business practices, corruption of government at the highest levels, and the creation of one of the most successful and enduring cartels the world has ever seen. Then as now in the US, government and Big Oil were closely interlinked. Rockefeller had agents all over the world, forming a semi-official diplomatic structure that negotiated trade deals directly with national governments. Today, the links are even closer, with former oil executives occupying many of the top positions in the current US administration, and taking policy positions highly favourable to the industry in which they made their fortunes.

As the thirst for oil, and the vast profits it offered, enticed companies beyond their national borders, British, French and US oil multinationals have sought to exploit oil resources overseas, and have not hesitated to corrupt or subvert governments, be they in Africa, Asia or Latin America, in order to gain control of these valuable assets.

Today, oil multinationals are accused of crimes spanning most of the world's continents. Unocal has been ordered to pay compensation to Burmese villagers forced to work as slaves on a gas pipeline to Thailand. TotalFinaElf, which co-financed the pipeline, is being tried in France. ExxonMobil is accused of complicity in the Indonesian army's killings in Aceh.

The "oil wars" fought over ownership of oil reserves were motivated by greed. The first one started as early as 1932, when Bolivia invaded Paraguay to gain possession of the supposedly oil-rich Gran Chaco. Oil wars have continued ever since, right up to the Iraqi invasion of Iran in 1980, starting the Iran-Iraq war (1980–8), and Kuwait in 1990, and, arguably, to the US-led attack on Iraq in 2003, all of which were in part or wholly attempts to seize more oil, and thereby alter the global balance of power.

Governments' interest in oil, and securing it at almost any cost, really came into its own after World War I, when its strategic and military importance became crystal clear to the world's main industrial and military powers. Without oil, they realized, an army's aeroplanes were grounded and its trucks, tanks and battleships forced to a standstill. Germany discovered too late that oil can be decisive in winning or losing a war when its supplies were blockaded in 1918, and again in its disastrous push towards the Caucasus oilfields during World War II.

If deprived of oil today, the economies of industrialized countries, and those in the process of rapid industrialization like China and India, would go into meltdown. Consumption of oil is still increasing rapidly, but there have been few new finds in recent years. Fears that we will shortly reach "Peakoil", the point at which oil production peaks and starts to decline, are growing, although estimates of when it will occur vary from three to five years, to fifteen years, to decades. As a result, competition over existing resources is intensifying, and as oil prices rise and supplies dwindle, regional tensions look ever more likely to spill over into war.

The Middle East, with two-thirds of global oil reserves, remains the primary source of the world's oil. Yet with tensions still high since the 2003 war in Iraq, major oil importers, including the US, Europe, Japan, and increasingly China and India, are seeking new sources. In a rerun of the race to colonize the developing world in the 19th century, these major powers are now competing for access to the oil of West Africa and Central Asia. Another flashpoint is the South China Sea, where six countries have laid claim to the oil-rich Spratly Islands. As soaring demand collides with diminishing supply, we will see "oil wars" increasing in frequency and violence.

Chapter One: The Birth of the Modern Oil Industry

As far back as biblical times, the mysterious flames from natural gas and oil seeps were treated with religious awe. Native Americans collected seep oil for medicine and drank it to cure digestive problems, while the Spanish conquistadors caulked the hulls of their ships with the tar that washed up along the Texas shores.

Seep oil was used in warfare: the ancient Greeks struck fear into their enemies with flaming oil torches fixed to the prows of their warships, and both Greeks and Romans doused pigs in oil then set fire to them, sending the terrified animals to run amok among opposing armies. Centuries later, "Greek fire", an explosive oil-based cocktail, was used to protect the garrison towns of medieval Europe.

It was not until the 20th century that people started going to war for oil. This was the era in which oil became vital first for defence, and then as the fuel upon which modern industrial societies depended. In the 20th century, governments realized that without oil they would have to change their way of life, their economies would founder, and they would be unable to defend themselves.

Why did oil suddenly become so important? From the Industrial Revolution to the late 19th century, coal had been the fuel of choice in Europe, America and the industrial regions of the Far East. Coal, cheap and plentiful, was burned in factories, in domestic fires and in the furnaces of coal-powered trains and ships. There was a relatively small market for oil, which was mainly sold as kerosene for oil lamps, or in medicines such as Seneca Oil, a cure for rheumatism, colds and other minor ailments.

The rise of oil to global dominance was partly due to technical advances – new drilling techniques and the invention of the internal combustion engine – but it was also a deliberate policy on the part of the oil companies to create a captive market. The world was to become so dependent on oil that demand would never dry up, and ultimately states would go to war to secure their supply.

Rockefeller Builds his Personal Oil Empire

Until the 1850s, no one had been able to extract oil in large quantities. Early attempts at drilling or digging pits for oil in China, in Baku (Azerbaijan), and in Poland's Carpathian mountains had created thriving local oil industries. Oil-burning lamps lit the streets of Krosno in southern Poland back in the 1500s. The small scale of these operations, however, meant that oil was too expensive to be widely used.

That all changed on August 27th, 1859, when the first modern oil-well was drilled in the US. In 1857 the Seneca Oil Company had hired engineer Edwin Drake to investigate suspected oil deposits near Titusville, a town in the industrial heartland of west Pennsylvania. A retired railway worker and self-styled colonel, Drake was selected for the job mainly because he was entitled to free rail travel. Once he arrived in Oil Creek, he started drilling, using a new method similar to that used by salt drillers.

Progress was excruciatingly slow. Once the drillers hit bedrock at 10 metres, they descended by less than a metre a day. The Seneca Oil Company had long since abandoned the effort, and the friends Drake had persuaded to finance him were rapidly backing out too. Crowds of local people came to jeer, nicknaming the well "Drake's Folly". Then suddenly, at just over 20 metres, the drillers struck crude oil. With Drake's new technique this could be extracted in far greater volumes than ever before. Within a day of the discovery, other engineers were copying Drake's well, and the Pennsylvania oil boom had started.

Rig hands, engineers and businessmen flooded into the new oil boom towns – among them Oil City, Pithole City and Petroleum Center. Many of the workers were soldiers returning from the US Civil War. Scenting the money to be made, pickpockets, prostitutes and criminals of all descriptions followed them to the oil belt, to prey off the bulging wallets of the oil workers. Among the derricks and shanty towns were street after unpaved street of brothels and gambling salons where drillers might lose in a few hours the proceeds from their oil finds. Some crooks and gangsters became notorious even in the wild new cities of the Pennsylvania oilfields: Stonehouse Jack, who tried to burn down Titusville, and gambler and prize fighter Ben Hogan, who dubbed himself "the Wickedest Man in the World" and "would give anything a try so long as it might pay well, be dubious and on the wrong side of the law ... he never got involved in oil except by filching other people's royalties." (Pees, www.oilhistory.com)

Fortunes were quickly made and lost in the oilfields of Pennsylvania. Pithole City had a population of 15,000 in September 1865, four months after it was founded, but a year later that had dwindled to 2,000, and soon it became a ghost town, as the oil ran out and drillers moved on to new sites. In the heady early days of the oil industry, as one well ran dry, another would be found to take its place. Drake himself died almost penniless in 1880. After his invention, which he failed to patent, took hold, oil supply raced ahead of demand. The price of oil fell from $10 a barrel in January 1861, to 50 cents in June, and to 10 cents by the end of the year. Unable to make a profit, the prospectors melted away as rapidly as they had arrived, leaving behind them rusting derricks and railway sidings full of empty trucks.

It seemed to many that it would be impossible to make stable profits in the oil industry.

One man, however, saw a solution. At 26, John D. Rockefeller had already risen from the position of clerk to co-owner of an oil refinery in Cleveland. He understood that huge profits could be made by anyone who could control the supply of oil. Then, as demand rose, he would be able to hold the world to ransom.

Born on July 8th, 1839, Rockefeller grew up in a financially insecure family, the probable cause of both his obsession with money and his extreme caution. As a child he had once been left out of a school photograph because his suit was too shabby. Rockefeller was the son of a deeply religious Baptist mother, and William "Big Bill" Avery Rockefeller, an itinerant snake oil salesman and a bigamist. Big Bill would roll up at the house "riding new horses, wearing fine clothes and brandishing a thick wad of crisp bills," then proceed to cheat his sons at cards "to make 'em sharp." (Chernow, p.28)

Rockefeller started as a clerk, then went into partnership with two Englishmen, whom he finally bought out. He grew richer by looking at where he might make an extra profit, for example by finding new markets for the by-products of kerosene production, cutting waste and manufacturing his own barrels rather than buying them. Rockefeller was still a young man in 1870 when he established Standard Oil with $1 million capital, of which he owned 27 per cent. Standard Oil was to become the world's greatest oil colossus.

Rockefeller persuaded other refineries to combine with him so that they could transport their oil at the lower rate offered by the railways to companies shipping in large volumes. It is still a matter of debate as to whether the next step was initiated by Rockefeller or the rail companies, but he is known to have met with representatives of the three largest railways in Pennsylvania, who agreed to charge Standard Oil and its partners a lower rate, while setting higher prices for their competitors. He also undermined his competitors by temporarily undercutting their prices to put them out of business, and secretly investing in other oil-related companies such as engineering firms and the manufacturers of barrels and pipes.

Rockefeller continued to extend his reach, inviting other refiners to join with him in the "South Improvement Association", a shadowy, cartel-like entity. Any refiner that refused found the railways suddenly raised their rates so high that they could no longer make a profit; Rockefeller then bought them out. The whole operation was cloaked in secrecy. Refiners who joined with Rockefeller were told, "Don't even tell your wife," but eventually the secret leaked out, much to the fury of the independent oil producers.

One witness to their outrage was Ida Tarbell, the 14-year-old daughter of an independent oilman, who years later was to expose Rockefeller's business practices in her book, *The History of the Standard Oil Company*.

"Nobody waited to find out his neighbour's opinion," Tarbell wrote. "On every lip there was but one word, and that was 'conspiracy'. For weeks the whole body of oil men abandoned regular business and surged from town to town intent on destroying the 'Monster', the 'Forty Thieves', the 'great Anaconda', as they called the mysterious South Improvement Company." (Tarbell, p.71). The railway companies quickly announced that they had severed their links with Rockefeller.

But instead of backing down, Rockefeller rapidly bought up 20 of Cleveland's 26 refineries, in the so-called "Cleveland Massacre". It was a masterstroke and one which, according to his biographer Ron Chernow, Rockefeller thoroughly enjoyed.

"During the Cleveland Massacre, Rockefeller savoured a feeling of sweet revenge against some of the older men who had patronized him when he started in business," he wrote.

"This was especially true of his negotiations with Alexander, Scofield and Company, whose partners included his original boss, Isaac L. Hewitt. After Hewitt came to Rockefeller's Euclid Avenue home to plead for mercy, they strolled down Euclid Avenue together, and Rockefeller told him his firm would never survive if it did not sell out to Standard Oil. He made a cryptic statement to Hewitt that entered into Rockefeller folklore: 'I have ways of making money you know nothing about.' Disconcerted by such assertions, Hewitt and his partners finally sold out for $65,000, though they believed their business was worth $150,000." (Chernow, pp.146–7)

Rockefeller now controlled the lion's share of US oil supplies, and his buying power persuaded the rail companies to secretly reintroduce their rebate system. His company continued to devour small independent refiners and producers, as well as related manufacturers and railroad infrastructure such as tanker trucks and rail terminals. By 1875 around 95 per cent of the US's refining capacity was in his hands. With new finds in Texas, Oklahoma, California and other states, as well as Pennsylvania, US oil production expanded rapidly, and with it Rockefeller's fortune. Annual oil production in the US soared from 2,000 barrels in 1859, the year in which Drake drilled the first modern well, to 64 million barrels in 1900. Demand for kerosene and other petroleum products was increasing, for use in heating and lighting, for lubrication in the growing industrial societies of the US and Europe, in rail locomotives, and in the new internal combustion engines first produced at the end of the 19th century.

Standard's monopoly was virtually unchallenged in Pennsylvania. It was not until new finds were made in other states that it was finally broken. Five years after entrepreneur Edward L. Doheny drilled the first Californian well in 1892, 200 oil companies were operating around Los Angeles. As in Pennsylvania, these were rapidly consolidated as weaker enterprises were put out of business or gobbled up by their competitors, but when Standard Oil entered California in 1900, buying the Pacific Coast Oil Company, there were seven major oil companies, of which the Union Oil Company was the largest.

The following year, drillers in Texas made the most significant oil strike ever in the US, at Spindletop. The early drillers in Texas were looking for water, not oil, and saw oil zones as a nuisance in their search for underground freshwater reservoirs. While a number of small oil discoveries were made, the first major find in Texas was in 1894. Patillo Higgins, however, believed that industry would switch from coal to oil. He was also convinced that significant oil deposits lay under the salt dome known as "Spindletop" in south east Texas. Higgins, a one-armed mechanic and self-taught geologist, started drilling, and after two months, "all of a sudden, a noise like a cannon shot came from the hole, and mud came shooting out of the ground like a rocket. Within a few seconds, natural gas, then oil followed. The oil 'gusher' – greenish-black in colour, doubled the size of the drilling derrick, rising to a height of more than 50 metres." (*Spindletop, Texas*, The Paleontological Research Institution)

As in Pennsylvania 30 years before, oil workers and engineers flooded into Texas. The drillers became known as "wildcatters" because they shot the wildcats that harried the early prospectors and nailed the corpses to their derricks. Again, the familiar pattern of soaring supply and plummeting prices followed. By late 1902, oil was fetching three cents a barrel, while vendors in the Texas boom towns sold water for three cents a glass.

As oil rushes burst out around the country, with strikes in Oklahoma, Louisiana, Arkansas, Colorado and Kansas following Spindletop, there were winners and losers. Probably those who lost the most were the native Americans on whose land oil was found.

After the American Civil War and with the opening of the first transcontinental railroad in 1869, the West was opened up to settlers. The native Americans were forced further and further west, and eventually onto specially designated "Indian reservations". Even within their reservations, the Indians were not secure; they were still cheated out of their land, oil, water and other property rights. Until as recently as 1962, a century after the start of the US oil industry, the US Department of the Interior had mandated that it was "illegal, a violation of trust, for tribes to develop their own mineral property."

In the 1920s, oil was discovered on the Osage reservation in Oklahoma. This reservation had gradually been reduced in size in the early 19th century, as the Osages were forced to cede over 80 million acres of land, and relocated from Kansas to Oklahoma in 1871–2.

After the discovery of oil, the Osage rapidly became one of the wealthiest populations in the world. In his book *The Deaths of Sybil Bolton: An American History*, *Washington Post* journalist Dennis McAuliffe describes the killing spree by white men, who often married wealthy young Osage women before killing them and their families. Starting in the 1920s, this became known as the "Osage Reign of Terror". (McAuliffe, p.83)

"The Osages were the Kuwaitis of the 1920s. Oil had made the Osage Indians the richest people, per capita, in the world," writes McAuliffe. But for many, the enjoyment of this wealth was short-lived. "Up to sixty wealthy Osages – nearly 3 per cent of the tribe – were murdered for their money in the early 1920s before law-enforcement officials stepped in ... The going rate to hire a poor white to kill a rich Osage is $500 and a used Roadster." (McAuliffe, pp123–4) Among them was McAuliffe's grandmother, Sybil Bolton, believed to have been killed by her guardian.

While the oil industry was expanding, and other companies in western states had established themselves independently of Standard Oil, an attack was made on John D. Rockefeller's industrial colossus from another quarter.

The sheer size and ruthlessness of the Standard Oil empire invested it with sinister significance. In his book *Frenzied Finance*, Thomas Lawson describes the new company headquarters in chilling terms: "At the lower end of the greatest thoroughfare in the greatest city of the New World is a huge structure of plain grey stone. Solid as a prison, towering as a steeple, its cold and forbidding façade seems to rebuke the heedless levity of the passing crowds, and frown on the frivolity of the stray sunbeams which in the late afternoon play around its impressive cornices. Men point to its stern portals, glance quickly up at the rows of unwinking windows, nudge each other, and hurry onward, as the Spaniards used to do when going by the offices of the Inquisition. The building is No. 26 Broadway." (Lawson, p.5)

How far did Rockefeller's ambitions extend? At the height of his economic power, there was speculation that Rockefeller wanted not only to dominate the US oil industry, but to take over the country itself. They believed that John D. Rockefeller had founded a dynasty and made it the "invisible government of the US," a "predatory capital controlling the wheels of government behind a smoke screen," as Morris

Bealle describes it in his book *The House of Rockefeller* (p.69). The bribes and favours exposed by Ida Tarbell are attributed not to commercial expediency, but to boundless ambition.

The question of what was driving Rockefeller is an interesting one. He was the world's first billionaire, yet still adhered to the penny-pinching dictums of his youth. His biographer Ron Chernow describes how he used to save the paper and string from parcels sent to him. (Chernow, p.504) Married to a deeply religious woman, Laura Celestia Spelman, his home life was austere; his three children shared one tricycle between them.

Rockefeller's philanthropy and religious convictions were in stark contrast to his antipathy towards labour rights. Rockefeller believed that men are morally bound to use their wealth to promote public welfare, but he also believed there was nothing wrong in using whatever means necessary to maximize profits. On April 20th, 1914, detectives hired by the Rockefeller-owned Colorado Fuel and Iron Company shot and burned to death 20 men, women and children to break a miners' strike. This became known as the "Ludlow Massacre".

In the late 19th century it must have seemed that the empire Rockefeller had built up was impregnable. But a new generation of journalists, known as the "muckrakers", were taking on the US's industrial giants. Among them was Ida Tarbell, who, influenced by her experiences as a child in Pithole City, decided to use the case of Standard Oil to illustrate the growing concerns about the rise of monopolistic trusts in the American economy. "Out of the alarm and bitterness and confusion, I gathered from my father's talk a conviction to which I still hold – that what had been undertaken was wrong." (Tarbell, p.179)

Tarbell produced a compelling, meticulously researched narrative, that was also a damning critique of Rockefeller's business manoeuvres. "Our national life on every side is distinctly poorer, uglier, meaner, for the kind of influence he exercises," she wrote. "[Standard Oil] never played fair and that ruined their greatness for me." (Tarbell, p.41)

Tarbell's concluding character study is also revealing:

If Mr. Rockefeller had been an ordinary man the outburst of popular contempt and suspicion which suddenly poured on his head would have thwarted and crushed him. But he was no ordinary man. He had the powerful imagination to see what might be done with the oil business if it could be centred in his hands, the intelligence to analyse the problem into its elements and to find the key to control. He had the essential element of all great achievement, a steadfastness to a purpose once conceived which nothing can crush. The Oil Regions might rage, call him a conspirator, and all those who sold him oil, traitors; the railroads might withdraw their contracts and the Legislature annul his charter; undisturbed and unresting he kept at his great purpose. (Tarbell, p.42)

Exposés from fellow "muckrakers" such as Charles Francis Adams and Henry Demarest Lloyd helped create a tide of public feeling against Rockefeller and the other capitalist giants. Rockefeller never made a public statement against Tarbell, but in private referred to her as "Miss Tarbarrel" and "the poisonous woman". In any case, the damage had been done; there followed two decades of legal cases and investigations, at the end of which Standard Oil was ordered to divest itself of its subsidiaries. After years of legal wrangling, the US Supreme Court ruled that the firm was guilty of anti-trust violations. In 1911, Standard Oil was split into 35 separate companies.

John D. Rockefeller didn't seem perturbed by the Court's decision to split up the company he had founded. "Buy Standard Oil," he advised a friend when the news came through, then calmly resumed his game of golf. And it seemed that Rockefeller was right. The largest of these new companies, Standard Oil of New Jersey (later Exxon), took on an almost identical role to its much-criticized parent. Run from the old 26 Broadway building in New York City by many of the Standard Oil board of directors, Standard Oil of New Jersey still bought its oil from the producing ex-Standard companies and acted as their banker. All the ex-Standard companies continued to sell their oil at the same price – though at the time no one could prove whether this was collusion or just healthy competition. Among the larger ex-Standard companies were Standard Oil Company of New York (Socony, later Mobil) and Standard Oil of California (Socal, later Chevron).

Oil and Empire

As oil consumption increased in both Europe and the Far East, the resentment of the European powers at being dependent on a single

American company – Standard Oil – also started to grow. By the early 20th century, Standard still had the lion's share of the US oil market and profited enormously from rising oil sales in the US, Europe and the Far East. The invention of the internal combustion engine in the 1870s meant that the first motor cars were now on the roads, and oil was widely used for heating and lighting, in steam locomotives, and for lubricating machinery, while the waste products from oil refining were starting to be used in the chemical and plastics industries.

The high prices set by Standard gave European entrepreneurs an incentive to seek out alternative sources of oil, and encouraged the Rothschilds and other European banking houses to back them. These ventures often operated in a cosy partnership with their European governments.

Europe itself had few sources of oil: only in Poland, Romania and the remote, mountainous Caucasus, which had recently been absorbed into the expanding Russian Empire. The UK, France and the other colonial powers were accustomed to using their own empires as a source of cheap raw materials, from cotton to coal, and eventually oil. By restricting high-value manufacturing to the core of the empire, the European powers were guaranteed a source of cheap raw materials and a captive market for their manufactured products.

Standard Oil, which had made aggressive inroads into the European market, selling to the industrial economies of France, the UK and Germany, and exploiting the Romanian oil reserves, was locked out of South East Asia by the European colonial authorities.

The company credited with breaking Standard Oil's international monopoly is Shell Oil. Its founder, Marcus Samuel, grew up in the East End of London, where his father kept a small curio shop. On holiday at the seaside, Marcus and his siblings became fascinated with the shells they found and used them to decorate their lunchboxes. His father saw the commercial potential in selling shell-covered boxes and started importing exotic shells from the East. He died in 1870, leaving his sons a thriving import-export business and contacts across Asia.

Marcus Samuel took over the business after his father's death and continued to expand, starting to trade in kerosene and other oil products, mainly from the Rothschild oilworks in Baku. In 1890, he watched tankers in Constantinople being loaded with Russian oil to ship to the Far East, on a long journey round the southern tip of Africa.

To cut costs enough to compete with Standard Oil, Samuel wanted to ship oil through the Suez Canal, which until then had been forbidden for safety reasons. Samuel commissioned marine engineer Fortescue Flannery to find a way round this. Flannery built the *Murex*, a ship with novel safety features, including water ballast tanks to cut the risk of grounding. The canal authorities allowed the *Murex* to pass, and it started its journey on August 24th, 1892, carrying 4,000 tons of Russian kerosene.

Samuel started to develop a lucrative market for oil in India, made inroads in China, and sought out new sources in Romania, in the British colony of Borneo and in Texas.

After a period of spectacular success, Samuel suffered several reverses of fortune in the early 20th century. After the Boxer rebellion, a popular uprising against foreign influence in China in 1900, he was no longer able to sell oil in China. He also lost money speculating at Spindletop, the first Texas "gusher" oilwell, and the unpleasant smell of the oil from his new well in North Borneo put off customers who didn't want to use it to heat their homes.

Instead of addressing his business problems, Samuel, who was by then Lord Mayor of London, threw himself into ceremonial activities and socializing. Shell's weakness, meanwhile, aroused the interest of a relatively new player in the world oil market: Henri Deterding of Royal Dutch.

The son of a Dutch sea captain, Henri Wilhelm August Deterding was born in Amsterdam in 1866. He was passionate about figures, and as a young man he would study company balance sheets in his free time. His acquaintances described him as "dynamic" and "restless", with a "magnetic effect on those he worked with." (Sampson, p.64) Deterding started his working life as a bookkeeper for the Royal Dutch Company for Exploration of Petroleum Sources in the Netherlands Indies ("Royal Dutch").

Another Dutch oilman, Jean Kessler, had built the company, mainly operating in the Dutch East Indies (now Indonesia), into a major concern. Oil had first been drilled in large quantities in the Dutch East Indies during one of the most turbulent periods of that country's colonial history. The Dutch had retaken most of Indonesia from the British, and after 40 years of intense exploitation were only just starting to relax their regime when a former shopkeeper, Jon Reesink, started drilling at Cibodas in 1871 with financial backing from Royal Dutch. Reesink himself had little success, but other Royal Dutch ventures were much more encouraging, especially in Sumatra and Java. By 1911 Indonesia accounted for almost 4 per cent of world oil production. Deterding rapidly advanced through the company, being put in charge of selling oil throughout the Far East when he was only 29. When Kessler died in 1900, Deterding became interim manager, and remained in charge of the company for the next 35 years. Through an aggressive strategy of expansion and alliances, he extended Royal Dutch's oil holdings into a dozen countries.

British Lord of the Admiralty James Arbuthnot Fisher was later to describe Deterding as "Napoleonic in his audacity and Cromwellian in his thoroughness." (Marder [ed.], p.430) The Nobels, his main rivals in the Caspian, were less complimentary. They described him as "a terrible sort of being whose mission was to slaughter everybody and pick up the carcass." (Yergin, p.121)

Deterding was far more focused on business than Marcus Samuel. While Samuel was influenced by status and flattery, Deterding was single-minded in pursuit of money and power.

Competition with Shell was intense, but in 1903 the two companies put aside their differences to better compete with Standard Oil. This proved so successful that in 1907 they signed an agreement creating the Royal Dutch/Shell Group of Companies, 60 per cent held by Royal Dutch and 40 per cent by Shell.

"I cannot imagine any business built upon a surer foundation," Sir Marcus Samuel said of the merger.

Royal Dutch Shell was, however, unable to prospect for or produce oil in British-controlled India or in Burma (then administered by the British as part of the Indian subcontinent).

In 1886, 60 years and several wars after the East India Company first invaded, the whole of Burma, modern-day Myanmar, had been brought into the British Empire. "A New Year present to the Queen," Lord Randolph Churchill had said in London. The primary motive for the conquest appears to have been to protect India, the "finest jewel in the Empire's crown," from a possible invasion by the French from Indo-China or the Burmese themselves. Burma was also a treasure trove of riches, with precious metals, timber and oil.

In addition, the British invasion was sparked by the trade policy of Burma's new 19-year-old King Thibaw, who, ruled by his power-crazy mother-in-law, had started granting monopoly concessions to non-British companies.

Rangoon Oil Company, later Burmah Oil, had been the first foreign company to drill for oil in Burma, in 1871, and was given a monopoly on the production of crude oil. A Scottish syndicate, Rangoon Oil was run "with a mixture of adventurousness and meanness."

After its conquest by the British, Burma's army refused to surrender, melting into the jungles to wage a guerrilla war against the occupiers. Even in 1900, 15 years after the conquest of Burma, a 20,000 strong force of soldiers and military police was needed to prevent the guerrillas and Burmese bandits disrupting trade and administration in the country altogether.

Despite this insecurity, Burmah Oil continued to dominate Burmese oil production from 1886 until 1963, when the country became independent. With its discoveries of the Ychaugyaung field in 1887 and the Chauk field in 1902, the company remained extremely profitable.

The British and Dutch colonial powers gave the lucrative oil concessions within their empires to their own companies, preventing either the local populations or "foreign" companies from benefiting. This was a particular grievance for Standard Oil, which found itself blocked from the Indian market. According to one Standard Oil subsidiary, the Anglo-American Oil Company, the reason given was that "It is not desired by the Government of India to introduce any of the American oil companies, or their subsidiary companies, into India." (US Federal Trade Commission Report on Foreign Ownership in the Petroleum Industry (1923), p.105) This issue was to take on new significance after World War I.

Oil, Violence and Revolution: Baku and Mexico

Russia, too, was exploiting the oil reserves of its empire. As the Russian army advanced down through the Caucasus, Baku, now the capital of Azerbaijan, had fallen to the Russians in 1815. The city, 1,200 miles from Moscow and 287 miles north east of Tehran, was the site of one of the world's oldest oil industries. In the early 1870s, the Tsar opened up the Russian oilfields to private investment, and within two decades oil derricks had sprung up along the Caspian shore, and further north among the mountains of Georgia and Chechnya.

One man who made the difficult journey to Baku was Robert Nobel, the elder son of Immanuel Nobel, a Swedish businessman who created Russia's armaments industry. After running several companies of his own, all of which had gone bankrupt, Robert was now working for his brother, factory owner Ludwig Nobel, who followed him to Baku after Robert bought up several tracts of oil-bearing land. Working together, the Nobels exploited the oilfields ruthlessly.

By the late 1880s the Nobels became the "kings of Baku", with their workers calling themselves "Nobelites". As well as the Russian oil barons, the French banking family the Rothschilds and British oilman Marcus Samuel also flocked to invest in Baku oil. This became a particularly attractive proposition with the growth in popularity of the motor car, since the heavy Russian oil was less desirable than Pennsylvania oil for lighting, but was much more suitable for cars.

They created a modern city along the shores of the Caspian Sea, with elegant townhouses and the classical mansions of the oil barons. The *pièce de résistance* was the "Villa Petrolea", a complex of many buildings set among spacious, beautifully tended gardens and parkland. This was the Nobel headquarters in Baku.

The other side of the Caucasian oil industry was less attractive. Oil workers endured some of the worst conditions and were paid very little. Perhaps because of the contrast with the oil barons, Baku and Batumi (now in Georgia) were in a ferment of revolutionary activity in the early 20th century. Suddenly the oil industry was beset by a wave of strikes and sabotage. Among the workers' leaders was a young Georgian revolutionary, Joseph Stalin.

In 1903, a workers' revolt against the terrible working conditions started in Baku and spread not only through the oil regions, but throughout the whole of the Russian Empire.

In the first Russian revolution, two years later in 1905, another wave of strikes and sabotage flared up, and workers set many of the region's oilwells on fire. Later that year there followed bloody ethnic clashes between Azeris and Armenians.

A visitor to Batumi described the city as "a perfect hotbed of revolt," saying that: "When I arrived things were peaceable enough in appearance; although the state of siege was in force there were no patrols, and hardly any policemen. Yet not a day passed without murders being committed in the streets, and no murderer was ever arrested ... In the town itself the terror was so great that the least sound or appearance of disturbance caused an immediate panic." (Villari, p.53)

The strikers succeeded in driving out the Nobels, Rothschilds and most of the other international investors. By the beginning of 1906 two-thirds of the Caucasian oilwells had been destroyed and most of the rest were standing idle.

The same visitor to Batumi described the scene at the Rothschild oilworks. "Tall natives, mostly Adjar Mohammedans, armed with revolvers and kinjals (Caucasian knives) were standing about at all the entrances, and a group of Cossacks in very untidy déshabille were squatting on the ground playing cards outside the stable where their horses were quartered. Here and there a few workmen were seen looking after the machinery and the stores. But in spite of all these precautions no less than eighteen employees of the firm had been assassinated during the last few months, and the lives of all the others had been threatened and often attempted. The ex-workmen either did not wish to return to work or did not dare..." (Villari, p.54)

Although some of the foreign investors returned to Russia, they never recovered their former strength.

Oil Becomes a Military Necessity

The loss of Baku had raised for the first time the fear that oil might not always be readily available. Civilian demand for oil and oil-based products increased rapidly in the early 20th century, promoted by the main oil companies who marketed aggressively, seeking to increase dependence on their product.

Demand for kerosene had peaked in the 1880s, then declined as electric lighting became more popular, but new uses had emerged to take its place: oil-burning furnaces, and oil boilers for factories, trains and ships. The single most important development was the invention of the internal combustion engine. Previously, petrol had been discarded as a dangerous waste product from kerosene production. Now it had a potentially huge market as fuel. In the early 20th century, demand for the motor car increased and it was no longer seen as an expensive foible or passing fad. In 1894 there were two motorists in the UK. By the end of 1895, after more imports from Karl Benz and Gottleib Daimler in Germany, there were 14 or 15 cars on British roads, and that increased to over 700 by 1900, and carried on growing.

Although demand for oil was growing, it was not yet regarded as essential. If oil had remained simply a fuel used for heating, lighting and even the internal combustion engine, countries would never have needed to go to war for it.

"Many resources are needed to sustain a modern industrial society, but only those that are viewed as being vital to national security are likely to provoke the use of military force," writes Michael Klare in his book *Resource Wars*. (Klare, p.29)

The turning point, according to Klare, was when the British navy decided to switch from a coal- to an oil-powered navy – a move not just supported, but actually initiated by one of the leading oil companies, Royal Dutch Shell.

As tensions increased in Europe in the early 20th century, with the major powers aligning themselves in two major blocks, the UK, Germany and the other powers began to build up their military capacities. Germany was already building dreadnoughts, with the stated intention of overtaking the UK as the foremost naval power.

The British started designing bigger ships to stay ahead, encountering the difficulty of increasing firepower without cutting the space allocated for storing coal. It appeared that the navy would have to compromise either on size, speed and endurance – or on weaponry.

Marcus Samuel of Royal Dutch Shell then approached the British navy, proposing that they convert the British fleet from coal to oil. This, assuming Shell would be their supplier, would be a guaranteed large market for Shell's oil.

James Arbuthnot Fisher, then the First Sea Lord of the Admiralty, had already been considering oil as a fuel for the navy and seized enthusiastically on Samuel's suggestion, with such fervour, in fact, that he soon became known as "the oil maniac". Not a man to compromise, Fisher is credited as saying: "The essence of war is violence. Moderation in war is imbecility." (Michael Gove, *The Times*, March 23rd, 2003)

Fisher pointed out that big ships were slowed by the amount of coal they had to carry. An oil-powered ship would require less storage space, fewer stokers, and unlike a coal-powered ship, could be refuelled at sea. It could also increase speed more quickly, and since it would not need a funnel would be harder for enemies to see and would allow the guns on deck to target a wider angle.

Although trials of oil-powered ships and submarines had started back in 1903, the main problem holding back the switch to oil was that the UK had no oil (and plenty of coal). It couldn't afford to switch to an oil-powered navy without a guaranteed supply.

It was Winston Churchill, then the First Lord of the Admiralty, who found a solution. It was a solution that would not benefit Marcus Samuel at all. But it was to open up the world's greatest oil-producing region – the Middle East – to large-scale exploitation, and make the UK a leading force in the development of that region for the next half century.

Chapter Two: Carving Up the Middle East

At the turn of the 20th century, the Middle East was an undeveloped, neglected area, which attracted little attention from the outside world. Much of the region was under the Ottoman Empire, which had lasted for over 600 years but for a century had been in a state of stagnation. At the end of the 19th century it was heavily in debt to European banks and had lost territory to France and Britain, but Istanbul still ruled over modern-day Iraq, Israel, Lebanon, Palestine, Syria and parts of Saudi Arabia.

Persia, now Iran, was independent, though it was facing pressure from the Russian Empire to its north. With no bourgeoisie or commercial class, Persia was ruled almost feudaly by the Shah, while local despots held sway over illiterate peasant farmers. Nomadic tribes, like those in Arabia, roamed the eastern deserts. This unpromising region was to become the world's great oil producer in the 20th century.

The UK, in the pre-war years, was considering the switch to an oil-powered navy, but was afraid of becoming dependent on foreign suppliers to fuel its ships. Apart from the oil supply it obtained from Burma, on the other side of the world, all the oil used in the UK was imported either from the Caspian (now part of the Russian Empire), from Romania, the US or the Far East. It was looking for a supplier closer to home, and one that would be safe from rival European powers in the event of a European war.

In 1902, William Knox D'Arcy, a British entrepreneur who had already made a fortune prospecting for gold in Australia, bought a concession from the Shah of Persia to prospect for oil. D'Arcy had been inspired by biblical descriptions of eternally burning flames, which he assumed could indicate the presence of oil.

For D'Arcy and his chief engineer George Reynolds, progress was slow, but they continued with the help of finance from the Burmah Oil Company. In May 1908, seven years after they started searching, D'Arcy and his engineers struck a large deposit of oil at Masjid-I-Suleiman in south west Persia. The Anglo-Persian Oil Company (later BP) was formed in 1909 to develop the oilfield. Burmah Oil owned 97 per cent of the company.

After Anglo-Persian had entered a short-term agreement with Royal Dutch Shell, Deterding, Shell's chief executive, apparently decided to acquire Anglo-Persian. Charles Greenway, Anglo-Persian's new managing director, vehemently opposed this idea. As well as wishing to retain control of his company, Greenway personally disliked Deterding, and argued that his adversary was "non-British" (he was Dutch), the implication being that Royal Dutch Shell was not to be trusted.

Greenway had not only raised fears about the reliability of Royal Dutch Shell, he had also given a new idea to Churchill, one of the first to understand the military significance of oil. Churchill commissioned a study of the feasibility of the government taking over Anglo-Persian's claim, and they returned from Persia with an extremely favourable report. Although Persia wasn't in the British Empire, it was far closer than the East Indies, and near enough to India for troops to be rapidly dispatched there. Churchill gave the go-ahead for the Admiralty to buy a controlling stake of Anglo-Persian.

Floating to Victory "On a Wave of Oil"

World War I was the first war in which oil was of major military importance, and this became more and more apparent as the war developed. By 1918, in a single month the French army used 39,000 tons of oil, the British army 32,000 tons and US forces 20,000 tons. Before the war France had been importing 400,000 tons a year, but by 1918 it had to import one million tons.

Oil was not only needed in the navy. On the battlefields of Europe and the Middle East, oil was needed everywhere. Oil-powered trucks replaced horses, transporting men, weapons and supplies. They were quicker and more efficient; horses were a burden to an army, eating ten times as much as a soldier. The new oil-powered vehicles needed to store relatively little fuel, and the internal combustion engine later made possible new weapons of war – tanks and aeroplanes.

As the war progressed and oil became increasingly difficult to obtain, awareness of its vital importance grew. A *Daily Telegraph* article written on March 15th, 1915 commented:

> The Chancellor of the Exchequer was right when he said: "This is an engineers' war." We are seeing the impress of the engineer on every phase of the stupendous struggle now in progress throughout the world. No longer is engineering a sideline. It has become the principal feature of war, so much so that "Eye-Witness" has seen fit to call the present "the petrol war" in the course of his recent description of the part played by mechanical traction on the Continent. To call it "the oil war" would probably be more accurate since this term would also include the Fleet, so far as many of its greatest and smallest craft – as represented by super-dreadnoughts and submarines – are concerned.

The allies had relied on shipments from abroad – mainly from Standard Oil, but also some from the Far East by Royal Dutch Shell – but once German U-boats began targeting merchant vessels in February 1915, these dried up because the oil companies were unwilling to risk their ships. Both Standard and Royal Dutch Shell started selling their oil to the Far East instead of Europe. Countries on both sides in the war were running out of oil.

Germany, with no oil of its own, had access to Romania's oilfields through most of the war. Romania was not only richly endowed with fertile farmland, it was also the largest European oil producer after Russia. A traveller on the Orient Express in 1906 wrote about making "the final run to Bucharest through fields of maize and sun-flowers and past clusters of tall timber oil derricks." (Sir Roy Redgrave, *Orient Express Magazine*, 1986)

Romania, hoping to regain Transylvania as well as other territories, declared war on Germany and Austria on August 19th, 1916, immediately moving its troops across the border into Transylvania. German forces under Mackensen and Falkenhayn (two of the country's most successful generals) rapidly entered the country and routed its underprepared army. Bucharest was occupied on December 6th,

1916, leaving Germany in control of Romania's valuable resources.

When the British saw that Romania was about to fall, and realizing the vital importance of the Ploesti oilfields, they deliberately sabotaged the fields, burning or spilling some 800,000 tons of petrol. The Romanian Ambassador to the US, Constantine Angelscu, talked about Romania's losses in October 1917, including: "our enforced destruction of the oilwells in Romania, representing hundreds and hundreds of millions of francs in value, as well as of our stores of cereals and our factories, to prevent their falling into the hands of the invaders." (Horne [ed.] p.89)

Through most of the war Romania was under German rule and was heavily exploited, particularly the oilfields, which made a large contribution to the German war effort, though the Germans did not get them back to running at full capacity until almost the end of the war.

Britain and France were, for some time, equally strapped for oil. Deterding of Royal Dutch Shell was the first to offer more hope to the allies. Probably hoping to share in Anglo-Persian's concessions in Persia, he suggested to the British government in 1915 that he would turn Royal Dutch into a British-controlled company.

Deterding started selling oil at cost to the Indian government for the Indian railways, allowing the Burmah Oil Company to ship oil to the western front. He also moved Royal Dutch Shell headquarters from The Hague to London and became a British citizen. From 1916, the British government started to consider various schemes for making Shell a British rather than a Dutch company, and even for merging it with Anglo-Persian, though nothing came of these ideas.

It was, however, the supplies from Standard that made the real difference. Over the course of the war, US companies (chiefly Standard) supplied 80 per cent of the allies' fuel needs.

In 1917, the allied leaders were so desperate for oil that they asked the US President Woodrow Wilson for help, telling him that without it they would lose the war. "A failure in the supply of gasoline would cause the immediate paralysis of our armies," the French prime minister wrote in a telegram to Wilson. (Yergin, p.177) Under pressure from Wilson, Standard agreed to start supplying the allies in Europe – though on certain conditions. It wanted compensation for any tankers sunk by U-boats and for the tankers confiscated at the beginning of the war to be returned.

The agreement with Standard was crucial to the allies, particularly as it came just as Germany started to run out of oil. Without supplies coming in from the sea, the Germans had been dependent on supplies from Russia and Romania; the French Balkan campaign cut these oil lines. When Turkey seized the Baku oilfields in 1917, Germany was almost entirely cut off.

The allies, British Foreign Secretary Lord Curzon said after the war, "floated to victory on a wave of oil."

Why Europe Went to War in the Middle East

One question that historians raise in connection with World War I is why so much attention was paid to the Middle East, when the real theatre of war was in Europe. Prior to the 20th century, the entire region had been regarded as of little interest to the European powers. Indeed, the term "Middle East" was used for the first time in 1902. It was therefore surprising that so much attention was given to the region, resulting in so many deaths. It appears that it was only after the oil shortages in early 1916 that the UK turned its attention to Persia and Iraq. The diplomatic standoff between the UK and France at the end of the war indicates that both countries were planning to seize control of the oilfields for themselves.

Once oil had been discovered in Persia, the region took on more significance for the world powers. The intent of the UK, and to a lesser extent France, to take control of the oil-rich regions of Persia and Mosul (in present-day Iraq) became evident through various treaties designed to formalize their spheres of interests.

In 1913, the UK and the Ottoman Empire signed an agreement on their respective spheres of interest in Arabia. An arbitrary line was drawn to mark the easternmost point of Ottoman influence within Arabia, later referred to as the Blue Line after its colour on the map. In March 1914, the Violet line was added, to link the southern end of the Blue Line with the Ottoman border in south west Arabia. The lines separated British from non-British spheres of influence, and were effectively imposed by the British on the weak Ottoman government.

When war broke out the British and Ottoman Empires became enemies and the Anglo-Ottoman Agreement was declared null and void. The Ottoman Empire, which at the start of the war controlled the oil-rich Mosul oilfields, entered the war in support of Germany, and London immediately sent a strong force of mainly Indian soldiers to Basra. The Ottoman army was an unknown quantity, but allied to Germany it represented a serious threat to the British colonies of Egypt and even India.

This action was also intended to protect the 138-mile Anglo-Persian oil pipeline, which had been built in 1911 and ran from the oilfields at Masjid-i-Suleiman to the refinery at Abadan (both in Persia). Despite the threat to the British Empire, it appears that the British (and French) forces present in the Middle East were out of proportion to the threat in that region. The real reason for this action is more likely to have been the oil at Mosul, which the UK, perhaps, wanted to seize for itself.

"This should have been a sideshow," writes Stephen Pelletiere in his book *Iraq and the International Oil System*. "Yet Britain was almost constantly active in this arena. Moreover, operations carried on by the British in the Middle East were not negligible. Churchill conceived the idea of storming the Dardanelles with a great flotilla. That failed, as did Churchill's next big idea – to seize the heights overlooking the seaway by land. Some 40,000 Allied troops, mostly colonials, paid with their lives for this fiasco. One wonders what Churchill and Lloyd George were hoping to accomplish. A number of explanations have been advanced, but only one explanation carries weight, that the British were determined to take control of the area because of its oil." (Pelletiere, p.37)

The Dardanelles is the narrow strait overlooked by the high cliffs of Gallipoli between the Black Sea and the Mediterranean, which divides Europe from Asia. It was the route by which Baku oil used to be shipped from the Caucasus to Europe. The Gallipoli campaign of 1915 resulted in the deaths of over 200,000 men, many of them from the Australian and New Zealand Army Corps (the ANZACs). The British government had lost confidence that the invasion could succeed, and too few troops were sent, leading to failure to drive out the Turks and a British withdrawal.

The British also made considerable efforts to encourage local Arab populations to rebel against their Ottoman conquerors. They carried on two contradictory sets of secret negotiations. On one side they negotiated with Sharif Husayn of Mecca, promising to support Arab independence after the war, in exchange for the Arab revolt against Turkey. This is the story told in the 1962 David Lean film *Lawrence of Arabia*, starring Peter O'Toole. Even in the talks with Sharif Husayn, the British insisted that Baghdad and Basra must be zones of British interest with "special administrative arrangements" to "safeguard our mutual economic interests." (Henry McMahon, letter to Sharif Husayn, in Antonius, p.173). However, in 1916, the British and the French had carved up the region between them in the Sykes-Picot Agreement.

The UK's areas of control would be present-day Jordan, Iraq and an area around Haifa in what is now Israel. France would get south east Turkey, northern Iraq, Syria and Lebanon. The UK and France would also be free to draw up state boundaries within their areas of control.

The area which was later to be called Palestine would be under international administration, depending on the outcome of consultations with Russia and other powers. The borders of this area were to be the subject of great controversy in years to come.

The agreement was later expanded to include their allies, Italy and Russia, who were offered parts of the Ottoman Empire where it happened that no oil had been found. In return for accepting the terms of the Sykes-Picot Agreement, Russia would get Armenia and parts of Kurdistan. However, after the Russian Revolution, Lenin published details of the Sykes-Picot Agreement, as well as other confidential treaties.

By that time, the UK was already regretting the fact that under the Agreement northern Iraq had been allocated to France, probably because Picot was the more skilled negotiator.

British Foreign Secretary Arthur Balfour stressed the importance of becoming the "guiding spirit" in Mesopotamia (essentially, Iraq and part of Syria) in a talk to prime ministers of the British Dominions. "I do not care under what system we keep the oil. But I am quite clear it is all-important for us that this oil should be available," he said.

British forces had already taken Baghdad, and they took Mosul in November 1918, in violation of the armistice with the Turks a week earlier. "Control of these oil supplies becomes a first-class war aim," Sir Maurice Hankey, Secretary of the British War Cabinet, wrote to Balfour as British troops closed in on Baghdad. The French had been presented with a *fait accompli*.

Another race for oil was taking place a few hundred miles north east, in the Caspian, as German and Turkish troops closed in on Baku. After the 1917 revolution, Russia was forced to give the oilfields away to Germany as part of its peace settlement in 1918, but while the handover was being negotiated, the Turkish army set out to snatch the oilfields from its German allies. There followed a massacre of Baku's Armenian population, many of whom were oil workers, by the Turkish army and the Turkic Azeris. Exactly what happened and why it happened is unclear.

According to some historians, Azeris and Armenians lived peacefully side-by-side until the Russian invasion in the early 19th century. Despite their religious differences (Armenians are Christian and Azeris Muslim), there are many cultural similarities between the two ethnic groups, especially in music and cuisine.

So what provoked the 1918 massacre? One theory is that in the spirit of "divide and rule", both Tsarist and Bolshevik Russia promoted ethnic divisions in the Caucasus in order to safeguard their own position and prevent a unified Caucasian resistance. In 1918, the Bolsheviks are said to have incited the "dashnaks" (Armenian nationalists) to carry out pogroms against the Azeris.

Turkish control of Baku was short-lived. British forces entered the city in August 1918. The UK and France both sent troops to support the "Whites" in the civil war that followed the revolution – mainly to further their aims in World War I, but also because of a deep-rooted fear of the "Red" Bolsheviks and to protect their business interests in the former Russian Empire. Baku was of great importance to the British, and their White Russian allies, and the British force was designated to protect both the Baku oil and the stocks of cotton in Turkestan on the opposite side of the Caspian. By the end of 1918 there were over 300,000 foreign troops in Russia, from 11 European nations plus America and Japan.

The UK had already declared its support for the multiethnic "Central Caspian Dictatorship" (CCD), which had taken control after Soviet power collapsed in the region. Later that year, when the CCD split up, the UK recognized independent Azerbaijan and Georgia, both of which were hostile to the Bolsheviks. The British sent troops to Baku to protect the region's oil supplies and to cut the Red Army off from the oil that it needed.

The White Russian army held the Donetsk coalfields in the Ukraine, just north of the Caucasus. Without access to Caucasian oil or Donetsk coal, the Red-controlled areas suffered terribly that winter. People froze to death in their own homes in Moscow and St Petersburg, and trains with insufficient fuel broke down in remote provinces where their passengers died of cold or starvation.

After the British had been in Baku for a year, Azerbaijani and Turkish army corps entered the city, expelling the British. Then two weeks later came the Mudros armistice; the Ottoman Empire withdrew from World War I. Turkish forces evacuated the Caucasus and Baku, to be replaced by British forces, beginning the second allied intervention in the Caucasus, to the relief of the oil companies.

However, the British withdrew from Baku and Azerbaijan in August 1919, and the Soviets took over the Azerbaijan Republic in April 1920. The British, French and other European oil importers were temporarily cut off from supplies of Baku oil. But at the same time, their governments were seeking control of the oil in an even better endowed region: the Middle East.

The Spoils of War: Oil Over Self-Determination

After the war, the UK and France dismantled the empires of their defeated enemies, Germany and Turkey. Despite the rhetoric of self-determination at that time, the countries of the Middle East, newly liberated from Ottoman rule, became "protectorates" of the UK and France, with their resources firmly under foreign control.

Leaders of 32 states representing about 75 per cent of the world's population attended the Paris Peace Conference of 1919. However, in a trend that would continue through the next two decades, negotiations were dominated by the five major powers responsible for the victory: the UK, France, the US, Italy and Japan. Under the terms of the peace treaties, all the German colonies were to become League of Nations mandates, and the Ottoman Empire was reduced to the boundaries of present-day Turkey, while the UK and France administered the rest of its former territory.

The Ottoman Empire was carved up into "protectorates", states with some degree of autonomy but under the control of a more powerful state. Syria was partitioned into two French protectorates of

Lebanon and Syria, and the British protectorate of Palestine. Iraq and Transjordan became British protectorates. Unlike their colonies, the protectorates were not possessions of the UK or France, but in practical terms the relationship was fairly similar to the colonial one. Persia, then ruled by the Qajar dynasty, retained its independence, but political and economic life was heavily influenced by the Anglo-Persian Oil Company. In many ways Persia was treated as a subject nation by the British government in the interwar period.

While the word "oil" was hardly mentioned during the negotiations, both the UK and France paid particular attention to the regions of Iraq that were believed to hold enormous, as yet unproven, oil reserves. Furious at being outmanoeuvred in northern Iraq, French Prime Minister Georges Clemenceau is said to have almost come to blows with Lloyd George, only being restrained by US President Woodrow Wilson.

The next important step towards the oilfields came at the San Remo conference in December 1919, when shares in the Turkish Petroleum Company, which before the war had been granted concessions in Iraq, were reallocated to the victors.

The Turkish Petroleum Company was a syndicate put together by Armenian entrepreneur Calouste Gulbenkian, who owned 5 per cent of the shares. Anglo-Persian had just under 50 per cent, and Royal Dutch Shell and Deutsche Bank each had a little less than 25 per cent. At San Remo, Deutsche Bank's share was given to France, but Gulbenkian – later known as "Mr Five Percent" – refused to give up his share.

The US was furious that it had been excluded from the San Remo negotiations, and from the Iraqi oilfields, all the more so because the Shah had already granted Anglo-Persian a monopoly of oil production in neighbouring Persia. After months of heavy pressure, the US was finally offered first 12 per cent of the Turkish Petroleum Company, and later 20 per cent.

The new government of Iraq also signed an agreement granting the Turkish Petroleum Company a concession for the next 75 years. They did this reluctantly, since the terms offered in 1925 were considerably worse than those discussed at San Remo. Instead of a stake in the company and its management, the Iraqis were offered only financial compensation of four gold shillings per ton of oil.

All participants in the Turkish Petroleum Company also agreed only to seek new concessions in the former Ottoman Empire through the company. The deal was finally signed in July 1928. A few months later one of the world's greatest oilfields was discovered in Iraq, but the Iraqi people were not to benefit from it.

The denial of real independence and the exploitation of the country's resources created a breeding ground for Arab nationalism, not just in Iraq but also in neighbouring countries, that in the late 20th century helped to bring such anti-Western leaders as Saddam Hussein and the Ayatollah Khomeni to power. Getting in on the Iraqi action was particularly important to the Americans because it followed the first oil scare in American history.

Previously supply had so far outstripped demand that it was only by regulating supply that a market could be made at all. But after World War I, the US became anxious for the first time about securing future supplies, a pattern that was to follow every time a major conflict had passed.

"The vital role of oil in a modern industrial economy had vividly been brought home to the American people by World War I. Immediately thereafter, there developed a deep-seated fear that the United States was running out of oil," according to "The International Petroleum Cartel" (a report from the US Federal Trade Commission, 1952, pp37–46). This followed the huge foreign demand for US oil from its allies in Europe. "That it grew into a case of national jitters is not wholly surprising in view of the fact that the military importance of oil in modern war had been demonstrated. Oil supply took on a vital national defence complexion," said the report.

Fears were increased by gloomy estimates of future supply in the US and Mexico (where salt water had recently been discovered in some wells) from the US Bureau of Mines and the US Geological Survey.

"The position of the United States in regard to oil can best be characterized as precarious," said Dr George Otis Smith, Director of the US Geological Survey, in 1920. His colleague David White anticipated that within five years the US would need to import between 150 to 200 million barrels a year, adding that "a great slump in Mexican production ... seems sooner or later inevitable." (*Engineering and Mining Journal*, March 18th, 1922)

Relations between the US and UK had already cooled over the initial exclusion of the US from the Iraqi oilfields. After the war, Anglo-Persian controlled almost half the Turkish Petroleum Company, and had a monopoly position in Persia. It had also recently obtained an exclusive concession for all petroleum rights in eastern and western Macedonia, for an exploration period of five years, with an option for a 50-year exploration concession in some areas. Royal Dutch Shell and Burmah Oil had the sizeable oil reserves in Burma, Indonesia and Borneo.

In 1920 and 1921, the United States Senate demanded an investigation of the restrictions imposed on American citizens by foreign countries in prospecting for petroleum, and of the steps being taken to remove these restrictions, concluding that American interests were being systematically excluded from foreign oilfields.

"The British position is impregnable," wrote E. Mackay Edgar in *Sperling's Journal* in 1919. "All the known oilfields, all the likely or probable oilfields outside of the United States itself, are in British hands or under British management or control, or financed by British capital ... To the tune of many million pounds a year, America before very long will have to purchase from British companies ... a progressively increasing proportion of the oil she cannot do without and is no longer able to furnish from her own stores."

The Federal Trade Commission Report on Foreign Ownership in the Petroleum Industry of 1923 also pointed out that the US no longer had access to the East European fields. After the Russian Revolution, foreign interests, including the Baku oilfields, were expropriated and industry was nationalized. In the Romanian land reforms of 1918, large land holdings (especially those believed to contain oil) were expropriated from both Romanian and foreign owners, and surface rights were resold to peasants, with the government retaining the subsoil rights. In Poland, the government owned undeveloped lands, and strictly supervised exploration and exploitation. It was in this climate of growing insecurity that the details of the "Oilfields Group conspiracy" emerged. The US already feared that the UK was penetrating too far into their oil industry. Royal Dutch Shell rapidly expanded its exploitation in the US in 1919 and 1920, while, US officials alleged, conserving reserves elsewhere. According to Standard Oil of New Jersey's chairman Walter Teagle, a statement had been circulated among American oil companies in August 1919 to the effect that the British government had decided to use the Shell organization to develop the oil resources of the British Dominions.

In the early 1920s, American companies focused on obtaining oil concessions in the closer regions of Latin America, chiefly Venezuela (where Royal Dutch Shell already had significant holdings), Colombia and Peru.

It was therefore a shock to the Americans when it emerged that the British Controlled Oilfields Group had been buying up many of the oil concessions that the US companies had intended to exploit themselves.

Information on the BCOG is scant, but it was believed to be a subsidiary of Anglo-Persian, registered in Canada. BCOG's holdings included properties off Panama, leading to speculation that the UK was planning to use them as a base for attacking the oil-producing regions of the US. The intrigue and suspicion among the world's largest oil companies was to continue through most of the 1920s, as each company sought to improve their position and cut out their competitors. But all that was to change in 1928.

The "Seven Sisters"

In 1952, reports started to leak in the press about a highly critical report compiled by the US Federal Trade Commission on collusion between the world's largest oil companies. Initially President Truman's administration tried to suppress the report to avoid the damaging consequences of its publication, but as the rumours grew, the government made the decision to publish. Within hours, the report's explosive contents were being broadcast around the world.

Titled "The International Petroleum Cartel", the report confirmed a suspicion that many had harboured: that seven of the world's largest companies had been acting as a cartel for the past quarter century.

Three former Standard Oil companies – Standard Oil of New Jersey (Exxon), Standard Oil of New York (Socony, later Mobil) and Standard Oil of California (Socal, later Chevron) – had joined with the two British giants, Royal Dutch Shell and Anglo-Persian, and two other leading US companies, Gulf Oil and Texaco. Together, these seven companies held the world to ransom.

Each of them was richer and more powerful than many of the states in which they operated. By driving up demand for oil and promoting the automobile industry, they conspired to make the US, UK and other countries so dependent on oil that their governments would always support the oil giants, both in their activities abroad and in keeping rival companies out of their industry. They used their personal links with the highest echelons of government to push for intervention against any states that thwarted their aims.

How did the oil industry progress from the cut-throat competition of its early days to virtual elimination of any competition between the seven leading companies? In the early 1920s, rivalry between the companies was still strong. Demand for oil had increased rapidly during World War I and in peacetime continued to soar, especially in the US where the creation of the world's first consumer society was in progress. It was an exciting time, at least for the wealthy and middle classes in the US and the capitals of Europe. The bright young postwar generation reacted against the wartime gloom and misery, throwing themselves into the new fashions of the 1920s, jazz music and flapper parties, and an orgy of conspicuous consumption of everything now available, from the new domestic appliances to the automobile. Oil was now in demand for leisure travel instead of warfare, fuelling the huge ocean liners and cruise ships, as well as the aeroplanes that were just starting to be used for passenger and airmail flights. All these technologies were guzzling oil.

Nowhere was this more the case than in the richest country in the world, the United States of America. After World War I the US had turned in on itself, with an isolationist policy that protected its citizens from the danger of involvement in world affairs. Its economy was burgeoning, especially the oil and automotive sectors. From 485,000 in 1913, US automobile production soared to 3.5 million in 1924, reaching over 4.3 million in 1928. By the time of the Great Depression after the Wall Street Crash in 1929, one in five Americans already owned a car. Henry Ford's first automated assembly line was rolling out the Ford-T, a car so reasonably priced that even the workers in Ford's own factories could afford one, especially with the help of the new auto-driven consumer credit industry.

Labour-saving domestic appliances like washing machines and vacuum cleaners were transforming women's lives by freeing them from their domestic chores, but nothing had as great an impact on the American way of life as the motor car. Close-knit cities and villages were being transformed into suburban sprawls where people went from place to place by car. Highways lined with gas stations criss-crossed the country, and the freedom of owning a car was becoming an integral part of American culture and the American dream. This was also to lead to the eventual demise of America's public transport network, speeded on its way by an unholy alliance between Big Oil, car manufacturers and the tyre industry.

Since the motor industry was potentially the biggest peacetime market yet for their products, the oil companies were quick to throw their weight behind the auto-makers, lobbying the government to spend hundreds of billions of dollars of public money on road building in the 20th century.

General Motors set up the innocuous-sounding United Cities Motor Transit (UCMT) company in 1932. UCMT started buying up streetcar lines in towns all over the US, tearing them down and replacing them with buses. Standard Oil of California, together with GM and Firestone, followed this up with National City Lines, which continued UCMT's work. By 1956 the once popular and convenient electric streetcar systems had been replaced by buses in a total of 45 major cities. Often the bus services were badly designed and run, perhaps deliberately, meaning that for most Americans the only option was the private motor car.

As demand for oil grew, the major oil companies vied with each other to keep developing new sources of production and to sell their product against stiff competition from the others.

The early part of the 20th century had seen the three largest companies constantly seeking to expand their market share and take over new oil reserves. Shell's chief executive, Henri Deterding, had bought up oilfields in Egypt in 1908, the Russian Ural-Caspian oilfields in 1910, the Mexican oilfields formerly belonging to Lord Cowdray of Mexican Eagle in 1919, and started large-scale exploitation of oilfields in Venezuela in 1928 and – to Standard's great displeasure – in the US.

Walter Teagle, head of Exxon, had made the unfortunate misjudgement of secretly buying out the Nobels' Russian oil interests three years after the Revolution. (Alfred Nobel, a leading scion of the Swedish Nobel family, was later to found the Nobel prize, ensuring the longevity of the family name.) Since Standard was excluded from the east Texas oil find, Teagle had also bought Humble, one of the most prosperous Texas oil companies in 1919.

Anglo-Persian (later British Petroleum, or BP) had an exclusive concession in Iran as well as a quarter share in the Iraq Petroleum Company (previously the Turkish Petroleum Company). Standard of New Jersey and Socony also had a stake in Iraq.

Outside the US, these companies usually treated the countries in which they were extracting oil as conquered territories. Oil workers from the UK or the US did skilled jobs for high wages, while the local people contributed manual labour. After the early days of prospecting and exploration, the foreign oil workers lived in luxurious compounds, apart from the local population except for those who waited on them. The oil executives drove a hard bargain with the local governments, who were likely to only see a small share of the revenues from their oil.

Small wonder that the governments and local people resented the oil companies for their colonial attitudes and for stripping them of their resources. During the interwar period, several oil-producing countries were to take a stand against Big Oil, either renegotiating for better terms or driving the Seven Sisters out altogether.

The first taste the oil companies got of this was after the 1917 Russian revolution, when the new Communist government in Moscow confiscated their Russian holdings. Even though Soviet Russia had nationalized the oil industry, confiscating the Western companies' property in the Caucasus without compensation, the oil companies were initially very confident that the regime would collapse. The Nobel and Rothschild families, however, who had spent more time on the ground in the Caucasus, and were the first to develop the region, were less optimistic, and hastened to sell their holdings while they still could. Walter Teagle, the new head of Standard Oil of New Jersey, was so confident that he paid the Nobel family $11.5 million for the Caucasian holdings, some time after the Soviets retook Azerbaijan in 1920.

Then, to the further alarm of the oil companies, Soviet oil production started, flooding the European market with cheap oil. It was becoming apparent that the Soviets were there to stay. Despite the antipathy for the Soviets among the often aristocratic Western governments and business elites, in 1921 the Anglo-Soviet trade agreement was signed, and three years later Britain gave the USSR diplomatic recognition. Lord Curzon, the British Foreign Secretary, backed away from shaking hands with the Soviet Finance Minister, Leonid Krasin, only to be told sternly by Prime Minister Lloyd George to be a "gentleman". (Yergin, p.239)

The oil companies were just as anti-Soviet as Lord Curzon, and in July 1922 this led to one of the first attempts at collective action by the big companies. Teagle was joined by Deterding of Royal Dutch Shell, which had also lost a substantial investment in Russia, and together they created the "Front Uni", a bloc of around 14 companies that refused to trade with Soviet Russia unless it paid compensation for their lost oil holdings.

This became a salutary lesson for the oil industry on how far they could trust each other. Despite the supposedly united front, one company after another was seduced by the prospect of cheap Russian oil into signing a secret supply deal with the Russians.

Two years after the Front Uni was created, Teagle and Deterding met again and agreed to form a joint company that would negotiate with the Soviet government for a long-term contract. Negotiations between the Soviet government and the Liechtenstein-based company continued for two years.

Then there was another abrupt change of heart on the part of the oil companies, and Teagle and Deterding broke off negotiations. This was typical of the oil companies' mixed feelings about Russia. On the one hand they were furious at the confiscation of the oilfields and resented paying for oil they viewed as their own; on the other, Russia's oil was very cheap.

Deterding's attitude was compounded by his recent marriage to a White Russian woman. Just after the Front Uni had published its agreed policy, Deterding had happily double-crossed his cronies and signed a secret deal for the supply of Russian oil for Royal Dutch Shell to market in the Far East, where it was competing with Mobil. After his marriage, in a sudden about face, he wrote to Rockefeller, the grand old man of the oil industry, describing the Soviet regime as "anti-Christ" and asking Rockefeller if he wanted "bloodstained profits" for Standard Oil.

Meanwhile, cheap Russian oil continued to be placed on the

European market, compounding the problem of glut as supply contracted at the onset of the Great Depression. The failed Front Uni had shown the oil companies they if they were to find a common solution to the drastically falling prices, they would have to find a much more effective way to work together.

The Achnacarry Agreement

By the mid-1920s, it became apparent to Teagle at least that the intense competition between the leading oil companies was driving down prices and eating away at their profits, just like in the chaotic early days of the industry before Rockefeller's monopoly. Deterding too had for some years been trying to introduce some kind of cooperation between the top companies.

In August 1928, Teagle initiated a secret conference to discuss the oil industry. Despite their best efforts at secrecy, word of a mysterious gathering at Achnacarry Castle in the Scottish Highlands leaked out in the press. Owned by the Chief of the Cameron clan, once described as "fiercer than fierce itself", the castle had been lent to Deterding for the start of the grouse shooting season. There, Deterding was joined by Teagle and Anglo-Persian's head, Sir John Cadman.

It was an ill-assorted gathering. As well as representatives from Gulf and other companies, Deterding had brought along his new White Russian wife and her two nieces, who teased Teagle's German adviser Riedermann and played practical jokes on him. An irritated Teagle described the hunting at Achnacarry as "lousy", and criticized Cadman's fishing skills. (Gibb & Wall, p.261)

But the real business of the meeting wasn't hunting or fishing; it was in effect a "peace conference" between the oil barons. By the end of their stay, they had drawn up a 17-page document, the "Pool Association", later known as "As Is" or the "Achnacarry Agreement". This did, in effect, divide up the world's oil markets and resources between the major companies. It was based on the "As Is" principle – the competing companies would accept "their present volume of business and their proportion of any future increase in production."

The Achnacarry Agreement was, in effect, the greatest cartel the world had ever known, and its existence was not confirmed until the US Federal Trade Commission's report in 1952.

The loss of their oil interests in Russia had been a serious blow to the leading oil companies, and they were determined to hold their ground against challenges both at home and abroad.

Even after the Achnacarry Agreement was signed, it was not always easy for the Seven Sisters to get their way. During the 1920s and 1930s there emerged a number of challenges to their supremacy – from the myriad small producers in the US who chipped away at their markets during the Great Depression, and from radical new governments in states like Mexico and Bolivia, who sought to wrest control of the oil industry away from its foreign exploiters.

Nor were relations always harmonious among the Seven Sisters themselves. They continued to jockey for position where this could be done without being penalized under the secret cartel agreement. In 1928, around the time the Achnacarry Agreement was signed, Standard of New Jersey and Royal Dutch Shell were effectively at war, supporting opposing sides in the war between Bolivia and Paraguay over the supposedly oil-rich Chaco Boreal region (see Chapter 3).

During the negotiations leading up to the Red Line Agreement that shared out the oil resources in Iraq, both the UK and France had clung jealously to their shares in the Turkish Petroleum Company, and the US government had acted equally forcefully in order to secure a part of the company for its own oil producers. As a result, both Standard of New Jersey and Socony also took a stake in the company developing the Iraqi oilfields.

Before the Iraqi oilfields could be developed, the British army had to put down unrest among the Iraqi population, who had hoped to gain full independence after the disintegration of the Ottoman Empire.

Instead, Iraq became a British protectorate. Local outbreaks of violence against the British who occupied the country had already been recorded before the mandate was announced. After it was announced in late May 1920, Iraqi leaders met with Woodrow Wilson, but the US leader dismissed them as "ungrateful politicians". Shirazi, the grand Mujtahid (religious scholar) of Karbala issued a fatwa against the British and called for a jihad to drive them out of Iraq. Insurrections spread from Mosul through to the south, and the entire country was in a state of anarchy for three months, until the British managed to take back control after a bombing campaign, which included the use of poison gas.

This had been supported by Winston Churchill, by then Britain's Secretary for War and Air. Churchill was interested in the possibility of using new technologies to keep down the cost of policing the British Empire. In February 1920, just before the Arab uprising, Churchill wrote to Sir Hugh Trenchard, the pioneer of air warfare, asking if he could take control of Iraq and use "some kind of asphyxiating bombs calculated to cause disablement of some kind but not death" against the resistance.

"I do not understand this squeamishness about the use of gas. I am strongly in favour of using poison gas against uncivilised tribes," he said. (Gilbert, p.424-5)

Most of the British Cabinet were opposed to the use of gas, especially after it had been used to such devastating effect during World War I, and argued that the proposed gas would permanently damage people's eyesight and "kill children and sickly persons, more especially as the people against whom we intend to use it have no medical knowledge with which to supply antidotes." However, the gas attacks went ahead.

After the uprising was suppressed, the British put in place a provisional Arab government under the British High Commissioner for Iraq.

The British were also facing challenges in Persia – effectively, modern Iran.

The Shah of Persia had sought British protection against the expanding Russian Empire back in the 19th century, in return favouring British commercial interests. Feudal and backward looking, Persia would not have been able to resist the Russian army alone.

The Anglo-Persian Oil Company (later BP) was granted an oil concession in 1902. When the British government took over Anglo-Persian in 1914, the company also signed an agreement with the British Admiralty, guaranteeing the supply of oil to the Admiralty for 30 years at fixed prices. After the agreement, whatever the British government might claim, Anglo-Persian was not an oil company like any other; maximizing profits was not its sole aim. The agreement with the Admiralty was to have a significant effect on the company's revenues, which was a sore point for the Persians, who were receiving a part of the revenues in return for allowing Anglo-Persian to extract its oil.

The fact that Anglo-Persian was perceived as an arm of the British government was also an increasingly sore point for Persia. The Anglo-Persian Agreement proposed by Britain in 1919 would have made Persia a *de facto* British protectorate. Although the then Prime Minister Vosuq od-Dowleh and two members of his cabinet received financial incentives from the British to support the agreement, the Majis (parliament) refused to sign.

In 1920, the Persian government in Tehran made its first protest against the British domination of its oil industry, opening negotiations to increase the royalties paid to it by Anglo-Persian. In December 1920, Anglo-Persian agreed to pay Persia £1 million in settlement of Persia's claims. Then two months later, in February 1921, Reza Khan, an officer in the Persian Cossacks Brigade, together with Sayyid Zia ad Din Tabatabai, a prominent Iranian journalist, marched into Tehran and seized power, with the backing of the British government.

A new regime, under Reza Shah Pahlavi, came to power after the military coup of 1925, and as well as starting to modernize the country, it reopened talks on the revision of the Anglo-Persian concession in 1928. The Shah took a much stronger line against the British than his predecessors. He started by questioning the legality of the 1920 agreement, pointing out that it had not been passed by the Persian parliament. His chief negotiator in London, Court Minister Abdol-Hoseyn Timurtash, offered Anglo-Persian chairman Sir John Cadman a new 60-year concession in return for a reduction of the area of the Anglo-Persian concession, cancellation of the exclusive right of transportation, and certain other conditions.

Cadman and the British government assumed that Reza Shah Pahlavi and Timurtash were after money, and were optimistic that a compromise could be agreed. However, Reza Shah Pahlavi was also motivated by a desire to strengthen his own position by attacking rival power bases in the country. Just as he tried to undermine the clergy, he also wanted to diminish Anglo-Persian's power.

As Cadman and the British government considered Timurtash's proposals, the court minister returned to Tehran and stage-managed a visit by the Shah and his high officials to the oilfields. There, Reza Shah Pahlavi broadcast a cautionary message to Cadman: "The authorities of the company must know that neither the Iranian government nor the Iranian people agree with the D'Arcy concession ... Now, I explicitly notify the authorities of the company that they must rectify the matter and if they do not give it due attention, they will be responsible for any action which might result. No more can Iran tolerate the enormous profits from its oil going into pockets of foreigners while at the same time being dispossessed of its oil wealth."

Negotiations continued for several years, with Cadman making small compromises, while Timurtash continued to push for a better deal for Persia, and for Anglo-Persian to reveal its profits to the Persian government – a condition that the oil company vehemently opposed. Even when the Persian government was in severe financial straits, Timurtash held out against the idea of extending Anglo-Persian's concession, comparing the concession (which was not due to expire until 1960) to "an old and sick father who cannot be got rid of. We have to wait until he dies…" (Report of the meeting held in Sa'd-Abad on August 30th, 1931, dated September 5th, 1931, BP H10/174B)

When an agreement was drafted in 1932, the two parties hit a further snag. The agreement had been based on Cadman's estimation of Anglo-Persian's royalties for the year 1931, which was an extremely low figure, around one-third of the royalties received in 1929 and 1930, mainly due to the effect of the Great Depression. After Cadman refused to back down in 1932, Persia cancelled the concession altogether.

In an atmosphere of extreme tension, Cadman flew to Tehran to negotiate directly with the Shah.

Inside the royal palace, the Shah told Cadman that he would not let the Anglo-Persia officials leave the country until a new concession had been reached. Cadman had the backing of Anglo-Persian's majority shareholder, the British government, and to illustrate how close relations were to a breakdown he had his pilot taxi the plane around the airport in full view of the palace. After two days of meetings, agreement was reached on a new 60-year concession, but on much better terms for the Persians.

As well as receiving cheaper oil for the population, it was also now possible for Persia to offer non-British companies concessions in areas outside Anglo-Persian's control. Although through its tough negotiating Anglo-Persian had secured a good deal for itself, it had also created a high level of resentment against both the company itself and against the British government. Tehran allowed American companies to start drilling in the east of the country, well away from the British, but the deal fell through after the Americans found better prospects elsewhere.

Nazi Germany was also very interested in the Persian oilfields, and the resentment towards Anglo-Persian was certainly a large factor in pushing Persia, which was renamed "Iran" on March 21st, 1935, onto the axis side at the start of World War II. The harsh treatment of the Iraqi resistance, and the blatant exploitation of their natural resources, undoubtedly sowed the seeds for the sympathy that a significant proportion of Iraqis had for the Nazis.

Chapter Three: Riches and Revolution in Latin America

In Latin America, as in the Middle East and the Caucasus, oil companies have had to contend with the often turbulent politics of their host countries. Revolution, military coups, civil and interstate wars have all taken their toll on the Latin American continent since the early 20th century. Just as in Russia after 1917, the threat of expropriation was ever present in Mexico, Bolivia and other Latin American countries. The oil companies have struggled to keep their operations going through social unrest and political turmoil, and to stay in favour with the ruling regimes. But as in the Middle East and other oil-producing regions, the presence of oil has often been responsible for creating that turbulence.

Latin America was one of the earliest regions where large-scale oil exploitation took place. Mexico was already an important supplier of oil, mainly to the US, by the outbreak of the World War I. Venezuela, where Shell struck a major field in 1928, has been one of the world's leading oil producers ever since. Argentina, Brazil, Colombia, Ecuador, Peru and the islands of Trinidad and Tobago are all oil producers.

In most of these countries, the major oil companies operated in a very uncertain environment. In Bolivia, for example, the oil industry has several times been nationalized and then privatized, a cause of great insecurity to the oil companies. Seeking a secure economic environment and freedom from the threat of violence, they have tended to cooperate with repressive regimes such as General Gomez's in Venezuela, which has earned them the hatred of many local people.

Oil companies also sought to influence the political destinies of the countries in which they operated. In Mexico, Standard Oil is alleged to have backed the revolution against Portofino Diaz after the Mexican dictator appeared to favour British oil companies. The Huerta rebellion in 1923 is said to have been supported by the British companies Royal Dutch Shell and the Pearson Group.

In the Gran Chaco war of 1932–5, Bolivia and Paraguay went to war over the supposedly oil-rich Chaco Boreal region. Bolivia used a line of credit from Standard Oil of Bolivia to supply its army, while Paraguay is alleged to have received financial support from Royal Dutch Shell.

As well as the oil companies, the governments of both the US and UK had a strong interest in the outcome of all conflicts in oil-producing Latin America. After heavy lobbying from Standard, the US came close to going to war with Mexico in the early 1930s when the left-wing government nationalized the oil industry.

A similar situation followed in Bolivia. After the disastrous Gran Chaco war, a group of military officers staged a coup in 1936, introducing a military socialist regime under German Busch Becerra. In 1937, Bolivia charged that Standard Oil of New Jersey had defrauded the Bolivian government. Standard Oil had first entered Bolivia in 1920, buying a concession to explore and exploit the Andean foothill zone in the south east of the country, where it discovered several small oilfields. After the coup, Bolivia cancelled Standard's drilling rights and confiscated its facilities, to form the national Yacimientos Petrolíferos Fiscales. However, despite pressure from the oil industry, the US avoided military intervention and only put moderate pressure on Bolivia, by withholding loans and technical assistance. Aside from its oil reserves, Bolivia was of relatively little interest compared to Mexico since it did not share a border with the US.

Oil Companies in Revolutionary Mexico

The oil companies' rapacious drive for profits also contributed to the revolution in Mexico, one of the first countries outside the US where Standard Oil became active. Standard extracted oil from the estates of wealthy landowners, then shipping it to the US for refining and reselling to Mexico at a profit of up to 600 per cent. The firm's first real rival in Mexico was a British engineer, Weetman Pearson (later Lord Cowdray), who began selling Mexican Eagle branded oil in 1908 in alliance with Royal Dutch Shell, with the permission of Mexican dictator Portofino Diaz.

At this time popular opposition to Diaz was rising. The ruler of one of the world's longest-lasting dictatorships, Diaz held back economic development and protected the rights of the small urban elite and landowning class against those of the poor that made up the majority of the population. By 1910, the average Mexican was worse off than in 1810. Angered that Diaz appeared to be favouring British oil interests, Standard allegedly threw its weight behind his rival for the presidency, Francesco Madero, who, despite being born into one of the country's richest families, campaigned passionately for peasant rights and freedoms.

The extent to which Standard Oil supported Madero is still unclear, but it is said to have provided the revolutionary leader with considerable financial support. This was the accusation made in Ferdinand Lundberg's book, *America's 60 Families*. It is, however, likely that the revolution would have succeeded even without Standard's support, since Diaz had become very unpopular with the Mexican population. Although the economy had become more competitive, life expectancy was under 30 years, and a full 16 per cent of the population were homeless.

In a plan drafted in St Louis in the US, and widely distributed in Mexico, Madero called on the Mexican people to rise up against the government on November 20th, 1910. Madero and a small band of rebels entered Mexico, but turned back on finding no large-scale revolt against the government.

The revolution continued to gather momentum, however. Emiliano Zapata, the peasant leader, had recruited a peasant army in the province of Morelos. In January 1911, an insurrection broke out in the northern region of Chihuahua, led by Pascual Orozco, a local merchant, and Francisco "Pancho" Villa. Madero returned to Mexico to lead the revolution. After several months of fighting, Diaz resigned on May 25th, 1911.

The 1910–11 revolution was just the first in two decades of upheaval that would last until the Institutional Revolutionary Party (PRI) took power in 1929. Madero's rule was short-lived. In 1913, he was overthrown and then assassinated by General Victoriano Huerta. "General Obregon [who had been elected in 1920] charged that the Huerta rebellion [led by Adolfo de la Huerta] of 1923 against himself was backed by British oil interests, particularly the Mexican Eagle Company of the Royal Dutch Shell combine, and it is said that an

American oil baron, E.L. Doheny, lent Obregon five million dollars to suppress the revolt," writes Eugene Staley. (Staley, p.205) There is little hard evidence available to prove or disprove this theory, but the British immediately recognized the new president.

When Victoriano Huerta was forced out of office three years later, Lundberg claims that the new president Venustiano Carranza took office "on behalf of the National City Bank of New York." (Lundberg, p.125) (The National City Bank was a Rockefeller institution.)

While relations between the US and Mexico were strained throughout the revolutionary period, this was mainly due to fears that rebellion and instability would spread north across the border. US policy does not appear to have been influenced by the oil industry; in fact the US government often sided with the British against Standard Oil. The US ambassador was against Madero because he was a friend of the Guggenheims, who had extensive silver mining interests in Mexico. The UK, too, was interested in Mexico, not only to protect its oil interests, but because it had feared for over half a century that the US was planning to establish a protectorate over Mexico.

Most foreign companies in Mexico suffered damage to their business and property during the period 1910 to 1917, when no government was firmly in control of the country and foreign interests could not be well protected.

The foreign oil operators feared damage to their interests in the north east, but were less affected than they had anticipated due to their location in the Tampico-Tuxpán area, far from most military activity. Indeed, they may even have benefited because it was hard for the tenuous government 200 miles away in Mexico City to enforce taxation or corporate law. With much of the country in turmoil, control of foreign enterprises was not a priority. The oil-producing region was controlled instead by the regional leader Manuel Pelaez, whose driving motivation was money. He was therefore happy to sell protection to the oil companies.

Before the revolution, Mexico had been the most popular overseas destination for US oil companies. After the US, Mexico had been the world's no. 1 producer, with Standard Oil, Pan American Petroleum and Mexican Eagle vying for supremacy.

After several years of turmoil and rapidly changing regimes, in 1917 President Venustiano Carranza introduced the new Mexican

Constitution. The foreign oil companies were outraged by Article 27, which restored the traditional principle that below-ground resources (including, of course, oil) belonged to the nation. Based on old Spanish law, which stated that below-ground resources belonged to the crown, this had been abolished by President Diaz in order to encourage foreign investment. The new Constitution stated that:

> In the Nation is vested the direct ownership of all natural resources of the continental shelf and the submarine shelf of the islands; of all minerals or substances, which in veins, ledges, masses or ore pockets, form deposits of a nature distinct from the components of the earth itself, such as the minerals from which industrial metals and metalloids are extracted; deposits of precious stones, rock-salt and the deposits of salt formed by sea water; products derived from the decomposition of rocks, when subterranean works are required for their extraction; mineral or organic deposits of materials susceptible of utilization as fertilizers; solid mineral fuels; petroleum and all solid, liquid, and gaseous hydrocarbons; and the space above the national territory to the extent and within the terms fixed by international law.

The law did not ban foreign companies outright from involvement in the exploitation of Mexico's natural resources. Although only Mexicans and Mexican companies had the right to obtain mining concessions, Article 27 of the Constitution continued, "The State may grant the same right to foreigners, provided they agree before the Ministry of Foreign Relations to consider themselves as nationals in respect to such property, and bind themselves not to invoke the protection of their governments in matters relating thereto; under penalty, in case of non-compliance with this agreement, of forfeiture of the property acquired to the Nation."

By 1920, indeed, the Mexican government was edging towards a compromise with the foreign oil companies, since it needed their financial backing and expertise to make the oil industry profitable, at least until more local engineers could be trained.

However, the US oil companies active in Mexico, led by Edward Doheny of Pan American Petroleum, were lobbying the US government to intervene in Mexico. Even with the more conciliatory attitude of the Mexican government, Doheny and his cohorts were afraid of losing their oil interests in case of a change of policy, and were unwilling to invest without a better guarantee of security.

Edward Doheny was the ambitious son of an Irish labourer. After a failed mining venture, he was close to destitute, with a wife and young daughter to support. One day he noticed a wagon hauling blocks of a greasy, brownish substance past his hotel in the former gold rush town of Los Angeles. Catching up with the driver, Doheny discovered a hole dug in a nearby park, with the tarry substance welling out of it. He scraped together money to lease an adjacent plot of land and set up a derrick, discovering oil in 1893. Doheny, creator of the Los Angeles oil boom, went on to invest heavily in the "Golden Lane" area near the Gulf of Mexico.

The largest US investor in Mexico, Doheny was at the forefront of oilmen lobbying Woodrow Wilson's government to intervene in Mexico. During the period of unrest from 1910 to 1919, several hundred American citizens had been killed in Mexico and thousands had lost money. However, by 1919 Carranza (under pressure from the US State Department) had promised to protect the lives and property of Americans in Mexico. He said further that there was no intention of confiscating present holdings, but only of ensuring that from 1917 onwards natural resources would contribute to the national tax base.

This was not good enough for the oil companies, who were very keen to start exploring new fields in Mexico, where only a small number of the oil deposits had yet been exploited. They argued that their only motive was to protect their current holdings, and insisted that they were not seeking new concessions. They also claimed that the old Spanish laws did not apply to oil since it had never been mentioned as a property of the government. Most of the US and British oilmen in Mexico were afraid that the government was planning to make Article 27 retroactive.

In the US, the oil companies and other businesses involved in Mexico continued to lobby the government to take a tougher line with the Mexican government. They were calling for military intervention and the armed defence of foreign investments in the country. They also supported the traditional Mexican upper class, which was deeply resented by most of the Mexican population. As well as armed intervention, the powerful business lobby argued that the US should create a buffer state between the US and Mexico, to be made up of the slice of Mexico between the Rio Grande and the 22nd parallel.

The lobbyists won the support of Senator Albert B. Fall of New Mexico, and several other US senators. Fall considered the annexation of Mexico, but decided it would be preferable to keep the entire country as a peaceful buffer state, under US control, protecting the US from Latin America. In 1917, Fall called for a 500,000 strong army to be mustered, "ostensibly for the policing of Mexico, or for the invasion of that country."

By mid-1919 the country was divided over whether to go to war with Mexico. The oilmen were even more vociferous than Fall, launching a propaganda campaign to get the American people on their side. Newspapers ran reports of the chaos under President Carranza. Opposing them were the anti-interventionists, people like Samuel Guy Inman, a missionary and writer who published *Intervention in Mexico* in 1919, to very favourable reviews.

On June 24th Senator Fall proposed a resolution to break off diplomatic relations with Mexico. However, the then President Woodrow Wilson was a great exponent of self-determination, and opposed to intervention. He spoke out against Fall's resolution and it was abandoned. Instead, a subcommittee of the Senate Foreign Relations Committee was set up to investigate Mexican affairs, under the chairmanship of Senator Fall. In addition to Fall, committee members included Frank Brandegee, known as an ultranationalist firmly in favour of intervention.

When Inman appeared to present his evidence against intervention, he was continually interrupted and ridiculed by Fall. By contrast, the committee members treated Doheny as one of them when his turn came to give evidence. Not long after the investigation, Inman's book began to disappear mysteriously from bookshops. Unable to discover the cause from his publisher, the Associated Press, who was also reluctant to put out a second issue, Inman later heard rumours that the book had been bought off the market by oil interests, probably at Doheny's instigation.

A few months later, however, illegal collusion between Fall and Doheny in the US oilfields was discovered and the senator's committee was discredited.

The matter of intervention appeared to have been – temporarily at least – laid to rest. Relations between the oil companies and the governments of Mexico and the US warmed slightly as the situation in Mexico stabilized. When tensions rose again in 1927, they were defused before the US could decide to intervene militarily. In Mexico, though, there were very real fears of an invasion, and the then President Plutarco Elias Alles had ordered General Lazaro Cardenas (head of the armed forces in the oil-producing region) to be ready to set fire to the oilfields should the US invade.

In the mid-1930s things started to change. Lazaro Cardenas, now the country's president, was a puritanical, left-wing, nationalistic man. Having served as the military commander in the oil region, he was acquainted with the oil companies and their practices, and intensely disliked their attitude to Mexico and the Mexicans, considering that they treated the country as a colonized territory. American and British oil workers in Mexico lived in comfortable houses where their wives and children were waited on by Mexican servants. They played golf and cricket on their private grounds, and refreshed themselves from drinking fountains labelled "No Mexicans".

Lord Cowdray of the Pearson Group was the exception to this. A Yorkshireman who had turned a small building firm into one of the world's largest contractors, he had a strong social conscience and built schools, hospitals and missions in the areas in which he operated. He also earned the respect of his workers by being willing to get his hands dirty, and once nearly died working alongside his men in a tunnel under the Hudson river in the US.

While the men on the ground in the oil companies understood the difference between the Cardenas regime and those of his predecessors, where the oil companies had been able to use bribes to get their own way, their bosses in New York or London did not. Deterding ignored the local manager of Royal Dutch Shell when he tried to explain the situation, and branded Cardenas "half a Bolshevik".

The oil companies fought against nationalization as hard as they could. In 1935, Herbert Sein, a former member of the Mexican Consulate in New York, gave evidence to a Senate subcommittee investigating the oil industry in Mexico. Sein testified that American oil companies had paid bribes to bandits in the Mexican oilfields. They had, according to Sein, done this "with the full knowledge and even with the approval of the State Department." (*New York Times*, February

28th, 1926) Sein also reported that Edward Doheny too had admitted that his companies had paid bribes to bandits. Doheny had confirmed that the US State Department was aware of the bribery, and had even suggested it.

President Cardenas set up his own investigation into the Mexican oil industry, under the economist Jesus Silva Herzog, which reported back with the news that the oil companies were draining Mexico's resources while contributing nothing back in terms of economic development. With a wave of public sentiment against the (especially US) oil companies, combined with pressure from the unions to his political left, Cardenas, who had in any case intended to extend government control over the sector, declared in March 1938 that he was going to nationalize the oil industry. It would be better to destroy the oilfields altogether than allow them to hold back national development, he told his cabinet before making the public announcement. The news was greeted with a six-hour parade through the streets of Mexico City.

The oil companies once again lobbied their respective governments for intervention, but times had changed. Although the British government demanded that Mexico return the properties to their former owners – leading to an abrupt severing of diplomatic relations – in the US, intervention on behalf of the oil industry ran counter to the new climate in Washington, with President Franklin D. Roosevelt's New Deal and the Good Neighbor policy, under which the US was taking a more friendly and less interventionist line towards Latin America. Although some economic sanctions were put in place rather half-heartedly, Washington did not want to break with one of the world's leading and most conveniently located oil producers just when the dark clouds of war were once again gathering on the horizon.

Venezuela: The Darling of Oil Companies

After the difficulties in Mexico began, the oil companies cast around for a new source of oil, and they lighted on Venezuela. In the early 1920s it was still not certain whether exploration in Venezuela would be anything more than an expensive mistake. However, the country did have a pitch lake similar to the one near which Drake had started the first modern drilling operation some decades before, and a local drilling industry had been started in 1878, south of Lake Maracaibo.

Several of the Seven Sisters, led by Royal Dutch Shell, which had been introduced to the country by Calouste Gulbenkian – "Mr Five Percent" – just before World War I, were carrying out oil exploration expeditions in Venezuela.

Almost as important as the expectation of large finds was the regime of General Juan Vicente Gomez, which was extremely friendly to the oil companies. Gomez, who ruled Venezuela from 1908 to 1935, was originally from the *caudillo* class, which had ruled almost feudally over the disparate regions of Venezuela. Said to have fathered 97 illegitimate children, Gomez ruled through a tight network of family and cronies, the "Gomecistas". He dressed in a copy of US President Theodore Roosevelt's hunting gear until the start of the World War I, when he abruptly switched to a copy of the Kaiser's uniform.

When Gomez took power, he set about modernizing the country, not from a desire to better its impoverished population, but because he recognized that the only way to attain the wealth that he craved was to make his country rich. Gomez was cruel, cunning and almost illiterate, but he had an instinctive grasp of how to do this. He knew that Venezuela needed money to develop economically, and that this money could come from oil. Despite his desire for absolute personal power, he also knew that foreign companies would be more likely to invest in Venezuela if he could offer them a stable environment.

Encouraged both by Gomez's regime and by Royal Dutch Shell's obvious faith in the country, other companies, including Standard Oil of New Jersey, started buying up concessions in Venezuela.

Progress was slow. In the Venezuelan jungles there were no roads and barely any maps. Geologists travelling in the jungle by mule or canoe fell victim to tropical diseases or the arrows of hostile local Indians. In the early days of the Venezuelan oil industry, oilmen had to prepare as if for battle. Shell oilmen wrapped the cabins of their tractors in several layers of thick cloth to protect their drivers from arrows, while Standard Oil of New Jersey ordered all the trees to be felled within an arrow's range of their works.

Their efforts paid off in 1922, when Royal Dutch Shell's Barroso well in the La Rosa field on the shores of Lake Maracaibo started gushing out over 100,000 barrels per day, starting a frenzy of investment. Soon over 100, mostly American, companies had entered the market. By 1929, Venezuela was the largest oil producer in the world after the

US. As well as Royal Dutch Shell, Standard Oil of Indiana (Amoco) and Gulf Oil of Pittsburgh were among the major investors.

Gomez too was to benefit financially from the oil boom, mainly through the Compania-Venezuolana de Petroleo, a dummy company through which he and his cronies channelled oil money to themselves.

Gomez's regime, however harsh it was on his own people, was welcomed and supported by the foreign oil companies. They never had to fear that their holdings would be confiscated, or terms more favourable to the population would be introduced. Fears among Western oil companies only arose in Gomez's extreme old age. Worried about how Gomez's death would affect them, Amoco subsidiary Lago built its export refinery in Aruba, a Dutch island off the coast of Venezuela, rather than on the mainland. Royal Dutch Shell followed suit, building its refinery on the nearby island of Dutch Curacao.

After Gomez's death, the next two Venezuelan presidents were also Andean generals, though more liberal than Gomez, and it was not until the October Revolution in 1945, when a group of younger army officers joined with the populist Democratic Action Party to stage a coup, that there was a significant handover of power.

The Sisters at War: The Gran Chaco

The discovery of potentially huge oil reserves in Venezuela encouraged both the Seven Sisters and national leaders to expect further finds in Latin America. Until 1928 it would have been hard to imagine anyone going to war over the Chaco Boreal. A region of land around 100,000 square miles in size, the Chaco Boreal is divided between Paraguay, Bolivia and Argentina. While cattle can be grazed in the savannah to the east of the Paraguay River, most of the Chaco Boreal is arid, and among the hottest parts of the South American continent. Bordered by the Andes, the western region is a flat plain with little vegetation and almost no potable water; this semi-desert gives way to an almost impassable jungle of thornbrushes and dense quebracho trees. The few inhabitants of this inhospitable terrain were mostly Guarani Indians, who had braved the tropical diseases and deadly insects to eke out a living from cattle grazing and tannin extracted from the quebracho trees.

In the lower regions of the Chaco, Paraguay had started to produce mate, a type of tea that was also very popular in neighbouring Argentina. Bolivia, however, had taken no active interest in the region until 1928, when oil was discovered in the far west, in the foothills of the Andes, territory that had been allocated to Paraguay. Suddenly it looked as if an oil boom was about to start in the worthless Gran Chaco, and Paraguay and Bolivia speculated optimistically about the oil that might lie elsewhere under the Chaco plains.

The oil directly beneath the Gran Chaco was not the only reason for the mounting tensions between the neighbouring countries. Bolivia already had its own oil reserves to exploit, but after the War of the Pacific in 1883, it had to give up its entire Pacific coastline to Chile. Rather than shipping oil through Argentina, and losing a large share of its profits to foreign oil companies, Bolivia desperately needed access to the sea and its own pipelines.

Paraguay too had lost territory, and was determined not to give up the Chaco Boreal. When it first won independence from Spain in 1811, Paraguay was one of the larger South American states, but it too had lost over half its territory to Argentina, Brazil and Uruguay during the War of the Triple Alliance (1864–70). Although it had better access to the sea than Bolivia (via Argentina to the Atlantic), Paraguay was extremely impoverished and saw the oil find as its best hope for the future.

Border hostilities started between the two countries in late 1928, when Bolivian armed forces tried to strike through to the Paraguay River, which would give it access to the sea. Paraguay retaliated by destroying a fort on the Bolivian border.

After failed negotiations in the League of Nations, in June 1932, a large Bolivian consignment made a surprise attack on the fort of Vangaurdia, and full-scale war began. Bolivia was acting not only on its own initiative, but was actively encouraged by American oil companies already operating in the country, led by Standard Oil of New Jersey.

Although both sides were held back by the difficult terrain, almost impassable forests, lack of water and threat of disease, Bolivia started the war with a considerable military advantage. In 1930, it had spent the proceeds from its mines and a line of credit from Standard Oil of Bolivia to agree a major arms deal with Vickers. From Vickers, Bolivia had bought several tanks, mountain artillery, machine-guns and six

Vickers Type 143 Bolivian Scout aeroplanes, giving it undoubted supremacy in the air.

Meanwhile, Paraguay's army was ill-equipped and very short of money, although it is alleged to have received some support from Royal Dutch Shell, who was active in the country and didn't want to lose its concessions to Standard.

It was, some observers claimed later, a war of engineers, and it is certainly true that engineers played a vital role on both sides, not in warfare but in cutting roads through the dense forests, and most of all in locating water sources and digging wells – not for oil but for drinking water.

On the other hand, where military equipment was concerned, Bolivia's sophisticated tanks, planes and artillery counted for very little, since they were not at all suitable for the Chaco's terrain. The tanks in particular were useless unless roads were cut for them, and stuck altogether without supplies of increasingly scarce petrol.

The national morale within the two countries also counted strongly towards Paraguay's eventual victory. Apart from the government and the oil industry, few Bolivians had any interest in the Gran Chaco. The Indians and other indigenous people were conscripted to fight for a cause they had no belief in, for leaders they had no identification with. In Paraguay at that time, the population was more cohesive and ethnically mixed. They were also fighting for a part of their own country. While Bolivia relied on conscription, Paraguayans voluntarily signed up to defend their territory.

By the end of the war, in 1935, Paraguay had arrived in the Bolivian oilfields, at the fortress of Villa Montes, and had conquered all the disputed territory in the Gran Chaco; 80,000–100,000 people had died in Latin America's bloodiest 20th-century conflict. In the harsh Chaco climate, more soldiers died from malaria and other tropical diseases than in battle.

The peace treaty signed in 1938 gave Paraguay permanent control of three-quarters of the Chaco Boreal. Ironically, when the oil companies that had supported the war eventually gained concessions in Paraguay and started to explore the Chaco region, they found no significant oil deposits. The war appeared to have been fought for nothing.

Violence in the oil-producing countries of Latin America would continue for the rest of the 20th century, and still continues today. The US government and Big Oil wanted to ensure that they would keep their access to Latin American oilfields, despite the popular left-wing opposition to many US-backed regimes, and the perceived 'exploitation' by foreign multinationals. This resentment is kept alive by such scandals as the killing of 18 Colombian civilians in 1998 by a helicopter gunship allegedly paid for by the US company Occidental Petroleum, and ChevronTexaco's pollution of the Amazon rainforest. This will be explored in more detail in Chapter 9. Several major oil companies are still controversially paying private security firms and funding national armies or local militias to protect their operations. And there are strong indications that the US's current financial and military involvement in Colombia (see Chapter 8) is motivated as much to obtain oil as to prevent drug trafficking.

Chapter Four: The Thirst for Oil in Modern Warfare

In 1939, around 80 per cent of the world's known oil resources were located in countries controlled by or friendly to the US, Britain or the USSR, who would emerge victorious after six years of war. Oil – or the lack of it – often proved a deciding factor in World War II battles, from the siege of Stalingrad to the Battle of the Bulge. Yet several of the major US oil companies, in particular Standard Oil of New Jersey (Exxon) and Texaco, appeared to operate as a law unto themselves. They continued supplying oil to Germany and Japan during the war, and honoured their agreements with enemy nationals, weakening their own countries and probably prolonging the bloodshed. Meanwhile, behind the scenes of conflict, even when the war was at its height, the UK and US were jockeying for position in the oilfields of Saudi Arabia.

It also seemed that the allies did not take full advantage of the huge disparity in access to oil. Given that the axis powers, Germany, Japan and Italy, were so poor in oil, could an oil embargo not have been used to delay the onset of war? Why was it America did not deny oil supplies, and the UK and France not use their military and naval might to prevent Germany, Japan and Italy gaining access to this vital resource?

Abyssinia Betrayed

The first test of will came in 1935, when Benito Mussolini, Italy's fascist dictator, ordered his army to invade Abyssinia (now Ethiopia). The invasion followed a border dispute between Eritrea, already an Italian colony, and Ethiopia, but Mussolini's real objective was to create a new Roman empire in North Africa. Abyssinia was the perfect target for invasion. It would create a land bridge between Italy's other African territories, Libya in the north and Eritrea and Italian Somaliland in the Horn of Africa, and provide Italy with coal, gold, platinum and a small amount of oil. Conquering Abyssinia would also settle old scores. The failed colonization attempt in 1896 and Italy's defeat at the battle of Adowa still rankled.

After he took power in 1922, Mussolini crushed all attempts at resistance in Italy's African colonies. Troops were first sent to put down an uprising in Somaliland, then in 1929 the Fascists began a brutal campaign in Libya, killing many civilians and incarcerating others in concentration camps while their villages were torched.

A border dispute at the Wal Wal oasis on the border with Eritrea, in which over 100 Abyssinians and about 30 African soldiers under Italian command were killed, provided Mussolini with the excuse he needed to attack Abyssinia. In 1896 Abyssinia had been victorious. But in 1935, Italy struck with tanks, planes, armoured trucks and mustard gas against Abyssinian soldiers on foot and armed with rifles and machine-guns. Provided Italy had enough oil to keep its army moving, the Abyssinian people had little chance to defend themselves.

Abyssinia's emperor, Haile Selassie, appealed to the League of Nations, the international organization founded in 1919 in the hope that a global tragedy on the scale of World War I would never reoccur. Through collective security, it would protect the rights of smaller nations to self-determination, and settle international disputes with diplomacy rather than aggression.

By 1935, however, the League's reputation was somewhat tarnished. The US's isolationist policy at that time had led it to shun the League, and Japan had abruptly quit after criticism of its invasion of northern China. The League had conspicuously failed to do anything to stop Japan, and its two most powerful members, the UK and France, appeared to be more interested in furthering their own colonial ambitions than promoting self-determination.

Nevertheless, Haile Selassie made an impassioned appeal to the League of Nations. He described the terrible effects of mustard gas on his country's soldiers and civilians, and the "systematic extermination of a nation by barbarous means."

"Special sprayers were installed on board aircraft so that they could vaporize, over vast areas of territory, a fine, death-dealing rain," he told the chamber, describing how groups of nine to eighteen Italian warplanes would follow in waves so that the fog of poison gas would cover the land in a continuous sheet. "Soldiers, women, children, cattle, rivers, lakes and pastures were drenched continually with this deadly rain. In order to kill off systematically all living creatures, in order to more surely poison waters and pastures, the Italian command made its aircraft pass over and over again. That was its chief method of warfare."

Within a few months of Haile Selassie's appeal to the League, Italian forces had taken most of Abyssinia, entering the capital Addis Ababa on May 5th. All that the League had attempted were some half-hearted sanctions that left out Italy's single most vital import: oil.

Why was so little done? To the people of Abyssinia, the UK, France and other League members, the inaction was almost incomprehensible. What motive was there for the UK and France to ignore Italian war crimes and the unprovoked attack on Abyssinia? If a military response was not possible, why not deny Italy the oil it needed to continue waging war?

Mussolini certainly understood this. "If the League had extended economic sanctions on oil I would have had to withdraw from Abyssinia in a week," he said after the conquest of Addis Ababa (Ristuccia, p.7, originally quoted in Doxey, p.57).

But behind the scenes, the British and French leaders were playing a wider game. They had nervously observed the growing strength of Germany, and with memories of World War I still acute, were casting about for allies. While Mussolini seemed a natural partner for Germany's new fascist leader Adolf Hitler, he had opposed the attempted Nazi coup in Vienna in 1934, and invited the UK and France to join Italy in the Stresa Front against Germany.

The timing of Haile Selassie's speech had been exceptionally bad; only two days before Hitler had announced compulsory conscription in Germany and expanded the army from ten to thirty-six divisions. With Nazi Germany growing visibly stronger and more aggressive, they had no desire to antagonize Italy's ruler. In any case, both countries had dozens of colonies in Africa themselves. The conquest of landlocked Abyssinia by Italy hardly seemed very important.

It was only when public outrage at the reports from Abyssinia forced a response that the leaders of the UK and France allowed the

League to condemn the invasion and introduce sanctions against Italy. A poll of British voters found that only one person in 15 opposed sanctions, while three-quarters thought that military action should also be taken against Italy. Despite the depth of public feeling, the sanctions lacked bite. The League banned arms sales, but to both sides, which hurt Abyssinia more than Italy. Italy was still able to obtain steel, copper and other war materials. Its most crucial import – oil – was not embargoed at all. Mussolini had threatened war if sanctions on oil were imposed.

Meanwhile, British Foreign Secretary Samuel Hoare and Prime Minister Pierre Laval of France met in December 1935, developing the secret Hoare-Laval Plan, which would concede much of Abyssinia to Italy, and, they hoped, bring the war to an end.

Hoare's aim was to avoid war with Italy at all costs. He and Laval agreed that only limited sanctions (specifically not including oil) could be imposed, and that these must be economic rather than military, which ruled out blockading Italy or closing the Suez Canal to Italian shipping. Both Hoare and Laval also personally admired Mussolini and saw his regime as infinitely preferable to a Communist Italy.

An oil embargo would in any case not have worked without the participation of the US, Italy's primary supplier of oil. But the US was not a League member, and with an election coming up in the autumn, President Franklin Roosevelt knew he had to keep the millions of Italian-Americans sweet.

In fact, during the embargo period, exports of war materials, chiefly oil, copper, trucks, tractors, scrap iron and scrap steel, from the US to Italy increased. Even though the US Secretary of State Cordell Hull said in a statement in November 1935 that this trade in what he described as "essential war materials" was "directly contrary to the policy of the Government of the United States," there was no legal authority to prevent it.

The major US oil companies, led by the largest of the Seven Sisters, Standard Oil of New Jersey, had privately assured Mussolini that he could count on them. They knew that Rome would pay a premium for oil if sanctions were imposed. In the event, Mussolini agreed to the Hoare-Laval plan and an oil embargo was never used. The plan was later dropped after it was leaked to the media. Hoare and Laval both resigned in the face of public outrage at their betrayal of Abyssinia.

For the UK and France, the Abyssinian affair had been an unmitigated disaster. Abyssinia had been swallowed up into Italian East Africa. Their leaders had lost credibility with the public, suspicion had been aroused among less powerful allies who saw how Abyssinia had been sold out, and the League had lost credibility. Even the attempt to appease Mussolini and keep Italy on side had been unsuccessful. After Hoare and Laval's (admittedly mild) threat of sanctions, Mussolini abandoned the Stresa Front and from then on sided with Germany.

The Road to War in Europe

While Italy was taking over Abyssinia, Germany was building up its own armed forces. The UK, France and other European countries watched with alarm, and consequently started to increase their own military capacity. They were also confronted with the growing threat from Japan to their colonies in the Far East, but were in no position to take action without US backing. In 1937, first Japan, followed by Italy, signed the anti-Comintern Pact, aligning themselves with Germany.

Neville Chamberlain, the new British prime minister, believed that war could be averted by finding out what Hitler wanted and – within reason – giving it to him. With memories of the 1914–18 war still painful, much of the British population supported the strategy of "appeasement".

No one wanted another European war, so when Germany sent troops into the demilitarized Rhineland in March 1936, then annexed Austria on March 12th, 1938, no action was taken. Chamberlain met with Hitler, who assured him that he had no further territorial ambitions, apart from taking the ethnically German Sudetenland from Czechoslovakia. The Munich Agreement of 1938 was hailed as "peace in our time".

However, by the summer of 1939, German troops had overrun the whole of Czechoslovakia and were now massing on the Polish border. Both the UK and France had pledged to protect Poland, and they declared war on Germany on September 3rd, 1939, two days after the German invasion.

Stalling Japan

On the other side of the world, shipments of oil from the US and from the British and Dutch colonies in South East Asia were still making their way over the Pacific to another axis power, Japan, after war broke out in Europe. In Washington this was a growing dilemma for Roosevelt's government. The question was often asked – both at the time and subsequently – why the US continued to supply Japan with the oil that was later used in the war against its own soldiers.

By the early 20th century, Japanese society was torn between tradition and rapid modernization. Needing space and raw materials, and humiliated by the incursions of Western powers into its traditional sphere of influence, it started expanding into Russia in 1905, annexing Korea in 1910, and invading the northern Chinese province of Manchuria (renamed "Manchukuo") in 1931.

Japan was poor in natural resources and almost totally dependent on imports for its oil supply, importing 80 per cent of its oil from the US. After its invasion of the province of Manchuria in northern China, which furnished it with more land, coal, iron and other resources, Japan relied even more on the US. Japan had not been prepared for war against the Chinese led by nationalist leader Chiang Kai-shek. Even in the north, where they controlled the major cities, including Peking (Beijing), Shanghai and Nanjing, guerrilla action made the countryside virtually ungovernable.

The Japanese quickly understood that despite developments in synthetic fuel technology, they would need a guaranteed supply of oil if they were to wage war on a larger scale. (Ironically, the occupiers of Manchukuo were unaware that they were right on top of the huge Daqing oilfield north west of Harbin, which was not discovered until 1957.)

Although Japan's oil consumption was not high by US standards, almost all of this consumption was for military use. Its highly mechanized navy and armies needed either to count on oil from the US, or to look south to the oilfields of British Burma, the US-controlled Philippines and the Dutch East Indies.

As early as 1934 there was talk of an oil embargo – which would have hurt Japan badly. The big oil companies, led by Royal Dutch Shell and Standard Oil of New Jersey (Exxon), who between them held 60 per cent of the Japanese market, started calling for an embargo after the Petroleum Industry Law was introduced, giving the government the power to control imports. Deterding and Teagle hoped that the mere suggestion of an embargo would be enough to bring Tokyo back into line.

It was fairly obvious that Japan's aim was preparedness for war: one of the conditions for foreign companies doing business in the country was to maintain six months' worth of supplies over and above normal commercial levels. At that time, however, Cordell Hull said that the US would not support an embargo, even though the American public was outraged by footage of the Japanese attacks on Chinese cities, especially the bombings of Chunking in May 1939.

Why did the US not introduce an oil embargo? For Roosevelt and his government it was a Hobson's choice: allow Japan to stockpile oil reserves while it ravaged China and possibly prepared for a wider war, or cut off supplies and provoke Japan into invading South East Asia. The need for land and raw materials was a factor in Japan's expansionist policy, as was the growing nationalism within the country, but what Japan needed most was oil. Joseph Grew, the American ambassador in Tokyo, was strongly opposed to sanctions, believing that rather than falling into line with Western demands, Japan would go to any lengths to avoid losing face.

From 1939 US policy was directly opposed to Japan's expansionist intentions. And the US had, it seemed, the power to check Japan by denying it oil. Not only that, it was obvious by 1939 that Japan and the US could one day be at war. As early as 1934, Japan had demonstrated it was stockpiling oil, when it introduced new legislation that forced Shell and other international oil companies to stockpile additional supplies within the country if they wanted to do business in Japan. Japan had already started to look south, asking the government of Vichy France if it could send a military mission to the French colony of Indochina. Several allied colonies nearby, British Burma, the Dutch East Indies and the US-controlled Philippines, were threatened.

Some observers speculated that as a reaction to the rumours about Roosevelt's liaison with his social secretary Lucy Mercer, he had been trying to divert the country's attention to what was happening overseas. Others thought the only thing holding him back from taking a stronger line against Japan was the imminent presidential election.

If the war was seen as a move to protect Western interests in South East Asia it would be difficult to avoid accusations of going to war to protect the much loathed Standard Oil.

The US government moved slowly. In July 1940, Roosevelt had signed new legislation allowing plans to build a two-ocean navy to go ahead. But in 1941 the US was still providing Japan with oil for its own navy.

Then in mid-1941, US Under-Secretary of State Sumner Welles proposed that the US keep oil exports at the 1936–7 level, but stop exporting any oil or oil products that could be used for aviation fuel. All oil exports would need government-approved export licences. On July 25th, 1941, the US government froze all Japanese assets in the country. From August 1941 no more oil was exported from the US to Japan. The two countries were on the road to war.

Japan knew that a long war would favour the US, with their easy access to oil and other resources. The only way to win was to strike first. The Japanese high command knew the vital importance of oil, and knew too that bombing Pearl Harbour on Hawaii would deal a devastating blow to the US navy, knocking out the naval fuel dumps in the mid-Pacific.

"Hitler's Obsession Was Oil"

World War II was fought, as no war had been fought before, with machines and technology. In the 20 years since 1914–18, which had been called "the Engineers' War", the world powers had amassed armies of tanks, bomber planes, ships and submarines.

Within a year of declaring war on Poland, Germany had overrun most of Europe, with no country able to withstand its new technique of "blitzkrieg", lightning war.

Poland's army was destroyed within six days of the German invasion, as wave after wave of tanks and warplanes tore through the country. After them came the huge motorized army, consolidating positions and wiping out any resistance.

In April 1940, Germany struck again, invading Denmark and Norway on April 9th, 1940, then France, Holland, Belgium and Luxembourg on May 10th. The trapped British Expeditionary Force was evacuated from Dunkirk, leaving western Europe to Nazi occupation. The following spring, Hitler's armies invaded Greece and Yugoslavia.

Peace with the USSR had been secured through the Nazi-Soviet Pact, signed in Moscow on August 23rd, 1938. This left Germany free to fight the British air force in the skies above England. But there were many compelling reasons for Hitler to abandon the pact now that the rest of Europe was subdued. The defeat of Communism and the subjugation of the Slavs, who he regarded as an inferior race, were added to his distrust of Stalin and suspicions (incorrect) of a secret deal between the USSR and Britain. Above all, Russia could provide *lebensraum*, living space … and oil. The oilfields of Romania and Vichy North Africa were not enough; if Nazi forces could take the Caspian as well, the new German empire would be impregnable.

War in Russia

Hitler used the same strategy of "blitzkrieg" for Operation Barbarossa, a surprise attack on its former ally that destroyed most of Stalin's western armies. Plans for an invasion had been kept secret so successfully that Stalin refused to believe warnings of an attack from the Americans, British and other countries. When axis troops started pouring across the border, they intercepted Russian trains full of oil on their way to Germany.

Soviet forces moved back, withdrawing into the Russian steppe to stretch the German supply lines, while Soviet factories were dismantled and reassembled in the Ural Mountains, Siberia and Central Asia. The Germans had not expected to defeat Stalin's armies so quickly, or to advance so fast across Russia. They had underestimated the amount of fuel needed for the advance, and found they were running short of supplies.

Hitler made another mistake, ordering the greater part of his armies to go south, to capture the Caucasian oilfields, the Donetsk coal and the Crimea, from where Soviet bombers were targeting the Plotesi oilfields in Romania. He dismissed complaints from his generals, saying, "My generals know nothing about the economic aspects of war." (Shirer, p.1122)

Later, Hitler changed his mind and diverted forces to Moscow, but the German armies, in their three-pronged advance towards

Leningrad, Moscow and the Caucasus, became caught up in the Russian winter, and advance forces were defeated within sight of Moscow.

The following year, another great eastern push was launched, Operation Blau. German armies would capture the Caucasus, which Hitler's economists said was essential to continue with the war. From the Caucasus, they would fight on to take the oilfields of Iran and Iraq, and then India. Germany even put together a "Technical Oil Brigade", which was charged with getting the Caucasus oilwells up and running once they were captured.

By July 1942, German forces had taken Rostov, cut the oil pipeline from the Caucasus and taken the small westerly oilfield at Maikop. But Maikop proved to be little help to the German armies, who were already running short of fuel. The wells had been so thoroughly destroyed by the retreating Russians that they could not be used to provide petrol for the German panzer units. Even the captured Soviet fuel supplies were of little use; Soviet tanks ran on diesel.

Late in 1942, German forces had encircled the city of Stalingrad, starting a siege that was to last until February of 1943. The German Sixth Army dug into the snow during the winter of 1942-3 was slowly running out of food, clothing, fuel and ammunition, but Hitler refused to divert troops from the Caucasus to relieve them.

"It's a question of the possession of Baku, Field Marshal. Unless we get the Baku oil, the war is lost," Hitler told Field Marshal Erich von Manstein when he begged for help. (Yergin, p.338) In February 1943, the Sixth Army, starving and worn down by the freezing winter, surrendered to Soviet forces at Stalingrad, marking the turning point in the war between Germany and Russia. The battle of Stalingrad, lasting over 200 days, had claimed the lives of an estimated 850,000 axis troops; the Soviet losses were around 750,000 soldiers and over 45,000 civilians.

Trading Oil with the Enemy

When US soldiers stormed the beaches of Normandy in the D-Day landing, they were surprised to find the German troops facing them in Ford vehicles. It might also have come as a shock to Londoners huddled in air raid shelters or underground stations to find that the

German planes pounding their city were fuelled by Standard Oil, or to US airmen to find that their German counterparts were studying detailed reports on the American air force supplied by Texaco director Torkild Rieber's Nazi associates.

This cosy relationship between Big Oil and Hitler's Germany went a long way back. There are allegations, real or unproven, that several of the Seven Sisters made contributions to Hitler's campaigns in the late 1920s when the Nazis first started to emerge as a serious political force.

At the time this was not exceptional behaviour among foreign companies, and nor was it exclusive to the oil sector. Outside Germany, the world's aristocracies and business elites saw Russia as the real threat, and admired the way Hitler was dealing with Germany's Communists. Edward VIII, who abdicated the British throne in 1937 to marry the American divorcee Wallace Simpson, was fascinated by Nazism. After his abdication he and Mrs Simpson, now the Duchess of Windsor, visited Germany, where they met Hitler and dined with his deputy, Rudolf Hess.

The oilmen too were attracted by the new German regime and its anti-Communist stance, not to mention the motor car culture of the early 1930s in Germany. Shell's Henri Deterding had become vehemently anti-Communist after his second marriage to a White Russian. His third wife was his young German secretary Charlotte Knaack, herself a fervent Nazi, who he married just after his 70th birthday in 1936. This brought him even closer to the Nazis, who he believed offered the only solution to the threat of Communism.

It hasn't been proven whether Deterding – who had once been so keen to make himself and his company British – actually made contributions to the Nazi party, though it is widely suspected and there is circumstantial evidence that he did so, probably through his agent Georg Bell. The Dutch press has alleged that Deterding gave the Nazis, via Bell, four million guilders, when the party was preparing to take power. Deterding's biographer Glyn Roberts reports that Bell represented both Deterding and Hitler at meetings of Ukrainian Patriots in Paris. (Roberts, p.313)

In his book *Germany Puts the Clock Back*, Edgar Ansell Mowrer claims that Deterding provided an unspecified large sum of money to the Nazis before they came to power, on the understanding that they would give him better access to the German oil market. In 1935 he agreed to give Germany one year's oil supply on credit.

Deterding's Nazi sympathies did not, however, influence Shell's actions during World War II. By the mid-1930s, the other Shell directors became convinced that Deterding was not only pro-German, he was also on the verge of madness, and they acted quickly to oust him from the company he had led for 30 years, before he could become too much of an embarrassment.

Deterding lived out his final years on his estate at Mecklenburg in Germany. He became friendly with Hitler, Goering and other Nazi leaders, many of whom sent wreaths to his funeral. He died in early 1939, six months before war broke out.

After war was declared, both of the British "Sisters" retained close ties with the British government. For the American companies, especially Standard Oil of New Jersey (Exxon) and Texaco, it was a different story. Walter Teagle, now the Standard chairman, and his chief executive William Stamps Farish had signed a deal with Internationale Gesellschaft Farbenindustrie AG (IG Farben), tying Standard closely to the German chemical giant, which by the late 1930s was effectively the industrial branch of the Nazi party. Torkild Rieber, a Norwegian-American and the new Texaco chief executive, personally favoured the Nazi form of government, and even tried to persuade the Americans to cool relations with Britain and move closer to Germany.

Standard Oil and IG Farben

One lesson Germany had learned from World War I was that the country would need guaranteed supplies of fuel if it was ever to go to war again.

In 1913, just before World War I, a German scientist Friedrich Bergius had developed a way of extracting a liquid fuel (that could be used in internal combustion engines) from coal, by a process known as "hydrogenation". Germany had plenty of coal, but very little oil. In 1926, the German chemical giant IG Farben bought the rights to the Bergius Method.

Initially, reports of IG Farben's new fuel had greatly disturbed Standard. The company's head of research Frank Howard was so concerned that it could make Europe self-sufficient and destroy

Standard's European oil markets that after seeing the works in 1926 he immediately telegraphed Teagle to come over and see for himself.

A thoughtful Teagle met with IG Farben executives and agreed a deal, allowing Standard to build a hydrogenation plant in Louisiana.

Three years later, Standard and IG Farben made a wider agreement, giving Standard the patent rights to hydrogenation (which it initially planned to use on oil to raise gasoline yields) outside Germany. IG Farben received 2 per cent of Standard's stock, worth $35 million. The two companies agreed to keep out of the other's main areas of activity. "The IG are going to stay out of the oil business – and we are going to stay out of the chemical business," said one Standard official after the deal was signed. (Yergin, p.331)

Then in 1930, the two companies set up a joint venture. Standard had become IG Farben's largest shareholder, and, after the Rockefeller family, IG Farben was the largest shareholder in Standard.

Then IG Farben struck another agreement, this time with the Nazi party. While Hitler was still just the leader of a small party with a few seats in the Reichstag (German parliament), two IG Farben executives requested a meeting. Although in the past the Nazis had been quite hostile towards the company, the potential of the hydrogenation process to make Germany self-sufficient in fuel immediately captured Hitler's imagination.

The meeting ended with a commitment from IG Farben to continue their work with hydrogenation of coal and to start funding the Nazi party. In return, if and when the Nazis took power, they would provide a government subsidy for the chemical company – necessary since the process was not yet commercially viable; hydrogenation cost around ten times more than extracting oil. While the Brüning government offered only tariff protection, Hitler agreed to guarantee prices and markets for IG Farben on the condition it continued to increase production of synthetic fuels.

Corporate Traitors

By the late 1930s, IG Farben was almost completely "Nazified". The former director (not a Nazi) who had signed the original deal with Standard had been replaced, while his successors had rushed to join the party. The Jewish employees, who had once made up a large part of Farben's workforce, were driven out. But Standard continued to work closely with IG Farben, and to honour the companies' agreements on oil and synthetic fuels. "The history of the use of the IG Farben trust by the Nazis reads like a detective story," Roosevelt wrote to his Secretary of State Cordell Hull in September 1944.

After war broke out, a number of leading US companies continued to work with Nazi Germany. Investigations during and after the war revealed that banks, including the Rockefeller-owned Chase Bank, major companies like ITT, Ford and General Motors, as well as Texaco and several of the ex-Standard companies, worked in Germany (some using slave labour) or adhered to their agreements with German companies, and continued to supply Germany with oil and other materials necessary for war. (*Associated Press*, January 13th, 1999)

It also emerged that a number of US government officials, many of them in collusion with the oil companies, sought to prevent America entering the war or their supplies to Germany being stopped, by portraying Russia as the main threat and trying to discredit Roosevelt and his supporters.

After the worst excesses of Nazism emerged, the companies tried to make out either that they were forced to cooperate with the Nazis or that their dealings with Nazi Germany – to the extent of using slave labour – went on without the knowledge of the American corporate headquarters. Often, though, cooperation was not just with the knowledge of, but actually instigated by the American headquarters. Many major companies went to great lengths to keep hold of their assets in Germany, and continued to work with the Nazis even if it meant breaking the law in the US after America had gone to war.

IG Farben, which kept its ties with Standard Oil of New Jersey throughout the war, built a new plant near the Auschwitz concentration camp in order to use slave labourers from the camp. Some 27,000 prisoners were worked to death at IG Farben's plant.

The exact extent of the collaboration between Big Oil and the Nazis is still unclear. The Senate investigations headed by Harry S. Truman (later President Truman) in 1941–5 slowly uncovered Standard's operations, coming to the final verdict that the oil company was guilty of treason.

Later research revealed more details of IG Farben's use of slave labour from the Auschwitz death camp, Texaco's involvement in Nazi espionage, and Standard's attempts to hold back development of synthetic fuels in the US while subsidizing their manufacture in Germany. The 1998 Nazi War Crimes Disclosure Act was followed by the release of around three million pages of US intelligence files, and with them some of the last secrets of the war years.

A recent German investigation established that 26 of the 100 largest US firms were active in Germany in the mid-1930s. (Hamburg Institute for Social Research) In most cases this continued, not just after the war started in Europe, but after America joined the war.

The "Shadow" Suppliers

War means big business for oil companies. When war broke out in Europe in 1939, the US oil giants sent tankers across the Atlantic to feed Britain's demand for fuel. But several spotted that they could make even more money if they supplied Germany as well.

Since Britain had blockaded the Atlantic from the Arctic to the tip of South America, and was stopping any ship heading for Germany and seizing its contents, the oil companies had to act stealthily. After furious complaints from the British alerted the US government about the oil companies' help for the German war effort, they went under-cover, setting "shadow agreements" with partners in neutral countries to disguise their business with the enemy.

Texaco was among the first companies to start supplying Nazi Germany with oil. Before the start of World War II, Texaco's new chief executive Torkild Rieber had ignored the US government's Neutrality Act, which forbade US companies to supply either side in the Spanish Civil War.

In 1937 it was brought to Washington's attention that Texaco tankers supposedly headed for Belgium were changing direction mid-Atlantic and delivering oil to General Franco's armies in Spain. Even after the US Attorney General's warning that Texaco would be indicted for conspiracy, Rieber continued supplying Franco through Italy, sending a total of $6 million worth of oil on credit, to be paid for after the civil war.

It was through Franco that Rieber became closely involved with the Nazi regime. As the international climate turned against Germany, Rieber agreed to supply the country with oil from Texaco's operations in Colombia. From 1939, he avoided the British blockade by sending his tankers to neutral ports.

Standard of New Jersey had re-registered its entire fleet of tankers in Panama, transporting oil from the Americas to Tenerife. Standard's ships transferred their oil into German tankers stationed in the Canary Islands, who would take it on the final leg of the journey to Hamburg. Farish also organized shipments of oil across the Pacific to the Russian Far East, then across Russia on the Trans-Siberian Railway to Germany. After Hitler invaded Russia and the Nazi-Soviet Pact was defunct, Farish started shipping oil to Vichy North Africa.

A US Military Intelligence officer, Major Charles Burrows, reported to the US War Department in July 1941 that Standard Oil of New Jersey was using around half a dozen ships to transport oil from its refinery in Aruba off the Venezuelan coast to the Canary Islands, where it was being used to refuel German U-boats. According to Burrows, the ships were "manned mainly by Nazi officers." (Higham, pp.40–1)

Burrows also reported to the War Department that Standard was sending around 20 per cent of its fuel oil to Germany, and that unlike other American companies, Standard had not lost any ships to German torpedoes.

Opinion within the US government about supplying the Germans was divided. Roosevelt himself wanted to go to war, and also wanted to stamp out any connections between US companies and the Nazi regime. But there was strong opposition within the government to putting the US at risk by ending the interwar isolation policy. There were also those who secretly admired the Nazis or, like many oil executives and big businessmen, wanted to make money from them. They aimed to conceal the business links between the two countries, and to prevent laws forbidding trade.

It took the determined efforts of anti-Nazi officials – such as Sumner Welles of the State Department and William La Varne of the US Department of Commerce, and Winston Churchill's secret envoy to Roosevelt, William Stephenson – to uncover what the oil companies were trying to hide.

It was Welles who exposed Standard's deception, in a report published in March 1941. Standard Oil of New Jersey and Standard Oil of California topped the list of companies fuelling enemy ships and selling oil to Italian and German merchants from their refuelling stations in Central and South America. Similar deals between Standard Oil and the Japanese government for the purchase of tetraethyl lead were also reported. (Higham, pp.38–9)

La Varne uncovered details of Standard Oil's dealings with the Nazi airline, LATI. LATI aeroplanes were not subject to boarding searches by the British blockade, so they could be used to transport spies, propaganda and drugs across the Atlantic. All these dubious consignments were addressed to Sterling Products, whose director William Weiss was also on the board of IG Chimie along with Edsel Ford and James Forestal (later Under-Secretary of the Navy). La Varne pointed out that LATI must be receiving its fuel stocks from Standard Oil of New Jersey, since Standard was the only company with the high-octane fuel needed to make a trip across the Atlantic from Europe to South America without a refuelling stop.

A recently declassified British intelligence report on Texan oil billionaire Jean Paul Getty describes how Getty "returned from Europe in November 1939 talking breezily about his 'old friend' Hitler."

Getty was the controller of the Mission Oil Corp., the company that held the IG Farben and Standard patents. An intelligence report compiled after British forces apprehended a banker working for Goering in Trinidad links Getty to a network of financiers who were supplying fuel to Nazi Germany.

Among Getty's associates was Serge Rubinstein, the son of a banker working for the Tsar, who lost his business after the Russian Revolution. Rubinstein was an odd character, who "had a first class degree in economics from Cambridge but turned his talents to making money fast and illegally." (Peter Day, *The Daily Telegraph*, August 25th, 2003) Rubinstein claimed to be working for MI6, but was seen meeting with German agents in Cuba, the Ku Klux Klan and other far right groups.

Working with Rubinstein and Mexican presidential contender Juan Almazan, Getty is said to have sent one million barrels of oil to Germany, via Russia.

While some US officials were working to expose the links between corporate America and Nazi Germany, others within the State Department tried to block their efforts. One senior State Department official, William Bullitt, launched a personal vendetta against Sumner Welles, who was bisexual, persuading FBI director J. Edgar Hoover to investigate him. When Welles was travelling back to Washington after attending a funeral, Hoover hired two Pullman porters to flirt with him. Bullitt then put pressure on Roosevelt to dismiss Welles, which he reluctantly did.

Intrigue, Propoganda and Espionage

Texaco's involvement with the Nazis was equally deep. By the late 1930s Torkild Rieber had succeeded the company's founder Joe Cullinan as chief executive. Rieber was just as flamboyant a character as his Texan predecessor, arriving in the US as mate on a Norwegian oil tanker. After Texaco bought the tanker, Rieber rose rapidly within the company. Contemporaries describe him as "a stocky broad-smiling man with a thick Norwegian accent, a sailor's cap and a parting in the middle."

In many ways Rieber was a stateless individual, more at home on the sea than the land, and with no loyalty to any particular country. But like Deterding he had a great admiration for Hitler and the Nazi regime, becoming a personal friend of Goering. One German secret service agent described him as "absolutely pro-German" and "a sincere admirer of the Führer." (Jacques R. Pauwels, Labour/Le Travail, Spring 2003) He is said to have thrown a party at the Waldorf-Astoria Hotel to celebrate the fall of France in 1940. (Higham, p.97)

Under Rieber, Texaco continued shipping oil to Germany after 1939, dodging the British blockade. He faced the problem, though, of being unable to take money out of Germany. Goering offered him three tankers in return for the oil, but demanded that Rieber provide his diplomatic support as part of the bargain.

Rieber visited Roosevelt, as Hitler's envoy, in January 1940, and outlined Goering's peace plan, which involved a British surrender. Roosevelt rejected the plan and advised Rieber to abandon his German connections.

At around the same time, Dr Gerhard Westrick, a German lawyer who had represented Texaco and other American companies in Germany, arrived in New York, officially as a business consultant. In fact, his mission was to persuade American companies to stop selling arms to Britain. He argued that Britain was close to defeat, and after the war was over – on German terms – Germany would be

America's trading partner in Europe. Rieber funded Westrick's activities in the US, providing him with an office at the Texaco headquarters and a large house in Scarsdale, which Westrick used to entertain business leaders and promote the Nazi cause.

Another Rieber connection, Niko Bensmann, was arranging delivery of the tankers from Hamburg. Bensmann was an oilman who had worked for Texaco in Germany for years, but unknown to Rieber he was also a German intelligence agent. He used another agent planted within the Texaco headquarters to send reports from the US to Germany. Among these was a detailed and accurate report, from Texaco economists, on US aircraft manufacture.

News of Westrick's real activities in the US were finally leaked to the *New York Herald Tribune* by William Stephenson, who was working behind the scenes to bring America into the war and expose the companies breaking the blockade. Westrick left on a Japanese ship heading for Germany, where he continued his work with American big business by taking over as head of ITT's operations in Germany.

After the exposé, Rieber too was discredited. Although the US had not yet entered the war, feelings were running high against the Nazis. Texaco's board rapidly ousted their former chairman, and embarked on a series of goodwill gestures (such as their sponsorship of the Metropolitan Opera) in order to regain respect and bring their share price back up.

While Rieber was playing host to Westrick in the Chrysler building, Jean Paul Getty had gathered a bizarre cast of characters around him at the Pierre. Getty is rumoured to have bought the hotel on a whim because he wanted to sack a waiter who was rude to him. Many of the "guests" at the Pierre had Nazi or Vichy connections, among them Countess Mohle, who, according to the British intelligence report, "spent her time making herself attractive to US Army officers and was in a perpetual state of wide eyed curiosity about military affairs." The men Getty employed to manage the hotel included an Austrian baron and a former U-boat captain.

Unlike Rieber, Getty managed to re-establish himself, changing his stance after the US went to war against Japan and volunteering for navy service. This stood him in good stead after the war, when he went on to become the richest man in the world.

Standard Oil of New Jersey, too, was discovered to be distributing pro-Nazi propaganda by the US Legation in Managua, Nicaragua. Rockefeller public relations man Ivy Lee, in particular, is known to have carried out propaganda, espionage and intelligence work, and investigations by John Muccio of the US Consulate found that the operation was not limited to Nicaragua; Standard was distributing similar pro-German propaganda in countries around the world.

Synthetic Fuels: Holding the US to Ransom

Standard Oil and connected companies not only continued sending oil to Germany, they also held back US efforts to develop synthetic fuels and related products, while continuing to invest in similar operations in Germany and Japan.

The partnership between Standard and IG Farben had started back in the 1920s. Standard had shared its patents and know-how for synthetic rubber manufacture with the German chemical company. Although IG Farben was supposed, under the terms of the agreement, to disclose its own patents to Standard, it was less forthcoming, acting on instructions from the Nazi government.

When, in 1939, it became apparent that the US and Germany could one day go to war against each other, senior executives from the two companies met in the Netherlands to discuss how to continue working together. A letter from Standard, renewing its agreement with IG Farben, was turned over to the Truman Committee investigating allegations of treason. The letter "made it clear that the Rockefellers' company was prepared to work with the Nazis whether their own government was at war with the Third Reich or not." (Mintz & Cohen, pp.499–500)

At the hearings in 1942, a Texas oilman, C.R. Starnes, gave evidence that Standard had blocked his efforts to produce synthetic rubber after the bombing of Pearl Harbour. John R. Jacobs of the Attorney General's department testified that Standard had blocked production of synthetic ammonia, used in explosives, "paraflow", used for aeroplane lubrication at high altitudes, and restricted production of methanol. But General Motors in Switzerland was converting gasoline to methanol during the war without intervention from Standard.

Thurmon Arnold, the assistant district attorney who led the initial criminal investigation, wanted a $1.5 million fine for Standard, and demanded that Farish hand over the IG Farben patents for the duration of the war.

Farish didn't accept Arnold's demands. Instead, he pointed out the contribution that Standard was making to the US war effort through its supply of a high percentage of the fuel being used by the armed forces, and asking what the US would do without Standard. In effect, Farish was threatening to disrupt the US war effort by withholding oil supplies. Farish was acting on advice from two of Standard's lawyers, John and Allen Dulles. John Foster Dulles was later to become Secretary of State, while Allen Dulles became director of the CIA.

A fine of $10,000 was agreed, to be shared out among the top Standard executives, with Farish himself paying $1,000, a quarter of one week's salary.

But the matter was not dropped forever. A US Senate investigation headed by the future President Harry S. Truman, then head of the Senate's Committee on the National Defense, was launched in March 1942 to uncover the truth about Standard. Documents produced during the hearing included a Standard memo on the 1939 agreement with IG Farben, which Truman described "treasonable".

A final verdict on the case was not reached until 1947, following a lawsuit from Standard over the confiscation of its patents. Judge Charles Clark said: "Standard Oil can be considered an enemy national in view of its relationships with IG Farben after the United States and Germany had become active enemies."

War in the Middle East

The three great allied powers – the US, UK and USSR – were united in the need to defeat Hitler. But they were divided over how to do this. From 1942, both the US and USSR saw that the only way to deal a devastating blow to Nazi Germany was by opening a second front in western Europe, while the Soviets fought in the east.

For some time, however, the British resisted the idea of a second front, persuading the Americans to join them in an invasion of Vichy and German-controlled North Africa. Why?

With the Nazis occupying almost all of Europe, Winston Churchill was determined to drive them out of North Africa. In June 1942, the Afrika Corps, under Erwin Rommel, drove the British Eighth Army out of Libya as far as El Alamein, under 65 miles from Alexandria.

Churchill persuaded Roosevelt to support a joint US and British invasion of Vichy North Africa, Operation Torch, against the advice of the leading American generals, who argued that even if the operation was successful it would not have a significant impact on Germany, and would delay the opening of a second front in Europe. It would also do little to help the Soviet troops who were battling alone on the eastern front.

But by 1942, Britain had long realized that it was no longer the world's foremost naval power, and also that it would not be able to fight in Europe and the Middle East, maintain the Atlantic blockade, and prepare to defend India and its colonies in the Far East. It had to choose its priorities, and both the Chamberlain and Churchill wings in the Tory party agreed that maintaining Britain's position in the Mediterranean and the Middle East was crucial.

If allied forces could drive the Germans and Italians out of North Africa, they would secure the Mediterranean, protect the Suez Canal and – not least – block one potential route for the Germans to seize the Middle East oilfields. As in World War I, India was of prime importance to Britain, as was the continuation of oil supplies from Iran.

If Germany was able to break through the British Eighth Army in Egypt, there would be nothing to stop it striking through the Middle East to India, taking the Gulf oilfields on the way. Oilwells in the region were already being capped in preparation for a German invasion.

Britain was so determined to keep the axis out of the eastern Mediterranean that it even sent tanks from Britain to Egypt, at a time when there was a real danger of a Nazi invasion at home.

The British were already dealing with problems in the region, where nationalists in Egypt, Iran and Iraq were considering throwing in their lot with the Germans to free themselves from the British. Two other Middle Eastern countries, Syria and Lebanon, came under the control of the Vichy government after the fall of France.

Anti-British nationalists in Iraq, led by Rashid Ali al-Gailani, deposed the regent and set up a pro-axis government. The rebellion was short-lived; when al-Gailani refused to allow British troops to cross Iraq, an Indian force landed at Basra, and, with Arab troops from Transjordan, returned the regent to power.

Iran was another key Middle Eastern country that the allies were afraid of losing, especially as the German armies storming towards the Caucasus were getting closer every day. After years of exploitations by first Russia and then Britain, Iranian nationalists allowed Nazi agents to operate within the country. In 1941, the Iranian government refused to allow Britain to send supplies to the USSR across the country. Soviet and British troops invaded simultaneously, taking the whole country within a few weeks. Iran was divided into British and Soviet occupation zones for the remainder of the war, and the Shah's 23-year-old son was put on the throne.

By the time Operation Torch started in North Africa, General Bernard Montgomery, the new commander of the British Eighth Army, had massed a formidable army at El Alamein. On November 4th (four days before the "Torch" landing in Morocco and Algeria), British tanks broke through German lines and started to chase Rommel's armies back through Libya.

When Churchill and Roosevelt met at Casablanca in January 1943, they were not yet ready to open a second front. Instead, they decided to drive the Germans and Italians right out of North Africa. By May 1943, the allies controlled the Mediterranean and the whole of Italian and French North Africa. High among the reasons for the axis defeat were – as always – a lack of oil.

"Shortage of petrol! It's enough to make one weep," wrote Rommel in a letter to his wife. (Bullock, p.751)

But by the time the allies had taken North Africa, it was too late to start moving the troops to Britain and preparing to open a second front in western Europe. Operation Torch had driven axis forces out of North Africa and secured the Mediterranean in preparation for an invasion of Italy. Yet it was not until 1944 that a second front was opened in mainland Europe, with the D-Day landings on June 6th.

Running Out of Oil

The Germans fought bitterly to hold onto northern France, and for months the allies advanced by only a few hundred yards at a time. However, the destruction of the German Seventh Army at Falaise together with the allied breakthrough at St-Lô allowed allied forces in the north to link up with armies pushing north from Italy. Paris was liberated on August 25th, 1944.

It was obvious that Germany was losing the war. US and British forces had already taken the whole of Italy and were moving up through France and the Low Countries, while the USSR was pushing westwards. Soviet troops had already reached the Polish border in early 1944, taking Finland, Romania and Bulgaria. Allied planes roared overhead every night, dropping their cargoes of bombs on German cities and industrial areas.

During the war years, half of the fuel used by the German army was synthetic, produced, often by slave labourers, in the vast plants of IG Farben and other chemical companies. On May 12th, 1944, a combat force under the command of US General Carl Spaatz had bombed many of Germany's synthetic fuel factories, including IG Farben's plant at Leuna. Germany was desperately short of fuel.

In December 1944, the German army made its last major offensive in the west, making a surprise attack on allied forces in the Ardennes and attempting to capture the important port of Antwerp, in what later became known as the Battle of the Bulge. The offensive, planned by Hitler himself, targeted the allied fuel dumps near Stavelot in southern Belgium, where around 2.5 million gallons of fuel were stored.

The Germans had scrounged together just enough fuel for a heavy attack – the last "blitzkrieg" of the war. At 5:30 am on December 6th, 1944, 21 German divisions attacked five divisions of the US First Army. The US divisions were taken by surprise and quickly surrounded.

It was the heaviest fighting since the D-Day landings. The allies managed to launch a counteroffensive in the last days of 1944. Soldiers of the US First and Third Armies, their uniforms padded with newspapers to keep out the snow, tried to trap the German armies at the village of Houffalize.

Hitler responded with "the Great Blow", an air attack on all the allied airfields in Belgium, Holland and northern France, but the Luftwaffe's losses were worse than those inflicted on the allies, and on January 8th, 1945, German troops started withdrawing from the Bulge. Soldiers had come within a mile of the allied fuel dumps, but with out-of-date maps had failed to recognize them.

Overall, more than a million men fought in the battle, including 600,000 Germans, 500,000 Americans and 55,000 British.

Soviet armies had reached Germany's eastern borders. Allied

forces entering Germany from the west met soldiers and civilians flee-ing the Soviet advance. With fuel supplies cut off, the German war machine was useless. Allied soldiers found army trucks abandoned all along the roads, or being pulled along by donkeys.

In the Far East, the relentless drive south of the Japanese armies had almost succeeded in taking Port Moresby, Papua New Guinea, which would have put their navy within striking distance of Australia in 1942.

The battle at Port Moresby was the first successful battle against Japan, and the following month the US navy had another success, pre-venting the invasion of Midway Island and destroying four Japanese aircraft carriers.

Although for the US and UK, liberating Europe from the Nazis was the main priority, US and Australian forces started attacking Japan's captured territories.

Allied submarines and aircraft also attacked Japanese shipping, depriving Japan of the raw materials it had gone to war to obtain. If Japan could not import oil, steel and other materials it would no longer be able to wage war effectively. As US forces closed in on the Japanese mainland, fewer and fewer supplies got through.

When the Japanese fought back and captured most of Burma, cut-ting off allied supplies to the Chinese nationalist army, the allies began a huge airlift known as "the Hump", until Chinese, American and British forces could clear a passage through Burma.

Then the allies captured Iwo Jima, Okinawa and other islands close enough to Japan for aerial attacks on the country to begin. The first atomic bomb, the "Little Boy", was dropped on Hiroshima, completely destroying the city and killing its population or condemning them to a slow and painful death. On August 8th, 1945, the USSR declared war on Japan, and invaded Japanese-occupied Manchuria. On August 9th, another atom bomb was dropped on Nagasaki. The Japanese surren-dered on August 14th, 1945.

Seeking Supremacy in the Middle East

Even while British and American forces were driving the axis troops out of North Africa, a secret tussle for supremacy in the Middle Eastern oilfields was taking shape.

During the interwar years, the US had been slowly improving its position vis-à-vis the British, starting with its insistence on a stake in the Iraq Petroleum Company, and moving in on Saudi Arabia. At the height of the war, in 1943, Everette Lee DeGolyer, the foremost US geologist, arrived in the Middle East on a tour of Saudi Arabia, Kuwait, Iraq and Iran – the key oil-producing countries. His mission, set by the US president himself, was to evaluate how important the oil reserves of the Persian Gulf would be to the future of the world.

DeGolyer's report to Roosevelt concluded: "The centre of gravity of world oil production is shifting from the Gulf-Caribbean area to the Middle East and the Persian Gulf area, and is likely to continue to shift until it is firmly established in that area." (Nuruddin Mahmud Kamal, *Lebanon Daily Star*, March 4th, 2003)

It also alerted the US government to the increasing friendliness between its UK ally and the Saudi government; since the beginning of the war, the British had been subsidizing the king and his regime to the tune of around $20 million. Texaco, one of the main American firms in Saudi Arabia, raised further concerns when it pointed out that several geologists had been included in a British expedition to deal with a locust problem.

In February 1943, officials from Texaco Socal called on Harold Ickes to counter the British influence by providing Saudi Arabia with US lend lease funds. It is a measure of how seriously the issue was taken within the US government that Ickes (who was no friend to Big Oil) rapidly obtained the funding, leading to an orgy of extravagance and corruption within the Saudi government.

Aware that they could no longer be the world's power supplier, the US envisaged a relationship with Saudi Arabia similar to the British with Iran, and immediately after the war Roosevelt set out to visit the Saudi king. Their meeting was to set a foreign policy course that was to endure from World War II until today.

Chapter Five: The Oil-Producing Countries Take Control

After World War II, Europe was slowly rebuilding, but in the US, further removed from the theatre of conflict, a bold new consumer society was emerging. The technological leaps forward that had helped the US to win the war were now directed at civilian life as well. The end of rationing meant that Americans could at last spend the money accumulated from their war work, and the ensuing consumption bonanza continued until the early 1960s. The rest of the world watched with envy as Americans bought television sets, home appliances, leisure equipment and, of course, motor cars. This was gradually repeated in Europe, though not until around a decade later, and first the US, then other developed countries, saw a rapid increase in demand for oil.

Even as World War II ended, however, the threat of a new conflict began to grow. The Western powers and the USSR had been in alliance against the axis. Once the war had been won, relations between them became increasingly uneasy, particularly over the question of the Soviet occupation of Eastern Europe. In 1946, the British Prime Minister Winston Churchill warned that "From Stettin in the Baltic to Trieste in the Adriatic, an iron curtain has descended across the continent."

This was the start of a 50-year standoff between the two new "superpowers", the US and the USSR, as the Berlin Wall sealed off the Communist bloc from western Europe.

The UK and France fought hard against the loss of their great power status, but both countries had been battered and impoverished by the war and were for many years financially dependent on the US. The safe old colonial world, where Europe ruled over large parts of Asia and Africa, was coming to an end. Talk of a war fought for freedom, and the concept of the "free" West standing against the

Communist bloc, was not compatible with colonialism. The colonies in Africa and Asia were not prepared to be part of an empire any more. India won its independence on August 14th, 1947, the death knell for the British Empire, and European colonies first in Asia and later in Africa fought to drive out their colonizers. But even after they gained their independence, the oil-producing countries still found themselves taking instructions from the major oil companies, the Seven Sisters, who decided how much oil they would export and at what price. Oil had become even more important in this emerging consumer world, and the oil producers, sensing the winds of freedom, wanted a piece of the action.

Oil was more of an issue for the US and its allies than for the USSR during the Cold War. The USSR had substantial oil resources of its own in Siberia and the Caspian, but the Western powers became increasingly anxious about securing future supplies in case of war, and to preserve their way of living. They looked first to the Middle East, whose vast reserves dwarfed those of the rest of the world. But as the colonial age came slowly, and sometimes bloodily, to an end, the countries of the region started to assert themselves against their former colonizers, often with support from the USSR.

Iranian Prime Minister Mossadeq's attempt to nationalize the Anglo-Persian Oil Company brought him to a standoff with the British government, with both sides determined to control the Iranian oilfields. Soon after negotiations broke down, Mossadeq was ousted in 1953 by a *coup d'état* that is widely acknowledged to have been backed by the British and masterminded by the CIA.

A decade later, in 1963, the CIA intervened again, this time to remove General Qasim, the new Iraqi leader who appeared to be moving the country closer to the Soviet bloc. One of Qasim's would-be assassins, acting in close cooperation with US intelligence officers, was the future Iraqi leader Saddam Hussein.

After World War II, the UK and France, as well as the US, continued to be heavily involved in the Middle East.

During the interwar period, the British, who then ruled Palestine, had made tentative moves towards creating a Jewish homeland. These had been abandoned after the outbreak of World War II because of the need to keep Palestinian support. With the UK hampered by its commitments to Arab leaders, by 1946 the US had become the leading force in the creation of a homeland for the Jews who had survived the Nazi Holocaust. As Jewish refugees poured into the country, violence between Jews and Arabs increased. In 1947, the British government withdrew from its Palestinian Mandate, and the UN plan, championed by the US, for partition of Palestine started to go ahead.

The new state of Israel was created on May 14th, 1948, and immediately six Arab armies launched an invasion. Israel not only repulsed the invading armies, but also captured and annexed additional territory within Palestine. From the outset, relations between Israel and its Arab neighbours were poor, and there was a sense in much of the Middle East that Israel was a construct imposed on them by Washington. This created a growing resentment against the US for its interference in the region and its continuing support for Israel.

Egypt had become partially independent from the UK in 1922, but did not gain full independence until after World War II. In 1952, a military coup with widespread popular support deposed King Farouk, and two years later Gamal Abdel Nasser, the leading force behind the revolution, became president.

In 1956, Nasser nationalized the Suez Canal, which was the principal trading route between Europe and the Far East and a major route for oil to the western European economies. The journey from the Persian Gulf to the UK via the Suez Canal was 6,500 miles, compared to 11,000 around the Cape of Good Hope.

Relations between the UK and Egypt had worsened considerably after the coup. The UK withdrew its offer of funding for the Aswan Dam project in Upper Egypt when Cairo appeared to be seeking closer relations with the Communist bloc. Tensions between Egypt and Israel were also increasing, with both sides making frequent incursions into the other's territory.

On July 26th, 1956, Nasser announced the nationalization of the Suez Canal, and closed it to Israeli shipping.

The UK and France reacted by planning an invasion of Egypt at a secret meeting in Sèvres, near Paris. Many documents from the meeting were destroyed, but it emerged years later that an Israeli invasion of Egypt had been planned to provide a pretext for British and French intervention.

On October 29th, Israel invaded the Gaza Strip (formerly part of Palestine and now under Egyptian control) and the Sinai Peninsula, striking towards the Canal Zone. The UK and France offered to occupy the area, an offer that Nasser predictably refused. Air forces massed on Cyprus and Malta were then unleashed on Egypt.

Very noticeably, the invasion was condemned by the US, which had been accused of hypocrisy for criticizing the USSR's role in the 1956 Hungary crisis, while its allies attacked Egypt. With Moscow threatening to intervene in support of Egypt, US President Eisenhower put pressure on the UK and France to agree a ceasefire. This pressure was partly financial; Eisenhower planned to sell the US's pound sterling reserves, causing the British currency to collapse. The British Prime Minister Anthony Eden resigned, and the invading armies withdrew from Egypt in 1957.

Although it was a military success, the invasion and its denouement were a humiliating disaster which exposed the hollowness of the UK's and France's perceptions of themselves as major international players in the post-war world. From then on, the primacy of the US and USSR in the post-war world was undisputed.

Growing Arab militancy and resentment at US and British support of Israel later boiled over in 1967, when Egypt blockaded the Tiran Straits, again preventing Israeli shipping from reaching its markets in Asia. This precipitated the Six Day War (June 5–10th, 1967), when Israel again drove back Arab armies, this time capturing East Jerusalem, the West Bank, the Golan Heights, the Gaza Strip and the Sinai Peninsula. The Six Day War and the 1973 Yom Kippur War increased concerns about the stability of this vital oil-producing region, especially when OPEC increased oil prices during the Yom Kippur War to put pressure on Israel's Western supporters. The creation of OPEC, a cartel of oil-producing countries, in 1960, was a direct challenge to the Western importers who had previously relied on cheap oil. It coincided with a rise in strongly nationalistic leaders determined to set a course away from the West. Among them were Saddam Hussein in Iraq, the Ayatollah Khomeini in Iran and Colonel Gaddafi in Libya.

The Influence of Oil on US Foreign Policy

World War II marked the end of the era in which the US could fulfil the world's needs for fuel – or even its own needs. The US had supplied six out of every seven barrels of oil used during World War II.

At the start of the war, estimated reserves were 20 billion barrels of oil, but by 1942 it was using 4 million barrels per day, 1.45 billion barrels per year. At this rate, the US would use up its entire reserves in 13 years.

The solution was to look elsewhere, in particular to the Middle East, where the early 20th-century discoveries in Iran and Iraq were followed by new finds in Saudi Arabia in the late 1930s.

"The center of gravity of world oil production is shifting from the Gulf-Caribbean area to the Middle East to the Persian Gulf area – and is likely to continue to shift until it is firmly established in that area," said DeGolyer in the prophetic 1944 Preliminary Report of the Technical Oil Mission to the Middle East. This would become a major foreign policy direction in the decades to come.

Accordingly, President Roosevelt had met with the Saudi king, Ibn Saud, and assured him that the US would protect the Saudi government from attack from within or outside the country. Ever since the meeting, US government officials have considered maintaining access to Saudi oil to be a matter of vital national interest.

In the post-war years, pressure on oil resources continued to increase, to such an extent that there was much speculation that the oil companies were restricting supply deliberately to provoke panic buying and drive prices up.

In fact, demand was being driven up by the consumer boom in 1950s America. Consumption within the US tripled in the 25 years after World War II, rising from 1.8 billion barrels per year in 1946 to 5.4 billion in 1971.

Perhaps because the US had started out with ample oil reserves of its own, cheap oil was seen as part of the "American way of life". Cutting back would not only be uncomfortable, it would also entail giving up a part of the country's culture.

Once oil became a factor in foreign policy decisions, it was also a source of tension within the US government. While the Justice Department was working to uncover cartels within the oil industry, launching over 20 investigations and eventually exposing the secret Achnacarry Agreement, the State Department was promoting US oil interests abroad.

The State Department also had to reconcile its policy of protecting the new state of Israel, created as a Jewish homeland after the

Holocaust, with its need to maintain friendly relations with the oil-producing Arab countries in the Gulf.

The State Department's solution was, publicly at least, to abnegate responsibility towards the governments of the oil producers. Instead, the oil companies took on a quasi-diplomatic role. Through their contacts with the highest levels of government, and the huge economic power they wielded, they were able to influence policy. They were also responsible for the US dollars channelled into their host countries, which were used for government projects – often arms buying.

Within Saudi Arabia, this meant delegating authority to the Arabian American Oil Company (Aramco), a consortium of four major US oil companies: Socal, Texaco, Exxon and Mobil. The original two companies in Saudi Arabia, Socal and Texaco, had allowed the other two "Sisters" to join them when it became apparent that the Saudi oil reserves were so vast that alone they could not provide sufficient capital to exploit them.

Exxon and Mobil were still locked into the Red Line Agreement in Iraq, signed in 1928. Under this agreement, the consortium partners agreed not to develop oil concessions within the red line (comprising most of the former Ottoman Empire, except Kuwait and Egypt) except with the consortium as a whole. The two US members of the consortium, Exxon and Mobil, had equal shares in a 23.75 per cent stake, while Anglo-Persian (which became British Petroleum), Shell and Compagnie Française Petrole (CFP) each had a 23.75 per cent stake and Armenian entrepreneur Calouste Gulbenkian had the remaining 5 per cent.

However, Exxon and Mobil wanted to be released from their obligation not to extract oil within the Red Line except with their partners in the original consortium, so that they could share in the exploitation of the Saudi oilfields with Socal and Texaco. In 1946, Exxon and Mobil representatives arrived in London for negotiations with Shell and Anglo-Persian. The British oil companies' main fear was of being undercut by cheap Saudi Arabian oil. Exxon and Mobil managed to allay these fears with promises of long-term supply contracts; Exxon agreed to buy 800 million barrels of crude oil from Anglo-Iranian over the next 20 years, while Mobil made a similar commitment to Shell. However, the French company CFP (later

TotalFinaElf) and "Mr Five Percent" Calouste Gulbenkian were to prove less amenable, and launched a lawsuit against their partners.

The two American companies had to promise more investment in Iraq (funding two pipelines to the Mediterranean and further expansion of their drilling operations), as well as extra free oil in a concession to Gulbenkian to get out of the deal.

No sooner had the Red Line Agreement been cancelled in November 1948, than Ibn Saud, king of Saudi Arabia, started making demands on the American oil companies. He, like the other Eastern oil producers, had watched with interest as Venezuela's new leader Perez Alfonso had, in 1943, signed the first "fifty-fifty" agreement with Exxon, under which the Venezuelan government took a 50 per cent share of profits.

Unlike Alfonso, Ibn Saud was not a reformer, but he had a large appetite for luxury and state prestige projects like the Aramco-funded railway from Riyadh to the oil city of Dhahran. He too sought a 50 per cent share of the oil profits for his country.

Worried Aramco executives met with the US Assistant Secretary of State George McGhee. McGhee was, in fact, a Texas oilman and the son-in-law of the geologist Everett DeGoyler, who had been to investigate the region's oil reserves in 1943. As well as sympathizing with the oil companies' concerns, McGhee believed it would be a good idea to provide more money for the Saudis. He hoped to keep them friendly to the US rather than risking a drift towards the USSR, and to allow them to build up their military capacity.

The solution dreamed up by Aramco and the State Department became known as the "golden gimmick". Ibn Saud would receive his 50 per cent. But any money paid to the king by the oil companies would be treated as foreign income tax, deductible in the US under rules preventing double taxation, so the oil companies would end up paying no more than before.

The only loser would be the US Treasury, which lost $50 million in taxes the following year. The "golden gimmick" also fitted in with the State Department's plans, allowing it to subsidize Saudi Arabia without alienating Israel or needing to ask Congress for approval. In short, the US taxpayer was the loser – the agreement subsidized Saudi Arabia and the oil companies.

Oil and the CIA Coup Against Mossadeq

After the disastrous Suez invasion of 1956, the US and UK continued to work hard to maintain their influence in the Middle East. In the 30 years after World War II, the European colonial powers had been forced to give up their empires. India had won its independence in 1947, and other countries were eager to follow suit. This caused difficulties for the major oil companies, who often established quasi-colonial relationships with the oil-producing countries of the Middle East, though economic pressure could still be used to bring countries that resisted back into line.

Like Ibn Saud, Mohammed Mossadeq, the new prime minister of Iran, was impressed by the success of Alfonso's "fifty-fifty" law. Soon, Mossadeq became locked into a battle with the Anglo-Persian Oil Company (BP), backed by the British Foreign Office, not just for money but for overall control of the Iranian oilfields. In 1951, it became apparent that there was no possibility of a compromise, and Mossadeq nationalized the Iranian oil industry. It is no secret that his subsequent removal from power and the reinstatement of the Shah was (as stated above) a coup orchestrated by the British and the CIA. What is less clear – and still hidden among classified US and British archives – is the motivation behind the coup, and to what extent it was motivated by the politics of oil.

Anglo-Persian had profited greatly from Iranian oil, and it dominated the country's economic life. Anglo-Persian was the *de facto* ruler of the areas in which the main oilfields were situated, in the south western part of the country. Abadan, where Iran's oil-refining infrastructure is located, was run as a company town, where "natives" were kept out of company stores and clubs.

Iran also had concrete financial complaints. The British navy was still receiving oil at substantial discounts, while the Iranians themselves had to pay world market prices rather than local production rates for their own oil. The Iranian government received royalties of 10–12 per cent of the company's post-tax proceeds, while the British government received over double this amount, 30 per cent, in taxes from Anglo-Iranian. The amount Iran got depended on the British government; if London raised taxes, Tehran's revenues went down. Anglo-Persian itself made profits of £170 million in 1950. (Louis, p.682)

Diplomats from London perpetuated the colonial myth that Iran was "not ready" to exploit its own oil, and needed to be protected from itself. As Sir Francis Shepherd, the UK's ambassador in Tehran, commented, "it is so important to prevent the Persians from destroying their main source of revenue," (Foreign Office Papers, F. Shepherd to O. Franks, October 2nd, 1951, PRO, FO 371/91464) i.e. their oil, by trying to run it themselves. Shepherd and other influential British officials consistently portrayed the Iranians as "childlike", "overemotional", and unfit to run an oil industry.

Anglo-Persian itself claimed that Iran should thank the company for its "civilizing mission", investing in local infrastructure and creating new jobs, homes and "such amenities as swimming pools," but it failed to deliver on promises to promote Iranians to technical or managerial positions. While foreign oil workers were getting richer, the Iranian employees were stuck in low-paid jobs and substandard, overcrowded housing, a recipe for revolt that the British ignored.

"This is just the way all Iranians live," claimed one British official.

Iran wanted to renegotiate the treaty, addressing such issues as the length of the contract (it ran until 1992), the British insistence on paying royalties in pounds, and its refusal to show company accounts to Iranian auditors. But the overall grievance was that the UK treated Iran as a subject country, under the guise of supporting "stability". (Foreign Office Papers, G. Middleton to A. Eden, February 25th, 1952, PRO, FO248/1531)

Mohammed Mossadeq, an Iranian aristocrat and experienced politician, became the spokesman for the tide of public opinion demanding a change to the relationship between the UK, Anglo-Persian and the state of Iran. Specifically, he called for Iran to take control over its own oil industry.

His predecessors had enriched themselves with the proceeds from the Anglo-Persian operations, and therefore had a vested interest in keeping the company in Iran even while they negotiated for a larger share of its profits.

Mossadeq's National Front party was different. Even Ambassador Shepherd admitted they were, "comparatively free from the taint of having amassed wealth and influence through the improper use of official positions." (Foreign Office Papers, F. Shepherd to H. Morrison, March 15th, 1951, PRO, FO 371/91454)

Public support for Mossadeq was so great that in May 1951 Mohammad Reza Shah Pahlavi had to appoint Mossadeq as prime minister, as well as signing a bill to nationalize the oil industry.

Back in 1932, the Shah's father had threatened nationalization, but it had been apparent to the British that he could be bought off with promises of more money and a better deal from the oil company.

They recognized now that Mossadeq was serious about nationalization, and that the issue at stake was not money but control, the one thing they were absolutely unwilling to concede. Shepherd himself was privately willing to accept a 60/40 deal, or even to share the concession with the other Seven Sisters, provided the UK retained control over extraction, distribution and pricing. A Foreign Office memo written in 1951 states that: "Whatever new arrangements we arrive at, they should be such that we keep effective control of the assets ... we can be flexible in profits, administration, or partnership, but not in the issue of control." (Foreign Office Papers: FO 371/Persia 1951/91470)

The Americans got involved to help the two sides reach a compromise, but both Mossadeq and the British knew this would not be possible since neither side was willing to let the other control Iran's oil industry. The simple fact was that either Iran obtained control or it didn't. "It seems very unlikely we can do anything at all to meet him ... We must keep effective control," said Shepherd. (Foreign Office Papers: FO 371/Persia 1951/19606)

If Iran controlled its own oil industry, it could set production at whatever volume it wanted, and sell its oil wherever it chose. It was a large enough player to influence world prices, or, instead of feeding oil to the West, it might decide to keep its reserves underground, selling only the minimum needed to buy goods from abroad.

"This raises a problem: the security of the free world is dependent on large quantities of oil from Middle Eastern sources," a British official outlined the problem to the US State Department. "If the attitude in Iran spreads to Saudi Arabia or Iraq, the whole structure may break down along with our ability to defend ourselves..." (Foreign Office Papers: FO 371/Persia 1951/98608)

The British believed, almost right from the beginning, that the only solution would be to remove Mossadeq from power.

Their first strategy was economic: simply, to stop production of oil, Iran's main source of income. The British (Labour party) government of Clement Attlee put an embargo on Iran's oil exports, while Anglo-Iranian worked with US oil companies (who feared Iran would set a precedent for local control) to increase its output from non-Iranian sources.

All the Seven Sisters were concerned about the example Iran could set to other countries in the region, and needed Mossadeq to fail. Royal Dutch Shell was reported to be just as worried about the situation as Anglo-Persian, while in the US, Exxon and Socony Vacuum (formed after the merger of Standard Oil Company of New York and Vacuum Oil) were lobbying the State Department for support.

When economic sanctions yielded no results, the British looked at ways to install a "more reasonable" government. Their preferred candidate for prime minister was Sayyid Zia, a man with little popular support, whose main appeal was that he seemed eager to agree an oil settlement with the British.

Accordingly, the British began a public relations campaign to smear Mossadeq, planting articles in British newspapers and, with the cooperation of the State Department, in the US media as well. Shepherd himself variously described the Iranian prime minister as a "completely unscrupulous", "crazy", "wily Oriental", who "looks like a cab horse", is "short with bandy legs" and "diffuses a slight reek of opium," as well as having "a daughter in a mental home in Switzerland."

Most importantly – because it was vital to get US support if military intervention was to go ahead – Mossadeq was presented as a Communist threat. The evidence for this was tenuous at best. Although he was consistently popular among the poor Iranian majority (a popularity that grew as his stance against the British hardened), Mossadeq was more an Iranian nationalist than a Communist. As a wealthy landowner, whose father had served the Shah's grandfather, he opposed measures to break up large estates and redistribute them to poor peasants. He even called a halt to the Shah's tentative moves towards redistribution. He had been just as strongly opposed to the 1945 Soviet request for a concession in northern Iraq as he was to Anglo-Persian.

Mossadeq responded to the British campaign against him by expelling all the British Anglo-Persian employees in October 1951, and then closing down the British Embassy in October 1952, on the (perfectly correct) grounds that British officials were using it as a base for conspiracies against him.

Since 1951, the British had been considering another option; if economic sanctions and propaganda could not remove Mossadeq from office, he might be removed by force. To do this, they needed the help of the Americans.

Harry S. Truman, who considered Mossadeq to be a bulwark against Communism, was relatively unsympathetic to the British. The following year, though, everything changed with the election of the Republican President Dwight D. Eisenhower in November 1952, and a Republican Congress in the US. This coincided with the return to power, in October 1951, of Winston Churchill and the Conservative party in the UK.

Churchill's Foreign Secretary, Anthony Eden, sent a team of British officials to Washington to discuss plans for removing Mossadeq. Together, Monty Woodhouse, SIS station chief in Tehran, and Kermit Roosevelt, the US chief of Middle East operations at the CIA, came up with Operation AJAX.

Operation AJAX was devised to remove Mossadeq from power and replace him with General Fazlollah Zahedi, who would rule on behalf of the Shah. It started with an attempt to get the Majils (members of parliament) to vote Mossadeq out – by bribing them – which was thwarted when Mossadeq dissolved the parliament.

Since Mossadeq had never commanded complete backing among all sections of Iranian society, when Iran's politicians began to waver, the Shah seized the opportunity to appoint General Zahedi as prime minister. Unfortunately for the Shah, details of his plan were leaked, and on the night of August 15th, forces loyal to Mossadeq arrested the Shah's emissary just as he tried to present the royal decree dismissing Mossadeq.

The Shah fled the country, but Kermit Roosevelt quickly came up with an alternative plan. He worked with Iranian agents to immediately start agitating within the country. Within days, huge demonstrations in support of the Shah had taken over the streets of Tehran. Some 300 Iranians were killed during the coup.

It later emerged that these were not spontaneous popular demonstrations, but had been paid for by the CIA and British intelligence services. A British agent reported that $1 million dollars had been delivered to the US Embassy and a further £1.5 million was sent from the UK to British agents in Iran.

"That mob that came into north Tehran and was decisive in the overthrow was a mercenary mob. It had no ideology. That mob was paid for by American dollars," said a former CIA officer. (Lapping, p.274)

British agents also sent mercenaries into the streets to pretend to be members of the Iranian Communist Party, the Tudeh, and throw stones at mosques and priests. This would create a pretext for a coup in Iran, and the return of the Shah to power.

Oddly, Mossadeq did not order out either his National Front or the army to oppose the demonstrators, and he also turned down an offer of help from the Tudeh. A minister close to the prime minister claimed that, as an Iranian nationalist, he wanted to avoid civil war at all costs because he believed it would lead to a British and Soviet partition of Iran. (US Embassy, Tehran, dispatch, May 19th, 1953, PRO, FO 371/104566)

Together, the CIA and British intelligence forces had succeeded in reinstating the Shah. In December 1953 Mossadeq was put on trial. It was the US's first foray into regime change as a foreign policy tool, a process it was to repeat time after time in the ensuing decades.

The British motivation was clear: they wanted to keep control of the oilfields they had managed since the turn of the century. But why did the US get involved? This was the era in which the US saw itself as the leader of the free world, yet they had replaced a democratically elected leader with a hereditary monarch, who was to rule increasingly harshly in the years after the coup. Many Iranians thought that the US had betrayed the values it claimed to stand for by supporting the British government on behalf of Anglo-Persian. The coup led to speculation that the US had been motivated by a wish to secure Iran's oil for American companies.

After the coup the Shah and his new prime minister General Zahedi denationalized the oil industry, with 40 per cent of the National Iranian Oil Company going to a group of US oil companies. In theory, the National Iranian Oil Company was in charge, but the consortium of foreign companies managing oil production rapidly took control of production and distribution of Iranian oil, giving 50 per cent of profits to Iran. Forty per cent of controlling shares in the consortium went to Anglo-Persian, 14 per cent to Royal Dutch Shell, 40 per cent to the Americans and 6 per cent to the French state oil company CFP. The British, with a 54 per cent share, had got the control they wanted. The Iranians, meanwhile, had managed to control their own oil industry for a mere two years, since Mossadeq's nationalization in 1951.

US oil companies had certainly benefited from the coup, by getting a foothold in Iran, which had previously been a purely British domain.

The Eisenhower administration was openly pro-business, and the Dulles brothers, who both now had senior government positions – John Foster Dulles as Secretary of State and Allen Dulles as director of the CIA – were former Wall Street lawyers with links to the major oil companies. There are claims that the US's primary reason for getting involved in Iran was to take a share of the country's oil industry. A deal between British and US oil companies to divide up Iranian oil is also rumoured.

This assumes that US oil companies wanted to enter Iran. In fact, in the early 1950s the Seven Sisters had few reasons to seek out new sources. The American companies had even richer reserves in Saudi Arabia, as well as concessions in Iraq and Kuwait. Since the market was already saturated, going into Iran would require them to cut back production elsewhere, which would have annoyed the Saudi and Kuwaiti governments.

Iran, with its simmering nationalism and the threat of expropriation, was a far less attractive proposition. On several occasions, US oil executives told state officials that they had little or no interest in Iranian oil. The Truman administration even tried to persuade them to join an Iranian oil consortium by offering to scale down an antitrust suit the Justice Department was pursuing against them.

There are also indications that the US believed it was acting with good intentions, rather than simply to promote its own oil industry.

"Why can't we get some of the people in these downtrodden countries to like us instead of hating us?" Eisenhower asked his National Security Committee in 1953. (Mushahid Hussein, *The Monitor*, Issue 113) More important to the Eisenhower administration than oil was the global fight against Communism. It is more likely that oil was only important in so far as the US preferred not to allow non-Western oil producers like Iran to set their own agenda. They wanted to nip this in the bud before it created a precedent that could spread throughout the region, and end the era of cheap, plentiful oil the Western powers saw as their right.

Most of all, the US feared that the Tudeh was paving the way for a Soviet takeover in Iran. Eisenhower claimed that had the Tudeh attempted a coup, Mossadeq would not have been strong enough to resist it.

The USSR was clearly interested in Iran, which bordered the Turkmen Soviet Socialist Republic and two of the Caucasian republics. Soviet troops had remained in Iran after World War II, not pulling back until 1946.

A variation on this theory was that Mossadeq's government had become reliant on the Tudeh to rule the country, and the Communists were now manoeuvring him out of power.

Oddly, though, in March 1953 the US Embassy in Tehran said that although the Tudeh was continuing its attempts to infiltrate the Iranian government and state institutions, there was "little evidence" that the party had gained in popular strength. Mossadeq considered a greater danger was of a coup not from the left, but from the Shah and right-wing forces. In January, the State Department had speculated that should the Tudeh attempt a coup, this would be likely to unite the entire country against it, and end in the destruction of the Communist movement.

The most compelling evidence for the US's motivation being primarily anti-Communist is the coup's timing. The US first approved the plans to overthrow Mossadeq just two weeks after Eisenhower's inauguration speech.

Eisenhower ushered in a new era of a more actively anti-Communist foreign policy, known as the "New Look". The Republicans had accused Truman's government of being ineffective against the Communist threat, and they were determined to act more aggressively than their predecessors. As discussed, the coup in Iran marked America's first use of regime change as a foreign policy tool, and it went on to make similar efforts in Iraq, Guatemala, Egypt, Syria, Indonesia and Cuba.

After the coup, the Shah repaid the US for its help by dealing mercilessly with the Tudeh. In the next five years, the Shah's police tracked down Tudeh members, torturing 11 to death, executing 31, and sen-

tencing hundreds of suspected Communists to hard labour for varying terms from one year to life. The US was believed to have pressured
the Shah into such "un-Persian" actions.

As for the Shah, he had written to Kermit Roosevelt after the coup,
saying: "I owe my throne to God, my people, my army – and to you."
(*The Times*, June 16th, 2000) But his rule, which lasted for another 25
years, was tainted by his association with foreign interference in Iran,
and as his popularity fell, the regime grew increasingly authoritarian
and corrupt.

The coup also proved, in the long term, to have damaged most
other Iranian institutions. Both the monarchy and the army were now
associated with the CIA, the British intelligence forces and Anglo-
Persian. The secular parties, the National Front and the Tudeh, had
been wiped out. The only alternative to the Shah was the Ayatollah
Khomeini's religious opposition, which had learned an important
lesson from the coup.

"We are not liberals, like Allende (and Mossadeq) whom the CIA
can snuff out," said Ali Khamenei, who was later to become Leader of
the Islamic Republic. (Ervand Abrahamian, *Science and Society*, July 1st,
2001)

Putting Saddam into Power

Another CIA-backed regime change was to have equally devastating
long-term consequences. In 1958, revolutionaries in neighbouring Iraq
tore apart the *ancien regime*, killing the royal family and former government. The Iraqi revolution was unique in the Arab world for being
a popular revolt, albeit led by the army, and for bringing in a complete
change of regime. The monarchy was replaced by a republic, and
Brigadier General Abdul Qarim Qasim, leader of the revolution, became
its new ruler.

Qasim's hold over Iraq was never absolute. The revolutionary fervour that had swept away the monarchy still ran high among many
Iraqis, demonstrations were common, and from time to time popular
feeling and resentments exploded into excesses like the bloody Kirkuk
riots of 1959. The Communists and other groups held sway in certain
areas of the country for a time after the revolution.

Qasim set out to become Iraq's sole leader, much to the anger of the army leaders who had fought alongside him in the revolution. But only Qasim had the popular support needed to rule. Perhaps seeking insurance in case of revolt he allowed his supporters to form militias, and embarked on a programme of reforms to improve the Iraqi people's economic situation and raise them out of poverty.

Western observers found Qasim something of an oddity, noting that he lived alone inside the Ministry of Defence, and had no other home. He never married, which was very unusual for an Arab officer.

But within Iraq he was well regarded for his attempts to improve the lot of the Iraqi people, despite his increasingly dictatorial rule. The Iraqi historian Hanna Batatu says of Qasim that he, "did not feed the poor with words, he acted in a tangible manner." (Batatu, p.841)

Just as in Iran, the Iraqi oil industry had been controlled by a foreign organization. In Iraq, it was the Iraq Petroleum Company (IPC), a consortium of British, American and French companies, plus the Armenian entrepreneur Calouste Gulbenkian.

Qasim did not initially seek nationalization, just a better deal for his country and money to fund his reforms. He also wanted a more honest approach from the oil companies, and started discussions on allegations of sharp practices. He believed that the British companies – Shell and Anglo-Persian – were deliberately keeping production low, concealing the true size of the Iraqi oil reserves in the country from both the Iraqis and the Americans.

The companies were also alleged to be abusing a system of "discounts" to make more money out of Iraqi oil. The companies were claiming discounts to compensate them for selling Iraq's oil, but Qasim pointed out that due to the integration between the different companies, they were effectively compensating themselves for selling oil within their own organizations.

Negotiations continued, but the atmosphere worsened, until in September 1960 Qasim published the minutes from his talks with the oil companies, signalling a breakdown in their negotiations.

The companies wanted their dispute with the Iraqi government sent to arbitration, which Qasim refused. Instead, he expropriated certain oil-bearing lands and invited independent companies to bid for them. But Big Oil did not give up so easily. Despite interest from independent companies in the US, the State Department moved to discourage them from bidding for contracts in Iraq. Averell Harriman (a State Department official who had also lobbied Mossadeq) met with the CEOs of Standard Oil of Indiana, Sinclair Oil Co., and other companies to persuade them that it was "not in the interest of US business to encourage the Iraqis." (Blair, p.86)

Harriman's motivation is unclear, since it seems to contradict that of the State Department's own lawyers, who said that Baghdad was quite within its rights to reappropriate the lands, and considered IPC's actions as "dog in the manger". (Blair, p.86)

The US, however, decided to overthrow Qasim and replace him with a government more in tune with their interests.

While the oil was probably a factor, the country was also important to the US because it was regarded as a buffer state. The decision to overthrow Qasim seems to have been sparked by his decision to withdraw from the Baghdad Pact and decriminalize the Iraqi Communist Party.

Along with Afghanistan, Iran, Pakistan, Turkey and the UK, Iraq had been a member of the Baghdad Pact, a regional agreement aimed at resisting Soviet influence. Qasim pulled Iraq out of the pact in 1959, and immediately started buying arms from the USSR. Qasim also became isolated from his Arab neighbours after they sided with the UK against Iraq in a territorial dispute over Kuwait.

The US decided that Qasim must go.

That year, there was a CIA-backed assassination attempt on Qasim. The assassin was a young man from a village near Tikrit in northern Iraq: Saddam Hussein.

Saddam had been inspired to go into politics by his uncle, Kairallah Tulfah, a Nazi sympathizer who had been arrested during World War II. In 1956 he joined Iraq's Ba'ath Party, which combined socialism with Iraqi nationalism. But Saddam was a street thug as well as a rising politician. During his teenage years he had run a paramilitary gang, which was linked to the murder of Communist party member Saadoun al-Tukriti.

The attempted assassination, by a six-man team of Iraqis with CIA support, was later described by CIA members as "bordering on farce". One former CIA official claims that Saddam, then 22 years old, started firing early, shooting Qasim in the shoulder and arm, but not endangering his life. Another says the problem was that one of the assassins was given the wrong bullets for his gun and another's hand grenade got stuck in the lining of his coat. Qasim, only slightly injured, hid on the floor of his car and escaped from the would-be assassins.

The CIA and Egyptian intelligence officials helped Saddam escape to Tikrit, then via Beirut to Cairo. While Saddam was in Beirut, the CIA paid for his apartment there and gave him a brief training course. From there he went to Egypt, where he studied law at Cairo University, but spent much of his time playing dominoes in the Indiana Café in an upper-class district of the city, watched by CIA and Egyptian intelligence officials. During this time he was a frequent visitor at the American Embassy, supposedly meeting with CIA specialists, including Mike Copeland and Jim Eichelberger.

Four years after the attempted assassination, the CIA made another attempt to remove Qasim from power, and this time they were successful.

In 1963, the CIA masterminded a coup that was carried out by a group of military leaders, including General Ahmed Hassan al-Bakr, a relative and mentor of Saddam. Al-Bakr was later appointed vice president under the new president Abd al-Salam Aref.

The coup was far bloodier than the one in Iran a decade before. Demonstrators were crushed in the path of tanks. Qasim had made mistakes: he had never formed a party or armed his supporters, so when it came to the coup, his working-class supporters and the Iraqi Communists armed only with sticks were fighting the well-equipped Ba'athists. He surrendered after two days of fighting and was executed. Many of the Iraqi people refused to believe he was dead until his bullet-ridden corpse was shown on television.

Ba'ath Party Secretary General Ali Saleh Sa'adi said afterwards: "We came to power on a CIA train." (Cockburn & Cockburn, p.75) The CIA is believed to have coordinated the coup's plotters from its base inside the US Embassy in Baghdad.

Immediately after the coup, Saddam returned to Iraq, where he set about purging the country of Qasim's followers. The Ba'ath Party lost no time in hunting down the Iraqi Communists, working from lists provided by the CIA, which had contacted agents throughout the Middle East for information on who should be eliminated. Later, King Hussein of Jordan said that the lists of those to be killed were transmitted by radio from Kuwait to Baghdad. He also says that a secret broadcast was made from Kuwait on February 8th, on the day of the coup, relaying "the names and addresses of communists there so that they could be seized and executed." (Cockburn & Cockburn, p.76)

This resulted in an orgy of violence, with the killing of around 5,000 suspected Communists, and the imprisonment and torture of up to 10,000.

The US had little sympathy for them. "We were frankly glad to be rid of them. You ask that they get a fair trial? You have to be kidding. This was serious business," a former senior State Department official told the press agency United Press International. (Richard Sale, UPI, November 4th, 2003)

Once Qasim had gone, the Ba'ath party had trouble holding onto power. It was a relatively small group, and had never been a major political force in the country. The CIA appears to have backed it mainly because of its anti-Communist position. The new president, Abd al-Salem Aref, was more skilled at political manoeuvring than the Ba'athists, and managed to eject them from power and create a government that was more pan-Arabist than Ba'athist.

Aref died in 1966 in a helicopter crash that was almost certainly an accident. He was succeeded by his brother, Abd al-Rahman Aref, who continued his attempts to restore normality in Iraq and calm the population, but with little success.

The Iraqi Petroleum Committee was initially allowed back into the fields appropriated under Qasim, but after the 1967 Arab-Israeli war, Abd al-Rahman Aref reversed his position and introduced measures that the IPC found hard to accept. He gave all exploration rights to the North Rumalia field to the state-controlled Iraqi National Oil Company (INOC), and, since France had supported the Arabs during the war, gave the French organization ERAP an exploration and development contract for central and southern Iraq. He then further alienated the Americans by signing an agreement with the USSR. In return for access to Iraqi oil, the Soviets offered to provide technical assistance to help the INOC market their oil.

On July 17th, 1968 the Ba'athists launched their second coup, this time creating a regime that would last for almost 40 years. There is speculation that they again had the help of the CIA. However, if the CIA did support the coup, it did not succeed in installing a government favourable to US oil interests. (Eric Black, *Star Tribune*, February 9th, 2003) Once again, the Ba'athists clamped down on those that opposed them. Soon afterwards, the party moved sharply to the left, and its members started describing themselves as Communists or left-wing radicals. They also adopted many of the policies of the man they had deposed, Qasim.

They also went even further than either Aref or Qasim against the oil companies. In 1971 they started by nationalizing the entire oil industry and carrying out all Aref's anti-IPC measures. Then in 1969 they set up new barter agreements with the Soviet bloc countries, exchanging oil for commodities and expertise starting in 1973.

This is initially puzzling. Why was it that an anti-Communist party that initially came to power in a CIA-backed coup would a few years later be trading with the USSR and nationalizing major oilfields? The most likely explanation is that they sought CIA help during Qasim's rule because it was the easiest way to get control over the country. But without a strong manifesto, they needed to find a way to stay in power, and ended up adopting many of the policies they had been so bitterly opposed to under Qasim. But if they nationalized the oilfields and kicked out the IPC, they would be unable to sell their oil, at least while the Seven Sisters cartel had a stranglehold on world markets. Instead of accommodating the IPC, they looked to the largest alternative market, the USSR. Cleverly, the Soviets also offered infrastructure development, which the IPC had always denied the Iraqis.

There was, supposedly, one more throw on the part of Western oil interests in Iraq. This concerned support for the Kurdish revolt led by Mustafa Barzani in 1972.

As well as slaughtering Iraq's Communists, the Ba'ath Party had launched a terror campaign against the Kurds in the north of the country, who were demanding autonomy. Baghdad was carrying out forced relocation of thousands of Kurds, and later an "Arabization" of the region.

By mid-1972, Saddam had made an offer to Barzani for a compromise to end the fighting. This was better than any offer Barzani had received from the previous Iraqi regimes, and offered much more autonomy than was permitted to the Kurds in Syria, Iran or Turkey, although it did exclude the vast oilfields under Kurdish-claimed lands from the proposed Kurdistan Autonomous Region. It is most likely that the Ba'ath party was trying to placate the Kurds, since its hold on power at that time was tenuous.

Then the US President Richard Nixon appealed to the Shah of Iran to do more to protect US interests in the region, and the Shah, who had been funding the Kurdish rebels for a decade, persuaded him to help them to keep the fight going. The Shah met with the Israelis, who also wanted to keep the war going, since it was in Israel's interest to foster instability in her Arab neighbours. Together, they persuaded Nixon to give Barzani $16 million worth of weapons, but only if the Kurds would agree to continue fighting.

This followed almost immediately after the Ba'ath party's announcement, in 1972, that it planned to nationalize the IPC. Only a few months later, the Shah, the Israelis and the Nixon administration in the US all came out in support of the Barzani revolt against Baghdad. While oil company involvement has not been proved, it is certainly possible that the oil companies were involved.

Holding the World to Ransom: OPEC's Challenge to the West

Since the end of World War II, individual leaders in Iran, Iraq and other oil-producing countries had challenged the oil companies and the Western governments, to try and get a better share of the money from their oil, and also to exert control. Almost always in the past, the oil companies had made concessions, waited, and eventually found themselves back in control.

It was not until 1960, when OPEC, the Organization of Oil-Producing Countries, was set up, that the Seven Sisters were finally toppled as the masters of world oil production. OPEC was set up at the Baghdad Conference in September 1960. Its five founding members were Iran, Iraq, Kuwait, Saudi Arabia and Venezuela. OPEC's stated objective was "to coordinate and unify petroleum policies among member countries, in order to secure fair and stable prices for petroleum producers; an efficient, economic and regular supply of petroleum to consuming nations; and a fair return on capital to those investing in the industry." (OPEC website)

Specifically, OPEC was formed in response to the overproduction of oil in the late 1950s, which caused the price of oil to drop drastically. There was no benefit to the oil-producing countries in overproduction, but they were powerless to stop it since the oil companies determined the level of output.

The governments in the OPEC countries were no longer satisfied with the "fifty-fifty" agreements, under which they received 50 per cent of the value of the extracted oil, less the cost of production. Even after the Achnacarry Agreement was exposed, the Seven Sisters continued to work closely together, becoming ever more entwined through a joint ownership structure of their holding companies. The Seven Sisters had the power to set global prices for oil among themselves, preventing the oil-producing countries from setting the price for the sale of their own primary asset.

The creation of OPEC was sparked by the glut in world markets in 1960 and the corresponding fall in oil prices, which caused a fall in tax revenues within the oil-producing countries. The founding members were joined by Qatar (in 1961), Indonesia (1962), Libya (1962), the UAE (1967), Algeria (1969), Nigeria (1971), Ecuador (1973) and Gabon (1975).

At first, OPEC was absolutely not a political organization, and it was relatively cautious in its economic aims.

In the early 1970s, OPEC started to increase prices in response to rising world demand for oil, and the falling dollar. Several of its member countries (Iran in particular) also needed more weapons for their ambitious new defence programmes, as tensions increased in the Middle East. OPEC was likely also inspired by the success of the new revolutionary government of Colonel Muammar Gaddafi in Libya.

Libya had become the favourite source of oil for consumption in Europe, since Libyan oil was cheap to extract and only needed to be transported a short distance across the Mediterranean. No other countries offered a similar resource, especially after the Biafra war started in Nigeria; in any case, the Nigerian oilfields were over 2,000 miles further south.

Despite the low cost of shipping oil to Europe, the oil companies operating in Libya didn't take this into account when fixing a price with Libya's government, the corrupt regime of King Idris. If anyone had been inclined to complain, the memory of what had happened to Mossadeq would most likely have deterred them.

Then in September 1960 a group of young army officers led by Colonel Muammar Gaddafi overthrew the king. Gaddafi's first prime minister, Dr Suleiman Maghrabi, had an intimate knowledge of how the oil business worked. He had worked as a lawyer for Exxon, later being jailed for organizing a strike, and had no doubt that the oil companies had cheated Libya.

Gaddafi and his cabinet were not only determined to stop the oil companies from – as they believed – cheating Libya, but also planned to use oil supply as a lever against the West and Israel.

Gaddafi told the 21 oil companies operating in Libya to raise their prices. At the same time, to show them he was serious, he made contact with Moscow.

The oil companies might have held out against Gaddafi if they had preserved a united front or modified their demands. (Even the US State Department supported an increase in prices if this would avert a similar crisis all over the Middle East.) But Exxon and the other companies were divided by their greed, allowing the Libyan negotiators to pick them off one by one.

Within a few months, the "wild men of Libya" had shattered the myth of the invincible Seven Sisters. Big Oil was now operating in Libya on Gaddafi's terms.

Inspired by the Libyan success, other Middle Eastern countries rapidly started raising their own demands, meeting in Caracas in December 1970 in a newly militant mood.

At the same time there were now the first signs since the formation of OPEC of a world shortage of oil. For OPEC, 1970 was a turning point, with the buyers' market turning to a sellers' market.

Then, on October 6th, 1973, the second Arab-Israeli war broke out; Egypt and Syria had invaded Israel seeking to reclaim territory given up after the 1967 war. Israel rapidly drove back the Arab forces.

For the first time, the Arab oil producers decided to use their oil as a political tool. OPEC increased oil prices by 70 per cent, to $5.40, on October 16th, as well as introducing an embargo on sales to the US and the Netherlands (because of their history of friendship with Israel and because they had allowed the US to use Dutch airfields to carry supplies to Israel) and a cut in global production. To the US's chagrin, its old ally the Shah was among the most vocal OPEC members.

The organization threatened to follow this with additional further cuts in production unless Israel withdrew from the conquered territories. Oil prices soared to nearly $11 a barrel, nearly four times its previous level, and the uncertainty kept prices high even when the embargo was lifted.

Certain observers have proposed that the creation of OPEC was either instigated or supported by either the major oil companies, or by the US government. Apparently, the OPEC countries themselves were suspicious that one of their number might have struck a deal with the US or the oil companies.

The economists Peter Odell (Odell, pp257–8) and Christopher T. Rand (Rand, p.84), for example, believe that the oil companies had already decided to accept a rise in the price of oil, because this would indirectly benefit them and make them richer. It would also ensure that more money would be going to the producing countries, and ease their demands for royalties. The companies operating in Saudi Arabia certainly did well immediately after the first oil shock, maintaining a close relationship with the Saudi government and raking in even larger profits than previously. A rise in prices would also reduce the gap between the posted and spot market price, which would damage the independent oil producers.

Odell and Rand also believe that the oil companies would have had the tacit support of the US government in this conspiracy. The US government had introduced a tariff on oil imports to stop companies drilling for oil inside the US being undercut by cheap imports from abroad. This meant that US consumers paid a higher price for oil than other importers such as Europe and Japan. This could explain why the US did not take action to back up the oil companies against OPEC.

On the other hand, there are equally compelling reasons to believe that neither the US government nor the oil companies would have supported OPEC – not least because the oilmen were reportedly furious about the oil producers' demands.

The key issue here is control. This was the thing at stake in Iran, before the coup against Mossadeq, and it was the one thing that Anglo-Persian and the British government were adamant they were not going to give up. OPEC allowed the oil producers to take that control because they became the price setters. The oil companies were not about to give this up voluntarily.

Also, once they had lost control the oil companies could not stop the producers from going further. First they might raise prices, but who was to say they might not choose to expropriate the oilfields and cancel their concessions next?

The main victims of the price shocks were the world's consumers.

The US was not hurt initially, because much of OPEC's profits found their way into American banks, but in the long term it was damaging for the economy.

Cashing In on the Middle Eastern Arms Bazaar

After prices went up, the oil-producing countries were awash with cash that their relatively small economies could not absorb. Their rulers, suddenly stupendously rich, started pouring money into public construction projects, importing cars, building palaces and shipping in millions of dollars worth of luxury goods. But above all, they bought arms.

This tended to be encouraged by the Western countries, who were eager to sell their products, and just as keen that the Middle East should be able to protect itself now that it was a region of such huge strategic importance.

Between 1972 and 1976, Iran alone bought $10 billion worth of US arms. Indeed, the OPEC countries as a whole proved to be such pro-lific spenders on weaponry that it has even been suggested that the US created the oil shock as a device to provide the oil-producing companies with money to buy arms.

In the early years of the Cold War, the US had been giving arms to countries that needed support against the Communist bloc. But by the early 1960s, the emphasis had shifted to selling US arms to fund the country's own expensive weapons programmes.

In 1961, the International Logistics Negotiations (ILN), a government agency devoted to increasing sales of America's military hardware, was set up. The Pentagon, meanwhile, launched the Military Assistance Credit Account, which guaranteed financing for arms deals. The money in this account mounted up rapidly, since any credit was paid back into the account, rather than to the Treasury. Unfortunately for the Pentagon, in 1967 Congress found out about the account and closed it down. The Pentagon needed a new source of revenue for its arms sales.

It was also seen by many in the State Department as being in the US's interests to sell arms to the Middle Eastern countries to enable them to defend themselves and their oil against Communism. On the other hand, they didn't want to be seen to be giving arms or aid to the Arab world when it was on the brink of war with Israel.

So when the Shah (who had been appointed as the US's representative in the Middle East) offered to start buying arms from the US, Nixon jumped at the chance to finance America's defence establishment, cutting Congress out of the picture.

The US rapidly embarked on selling state-of-the art equipment to Iran, despite the reservations expressed by Pentagon generals, who pointed out that the Shah was buying equipment that was far too sophisticated for his untrained army to use, and also that he was buying far more than he needed, often duplicating purchases. Nixon and Kissinger did not appear to be concerned, possibly considering that if the Iranian army could not use the arms it was buying, it wouldn't be able to do any damage with them.

Meanwhile, the sales to Iran and elsewhere were making the US's balance of payments look healthier, and as opposition to the Vietnam War grew, and Congress sought to rein in the Pentagon, they proved a useful source of revenue for the US's own defence programme.

Did the Pentagon encourage the oil shocks in order to create a market for US arms and provide the Middle East with the cash to arm itself? While the arms sales that followed the cash influx to the oil producers certainly benefited the US's defence industry, overall their effect was highly damaging to the US's economy. Europe and Japan also paid a high price. It is also unlikely that the US would have encouraged the oil producers to assert their independence. The oil shocks showed the oil producers that they could hold the world, and especially the US, to ransom by withholding supplies. But the attempt to persuade countries in the region to spend their money on arms after the shock was certainly successful. In total, the OPEC countries as a whole went from a $67 billion trade surplus in 1974 to a $2 billion deficit four years later.

Overall, the oil price shock and the creation of OPEC had deep and long-lived effects. It damaged the Western economies, plunging the US into recession. Europe suffered less initially; the UK and France had forbidden the US to use its airfields for attacks in support of Israel, and soon after the oil crisis the European Community released a statement that was widely perceived as pro-Arab. However, the oil price rises caused a rampant inflation across Western Europe (in the UK, for example, inflation reached almost 30 per cent) and forced many to think seriously for the first time about conservation and energy efficiency. They were also looking to new sources of oil, which was to trigger confrontations in new areas of the world in the decades to come. Most importantly, the sway of the Seven Sisters, which had lasted since the 1928 Achnacarry Agreement, was finally broken. The OPEC countries could use their oil wealth not only to increase their revenues, but also to exert political pressure on their international opponents.

Chapter Six: The Cold War "Proxy Wars"

In the 45 years from 1945 to 1990, neither the US nor the USSR, both of which had nuclear arsenals large enough to plunge the world into nuclear winter and kill everyone on it several times over, ever attacked each other directly. When wars did erupt – in the Middle East, in Africa, in Korea and Vietnam, in Latin America – these "hot wars" often became proxies for the hostility between the superpowers, who supplied the belligerents with arms, money and combat training. Where oil was at stake, the conflicts became even more vicious.

This chapter looks at four wars during the later years of the Cold War. Two were in Africa, the Biafra war in Nigeria (1967–70) and the Angolan civil war (1975–92), and two in the Middle East: the Iran-Iraq war (1980–8) and the Soviet war in Afghanistan (1979–89).

Angola was at war for almost half a century. The 14-year war of independence against the Portuguese colonists was followed by a civil war between three of the national liberation groups: the Marxist MPLA, UNITA, and the US-backed FNLA. Each side was vying to take over more oil and more diamonds, which would allow them to buy more arms and mercenary soldiers. Fighting continued for over a decade after the Cold War ended, finally coming to an end in 1992, although it again broke out in the late 1990s.

The Biafra war was very unusual for a conflict during the Cold War era in that the Nigerian federal government was backed by both the UK and USSR. The USSR was hoping to win Nigeria over with military aid, but the issues at stake in this civil war were autonomy for the culturally distinct Ibo people, and control of resources, primarily oil. While the British Cabinet debated whether to continue supporting General Gowon in Lagos, Shell, BP and other oil companies were doing business with the regime in Biafra.

In the oil-rich Middle East, the region's extreme strategic importance meant that the US and USSR had a constant covert presence in the region and an active interest in any conflicts between states there. The CIA funded resistance to the Soviet invasion of Afghanistan – allowing the extremist Taliban and Osama Bin Laden's terrorist groups to become a viable force for the first time – suspecting that the USSR had designs on the Persian Gulf. Not long afterwards, the US became embroiled in the Iran-Iraq war, at least partly because it involved the countries with the world's second and third largest oil reserves.

A number of scandals have emerged concerning the US and its ally the UK's actions during the Iran-Iraq war, which conspiracy theorists attribute to the darkest commercial motives. In the Iran Contra affair, the Reagan administration's secret arms sales to Iran were exposed. Proceeds from these sales were diverted to the Contra rebels (who were already receiving substantial financial contributions from Texas oil barons and other business leaders) fighting to overthrow the leftist and democratically elected Sandinista government of Nicaragua. There followed the Matrix Churchill affair in the UK, this time over illegal arms sales to Iraq in the 1980s.

The Cold War in Africa

One of the most surprising things about Africa in the second half of the 20th century is that there have not been more wars. Almost all the national boundaries on the continent were drawn up by the colonial powers (in 1957 only three African countries, Ethiopia, Liberia and South Africa, were independent), who ignored cultural or linguistic factors when dividing it up.

The Biafra war was the first of a handful of wars of secession on the continent, where the Ibo people of the oil-rich Biafra region tried to split from Nigeria and create a separate state. Largely, respect for established boundaries has been a central part of pan-African agreements aiming to promote stability and economic development.

Where conflicts did break out during the Cold War era, they were often exacerbated by interference from one or both of the superpowers or their allies. The USSR and "Red" China saw post-colonial Africa as ripe for conversion to Communism, and they had some success in Angola, Ethiopia and elsewhere.

Soviet and Cuban aid was instrumental in helping Ethiopia to drive back the Somali invasion of the disputed Ogaden region in 1977, while Soviet military aid also enabled the Ethiopian dictator Mengistu's forces to quash the Eritrean secessionists of eastern Ethiopia.

In two of the former Portuguese colonies, Angola and Mozambique, civil war has been raging for most of their existence as independent states. Mozambique's right-wing Mozambican National Resistance (RENAMO), with support from white South Africa, fought for 25 years to remove the Marxist government.

In Angola, three factions emerged to fight for rule of the country: the Marxist Popular Movement for the Liberation of Angola (MPLA), the US-supported National Front for the Liberation of Angola (FNLA) and the National Union for the Total Liberation of Angola (UNITA), which had support from China and South Africa. It was only after the Cold War was over, in 1990, that the US and USSR started to work together with the Portuguese mediators to bring peace to the war-ravaged country. One of the reasons that fighting could go on for so many decades was that Angola is extremely rich in natural resources, particularly oil and diamonds.

Angola's Civil War

Portugal had been the first country to create an empire in sub-Saharan Africa, and was the last to leave. Angola became independent on November 11th, 1975, 400 years after it first became a Portuguese colony in 1575. Angola was a rich prize for Portugal; it has the second largest oil reserves in sub-Saharan Africa (after Nigeria), and in the early 1970s was extracting almost 9 million tons a year (180,000 barrels per day). Portugal had relied heavily on Angolan oil when OPEC countries cut off exports after it allowed supplies for Israel to pass through its territories.

Until war broke out in 1975, Angola was also the world's fourth largest producer of diamonds, and had undeveloped reserves of other valuable minerals, including gold, zinc, copper and uranium. The country also had a 1,600-kilometre coastline teeming with mackerel, tuna, shellfish and sardines, and it was one of the world's top producers of coffee and other cash crops. Luanda, the capital, was larger than any city in Portugal itself, with a Manhattan-like skyline of high-rise offices, and Portuguese seafront cafés along the Atlantic coast.

Portuguese occupiers finally withdrew in 1975, after Salazar's government in Lisbon was toppled in a coup by young army officers who wanted to end the country's colonial wars. Several Angolan armies had been fighting for independence for 14 years.

The new rulers in Lisbon planned to hand power over to one of the groups fighting for national liberation, the Marxist MPLA. The MPLA was immediately challenged by the FNLA and UNITA, who tried to take Luanda before the MPLA could form a government, and war broke out soon after independence.

In July 1975, rebel forces invaded – UNITA from their bases in South Africa and the FNLA from Zaire. Holden Roberto, leader of the FNLA, was the brother of Zairean president Mobutu Sese Seko, who had come to power via a CIA coup (the US's role in Zaire is explored in Chapter 10). The CIA was involved in both attacks, and US State Department documents reveal that the US authorities knew about the invasions beforehand, and that they helped to airlift men and equipment to the front line.

CIA operatives sent to help the FNLA and later UNITA soon discovered that one of the problems they faced was that the forces of both factions were inadequate. Although the top CIA officials in the country had reservations, they decided to hire mercenaries. The results of this policy were mixed, with some soldiers simply incompetent and others dangerously psychopathic. A Greek Cypriot soldier, Costas Georgiou, who executed 14 of his own men for alleged cowardice in 1975, was one of the most notorious examples. He and four of his fellow mercenaries were sentenced to death at a military tribunal in Luanda, and executed by the MPLA. A British mercenary who deserted said the raids in Angola targeted not only the military, but "anything that moved, including women and children." (Bruce Kennedy, CNN, 1998)

The revelation that the CIA had provided covert support to both the FNLA and UNITA sparked a heated debate within the US Senate. Daniel P. Moyniham, the US ambassador to the United Nations, argued that if the US stopped aid to the anti-Communist groups, the "Communists will take over Angola" (New York Times, December 30th, 1975) and would not only control Angola's oil reserves, but also be in a position to threaten key shipping routes. The US was already concerned about the threat posed by Soviet bases in Somalia to oil traffic off the East African coast. If, for any reason, the Suez Canal could not be used, Angola was situated on the main alternative shipping route between the Persian Gulf and Europe.

In December 1975, however, the US Senate voted to cut off funding for covert arms shipments to Angola. The US, which was trying to withdraw from South East Asia after its humiliating defeat in Vietnam, did not want to commit to a war in Angola.

The FNLA was rapidly defeated, and the civil war ended in 1976, but UNITA controlled the northern part of the country, and continued to wage a guerrilla campaign against the MPLA, which was now established in Luanda. Conservatives in the US urged against a resumption of diplomatic relations between Washington and Luanda due to the presence of some 11,400 Cuban soldiers and technical advisers in the country.

Attempts to rebuild Angola after the civil war, and continue the fight against UNITA, were almost wholly dependent on oil, which in May 1976 was responsible for 80 per cent of the country's foreign exchange.

Gulf Oil, which had been operating in Angola since colonial times, briefly closed production and, under pressure from the US government, placed its royalties for Angolan oil in an escrow account for the duration of the war. By August 1977, however, it was producing 123,000 barrels a day, almost up to pre-war levels. It seemed that Gulf was just as happy to do business with the Marxist MPLA as it had been to work with the colonial Portuguese administration.

Ironically, Cuban troops were now protecting Angola's oilfields and infrastructure in the Cabinda enclave on the border with Zaire, so that Gulf Oil could do business there. (Marvine Howe, New York Times, May 30th, 1976) By 1985, Gulf had invested $100 million in Cabinda.

The US government's reluctance to reopen diplomatic relations did not extend to the business community, and by 1984 the US was Angola's largest trading partner, buying 53 per cent of Angola's exports (chiefly oil). A few years after the war, American banks were providing almost all the long-term financing for the state oil company Sonangol, which had a 51 per cent stake in Cabinda Gulf. US banks lent over $200 million to Angolan companies in the decade after independence, and a further $230 million was lent by the Export-Import

Bank, an arm of the US government that guarantees loans to encourage foreign companies to trade with the US.

Foreign banks and Gulf officials reported an excellent working relationship with the Marxist government in Luanda. "It is a question of business," said Lucio Lara, a member of the Angolan Politburo. (Steve Mufson, *Wall Street Journal*, November 13th, 1985)

This situation was to change in January 1981, when the new Republican President Ronald Reagan took office. Many US conservatives had maintained links with the UNITA leader Jonas Savimbi, and hoped to overturn the 1976 Clark Amendment banning support for anti-government groups in Angola.

In February 1981, White House officials announced that the Reagan administration was considering asking Congress to lift the ban, which many of Reagan's advisers blamed for the success of Angolan government forces, backed by Soviet and Cuban aid. They hoped Congress would allow them to back UNITA, despite the advice from Africa experts within the State Department, who warned that there was no indication that UNITA was on the verge of a breakthrough, and of the dangers of supporting a "surrogate" army when the US had no control over their actions.

Savimbi's right-wing supporters in the US also tended to ignore the fact that UNITA was originally a Maoist group, receiving aid from China as well as South Africa. Savimbi also stated that he had no ideological differences with the MPLA.

"I am not a capitalist. Some of my American friends were puzzled when I told them I was not a capitalist, and I don't intend to become one. So friends of mine, like Sen. Jesse Helms were absolutely shocked," he said in a 1982 interview. (Williamson M. Evers, *Wall Street Journal*, February 11th, 1986)

US State Department officials also pointed out that, contrary to UNITA reports, the number of Cubans in the country had recently decreased. Angolan government officials claimed that Cuban soldiers were still needed to deal with South African incursions in the south of the country, where they were targeting SWAPO (South West Africa People's Organization) bases for guerrillas fighting for independence in Namibia.

While Congress debated lifting the Clark Amendment, Chevron (Standard Oil Company of California had taken over Gulf Oil in 1980 and the merged company was renamed Chevron), Texaco, Elf and other Western companies were increasing their investments in Angola. A growing divide was opening up between the oil companies who were willing to do business with the MPLA (and even wanted the regime to continue for the sake of stability), and the anti-Communists in Washington who wanted a UNITA victory. The right-wing lobby group Conservative Caucus even had Wild West style "Wanted" posters featuring Chevron chairman George Keller printed.

UNITA announced that it would step up its campaign of economic sabotage, targeting the oil industry, unless multinationals operating in the country used their influence with the MPLA to end the war. Shortly afterwards, UNITA blew up part of Chevron's 25-mile overland pipeline, killing ten people. This was the sixth time since independence that the pipeline had been cut. In May 1985 there was a more serious attempt at sabotage; a South African commando was arrested trying to blow up the Gulf storage depot at Malongo.

"We were not looking for ANC or SWAPO, we were attacking Gulf Oil. But by that action we hoped to reduce Angolan government aid to those groups," Winan Petrus du Toit, the captured commando, said. (Patrick Reyno, Associated Press, May 28th, 1985) According to Paulino Pinto Joao, the Angolan information minister, had the sabotage attempt succeeded it would have cost Angola $30 million in crude oil, $200 million in equipment and a further $250 million in lost production during reconstruction.

In the mid-1980s, UNITA carried the civil war further into Angola with South African support, launching a campaign of economic sabotage aimed at frightening away the Western technicians and businesspeople cooperating with the MPLA government. They received a boost on July 10th, 1985, when the US Congress voted to drop the Clark Amendment, ending the decade-long ban on US military assistance to UNITA. Although there was now a Democratic majority in Congress, this was a symptom of the more hawkish stance in US politics at the time.

After the amendment was lifted, both Savimbi and the US State Department started to put pressure on Chevron and the other oil companies to close down their Angolan operations. Conservatives within the State Department considered that Chevron had gone too far by lobbying Congress against destabilizing the MPLA's regime. On

January 31st, 1986, Savimbi threatened to sabotage Chevron's facilities in Cabinda unless the company closed them down.

"It is a target," Savimbi told a Washington press conference. "Gulf is helping the war to continue by supporting the Angolan government with money from its operations in Cabinda." (John Fogarty and Jeff Pelline, *San Francisco Chronicle*, February 1st, 1986)

In an interview with the *Washington Post*, Savimbi accused Chevron/Gulf of "making a lobby against me … if they don't want to get hit, they don't make politics." (*Washington Post*, February 4th, 1986)

However, the State Department stopped short of ordering Chevron to withdraw from Angola.

In 1991, with the end of the Cold War, the MPLA and UNITA agreed to turn Angola into a multiparty state. Washington and Moscow had both joined in with the peace negotiations. However, when the sitting MPLA leader José Eduardo dos Santos won the UN supervised elections, UNITA claimed there was fraud, and the fighting resumed. Chapter 8 will look at how the world's major oil companies, now allowed to operate in Angola, cooperated with the rival factions and contributed to keeping the fighting going.

The Biafra War

Nigeria's Biafra war, between the secessionist Ibos of the oil-rich Biafra region and the federal government, was one of the bloodiest conflicts of the Cold War era, with 100,000 military casualties and up to two million civilian deaths from the federal government's deliberate policy of starvation.

Unusually for a Cold War-era conflict, both the UK and USSR gave their support to the federal government. Both London and Moscow anticipated that the federal government would be victorious, and that countries which supported it would have preferential access to Nigerian oil. There were other issues at stake, though. The USSR, itself an oil producer, wanted to win Lagos over to its side in the Cold War, while the UK was afraid of a fragmentation in many of its former colonies in Africa if the Biafran separatists set a precedent.

Oil was only discovered in the Niger Delta in 1958, two years before Nigeria gained its independence from the UK. Most of the oil was concentrated in the southern Niger Delta within the Biafra region, the home of the Ibo people. Since then, oil had rapidly come to dominate Nigeria's economy.

The causes of the Ibos' attempt to secede, only six years after Nigeria gained its independence from the UK in 1960, were both tribal and economic. General Gowon, Nigeria's president during the civil war, described it as a war of resource control (i.e. control of the oil in the Niger Delta), but it was more complex than that. Nigeria's borders had been drawn up by its colonizers, lumping together 60 million people and over 300 ethnic and tribal groups. The three major ethnic groups were the Ibo in the east, the Yoruba in the west and the Hausa/Fulani in the north.

The (Christian) Ibo often described themselves as "the Jews of Africa"; they were viewed with suspicion for their commercial success as much as for their religious differences with their neighbours. After independence Ibos took many of the top jobs in government and business, under the conservative political alliance between the leading Hausa and Ibo parties.

The Yoruba in the west were originally excluded from the coalition since the majority party in the region was the left-leaning Action Group. When a more conservative party emerged in the region, however, it formed a new political alliance with the Hausa, now excluding the Ibo from power.

In the 1965 elections, the Nigerian National Alliance, bringing together the Muslim north and conservatives in the west, won a resounding victory over the United Progressive Grand Alliance of the Christian east and liberals in other parts of the country.

After claims of fraud by the Nigerian National Alliance, left-leaning Ibo officers led by General Ironsi staged a coup. A few months later, General Yakubu Gowon replaced General Ironsi, after a counter-coup by northern officers. Ethnic tensions within the country increased, and there were reports of Ibos living in the Muslim north of the country being massacred. The Ibo authorities also feared that without a position in government, they would have no control over the oil produced in their region, and feared it would be used to benefit the north and west of the country.

The military governor of the Ibo region, Colonel Odumegwu Ojukwu, declared that the region had seceded from Nigeria, and would now be the independent Republic of Biafra. The government in Lagos refused to accept the secession because it would mean losing most of the country's oil reserves.

The Nigerian government immediately sent the army to recapture the Biafran territory and bring it back under Lagos' control. Initially, their efforts were unsuccessful, and Biafran troops drove back the government forces, crossing the Niger River and advancing far enough into federal territory to threaten its capital, Lagos. However, once the much larger federal armed forces were reorganized, they pushed the Biafran army back into the Ibo heartland, capturing the Biafran capital city, Enugu. A sea, land and air blockade of the Biafran region stopped arms or supplies getting through and prevented the Biafrans selling their oil.

By 1968, the two armies had reached a deadlock, with the Biafrans under siege, but preventing the federal army from advancing any further.

Only four foreign governments had recognized the Biafran regime, but as the war progressed, international sympathy grew. The federal army had been following a deliberate policy of sabotaging farmland and preventing food supplies from getting through to the Ibo, to starve the enemy.

"All is fair in war, and starvation is one of the weapons of war ... I do not see why we should feed our enemy fat in order to fight us harder," said Chief Awolowo, vice-chairman of Gowon's military government. (Hugh Nevill, Agence France Presse, January 16th, 2000)

Sympathy for the Biafrans grew further as pictures of starving children and civilians were broadcast round the world. Volunteer groups organized relief flights into Biafra, with food and medicines, though Lagos claimed that the volunteers were also flying in weapons, and that the Biafran government was hiring foreign mercenaries to fight for it.

The most significant outside support, however, was directed at the federal government in Lagos. The US had placed an embargo on exports of military goods to either the federal government or the Biafrans, but both London and Moscow allowed equipment to be sent to Nigeria. Most of Biafra's military supplies came from France, via the French-speaking African countries.

The UK had initially assumed that the federal government would be victorious and crush the rebellion quickly. Cabinet minutes from

1969 reveal that the government of Harold Wilson spent months debating whether to continue support for the Nigerian government, especially after it became apparent that General Gowon was trying to starve the Biafrans into submission. The government also faced political embarrassment after it emerged that the federal Nigerian air force was bombing civilian targets in Biafra.

It was, however, the first secessionist war in Africa, raising fears that allowing Biafra to break away could lead to wars of secession in many of the post-colonial African states.

"This created a dilemma for us. We appeared to have based our policy on prognostications of an early victory for the Federal Military Government, which had proved to be erroneous," Foreign Secretary Michael Stewart told the Cabinet. "We wanted the slaughter and starvation to cease, but the federal victory which we still appeared to regard as the desirable solution could not now – or so it seemed – be achieved without their continuation." (Giles Elgood, Reuters, January 1st, 2000)

Since Moscow was making overtures to the federal Nigerian government, the UK hoped to prevent Nigeria from going over to the Soviet side. Wilson, who visited Nigeria in March 1969 and found Gowon to be "a man of great sincerity and religious conviction," concluded that his policy was "the lesser of two evils." (Giles Elgood, Reuters, January 1st, 2000)

There were also less disinterested reasons for intervention: protection of British interests in Nigeria. This chiefly meant the largest British investment in the country: the joint Shell/BP venture in the Niger Delta oilfields.

Unlike oil executives such as Deterding or Teagle in the interwar era, the oil companies showed little political loyalty during the Cold War. They were prepared to work with satellites of either the Western or the Soviet bloc, provided they could improve their access to the world's oil reserves. If Gulf/Chevron and Texaco felt they would make more money doing business with the Soviet-supported MPLA in Angola, they would ignore State Department requests to pull out of the country. When the regime changed in the Biafra region, Shell, BP and the other companies in the Niger Delta started paying royalties to the Biafran regime, then in *de facto* control of the oilfields, rather than the Nigerian government in Lagos.

Shell had agreed to pay the Biafran government a "token payment" of £250,000, which the British Commonwealth Office initially supported because Colonel Ojukwu controlled the oilfields. (Aroyehun Gbenga, *Independent on Sunday*, January 4th, 1998) When Wilson reviewed the policy, he scribbled in the margin: "Dangerous argument – cf Rhodesia". Rhodesia (now Zimbabwe) had declared its independence from the UK in 1965, but the UK was still trying to prevent the new regime gaining international recognition.

The debate over paying oil royalties became irrelevant when General Gowon blockaded the Biafra region, preventing oil exports altogether. Already struggling with domestic economic problems, the British objective was to get the blockade lifted so it could continue importing Nigerian oil. While international relief organizations tried to get aid to the Biafrans, British and Egyptian pilots flew Soviet-made planes on night bombing raids against Biafran cities.

However, later in the war, pictures of starving Biafrans were broadcast around the world, causing the UK to step back from its support for Lagos. When General Gowon sought to import 12 jet fighter-bombers, 6 fast patrol boats and 24 anti-aircraft guns, the Minister of State at the Commonwealth Office, George Thomas, was sent to Lagos.

"If Gowon is helpful on oil, Mr Thomas will offer a sale of anti-aircraft guns," said the Commonwealth Office's note to Wilson.

Gowon, however, was not helpful on oil, refusing to lift the blockade. Most of the order was cancelled, but he managed to obtain the anti-aircraft guns as well as two patrol boats he had already ordered. During the war, these were used to enforce the embargo on Shell/BP's oil exports.

In December 1969, the federal army launched a four-pronged offensive on Biafra, with 120,000 troops. The *putsch* cut the rebel province in half, and the following month Biafran resistance collapsed. Ojukwu fled to the Ivory Coast. The war had caused the deaths of between one and three million people, either during the fighting or from disease or starvation. In the Biafra region, industry and infrastructure were devastated.

Initially, the federal government insisted on controlling all foreign relief efforts within Biafra, but it later allowed international experts to inspect the region (where they did not find evidence of genocide) and agreed not to treat the Ibo citizens as a defeated enemy. The exiled

Ojukwu and a small number of his close associates became scape-goats for the war, while ordinary Biafrans were reintegrated into Nigerian society.

Although the war was over, many of Nigeria's other minority ethnic groups in the Niger Delta resented the role that foreign oil companies played in taking their natural resources and often harming their environment. Chapter 8 will explore the continuing skirmishes in other parts of the oil-producing region, and the often tense relationship between local communities and the national government in Lagos.

Oil has also been a damaging influence in Nigeria in its contribution to corruption at all levels of government. It is currently estimated that 40 per cent of Nigeria's oil is stolen and sold on the black market. For the last three years, Transparency International has ranked Nigeria among the world's three most corrupt countries.

The Biafran war did not, in the long term, have severe consequences for world oil production. However, in the last decade of the Cold War, the 1980s, two other wars would erupt in the Middle East, an area of much greater concern for the oil companies and the oil-importing governments. The Soviet invasion of Afghanistan in 1979 was followed in 1980 by the Iran-Iraq war. Both of these would have far reaching implications for the future of the world's oil industry.

The Soviet Invasion of Afghanistan

Soviet forces first entered Afghanistan in 1979, the start of a ten-year operation that was to become known as "Russia's Vietnam". Over the ten-year duration of the war, and beyond, the conflict was to drag in other parties – the US, China, and Muslim nations such as Saudi Arabia and Pakistan – and eventually bring the fundamentalist Taliban dictatorship to power.

Armies from the ancient Persians, to those of Genghis Khan and Alexander the Great, to the forces of the British Empire, have all invaded Afghanistan, but none held its inhospitable mountain terrain for long. The importance of Afghanistan was, for all of them, mainly strategic, due to its location at the crossroads of the Middle East, Central Asia, India and China.

Afghanistan was in many ways still a feudal society, with rival leaders holding sway over different parts of the country, many of them virtually independent from the ruler in the capital, Kabul. In the 20th century, before the Soviet invasion, no less than eight rulers were removed by undemocratic or violent means. The longest-lived of these, King Zahir Shah, had made an effort to modernize the country, and his 40-year rule, from 1933 to 1973, was a period of unusual stability for Afghanistan. He was deposed by his brother, Sardar Mohammed Daoud, in a bloodless coup in 1973, then five years later Daoud and his entire family were killed in a Communist coup by the People's Democratic Party of Afghanistan.

Almost immediately the US stepped in to fund the "mujahideen" forces (a coalition of Islamic and nationalist resistance) fighting against the new Communist government under Noor Mohammed Taraki. For a year he struggled to put down the resistance as well as holding together his own increasingly fragmented administration. On December 24th, 1979, the USSR sent troops into Afghanistan.

Why did the USSR intervene in Afghanistan? At the simplest level, it was going to war to protect a fellow socialist government that had neither the money nor the weaponry to defend itself. This was what the then Soviet leader Leonid Brezhnev said, claiming that the USSR had the right to come to the aid of another socialist country.

But Afghanistan was also an interesting strategic target for the USSR. Getting Soviet troops into Afghanistan meant that only the lawless and sparsely populated Baluchistan region of Pakistan separated the area of Soviet influence from the Arabian Sea. This was on one side of the mouth of the Persian Gulf, the bottleneck through which most of the world's oil supertankers have to pass. At the start of the Afghan war, Pakistan had a right-wing government, but should the regime change, or Baluchistan make a bid for secession, Soviet forces would have access to Pakistani and/or Baluchi ports.

The presence of Communist governments in Ethiopia and the Yemen raised fears in the West of a planned "pincer movement" closing in on the Middle East.

The archive of General Vasili Mitrokhin, head archivist for the KGB's Foreign Intelligence service, reveals that the KGB increased its support for secessionist groups within Pakistan after the invasion. Certainly there were many in the West who saw the Soviet involvement in the war as a direct threat to world oil supplies.

However, if what Moscow wanted was control of Gulf oil, Afghanistan was hardly the obvious choice, other than that the difficulties of the leftist government in Kabul gave a pretext to send troops in. Why not target Iran or Iraq instead and get a result straight away? Taking the half step of invading Afghanistan would alarm and antagonize the Gulf states without getting concrete results.

It also ran counter to the Soviet attempts at that time to improve relations with Middle Eastern countries. A dispute between Saudi Arabia and the Yemen had recently been resolved and the USSR was encouraging Mengistu of Ethiopia to start negotiating properly with the Muslim Eritreans.

There was a certain amount of Soviet interest in the resources of Afghanistan itself. Since 1957 they had been exploring the natural gas deposits around the Amu Darya river in Afghanistan, and had agreed to provide technical assistance, with the aim of extracting Afghan gas and exporting it to Soviet Central Asia. There was no Afghan gas consumption at all until 1975, and after that around 2 per cent of output was used within the country. Since the 1960s, Soviet geologists had identified over 15 oil- and gasfields in northern Afghanistan, estimating the country's probable oil and concentrate reserves at 95 million barrels.

Another possible Soviet motivation, again confirmed in various speeches from Brezhnev, was that the Islamic revolution in Iran had sparked fears that this might spread to the southern states of the USSR (the five Central Asian states as well as Azerbaijan were all traditionally Muslim areas before 1920). Although the Ayatollah Khomeini and his followers had deposed a pro-US leader, Shah Mohammad Reza Pahlavi, they were no friendlier toward Communism. Brezhnev may have feared that the southern states might try to follow Iran's example and break away from the USSR.

Attacking Iran would have been difficult, since it was a country of some 65 million people, with all the sophisticated military hardware built up during the Shah's regime. But when a similar Islamic revolution looked like it might be fermenting in Afghanistan (right on the border of the USSR), this was a less daunting target.

The main reason for the US assumption that the Soviet invasion of Afghanistan was a threat to the Gulf was a CIA report, published in 1977, which claimed that the USSR was running out of oil. (Donald

L. Barlett & James B. Steele, *Time*, May 19th, 2003) The 14-page report, titled "The Impending Soviet Oil Crisis", pointed to the recent fall in oil extraction rates, and concluded that the USSR would soon cease to be self-sufficient in oil and become a major importer. "During the next decade: the USSR may well find itself not only unable to supply oil to Eastern Europe and the West on the present scale, but also having to compete for OPEC oil for its own use," said the report. This made the invasion of Afghanistan, two years later, particularly alarming to the US.

"Let our position be absolutely clear: An attempt by any outside force to gain control of the Persian Gulf region will be regarded as an assault on the vital interests of the United States of America, and such an assault will be repelled by any means necessary, including military force," said US President Jimmy Carter in his State of the Union address in January 1980.

In fact, the USSR had some of the world's largest oil and gas reserves, in the Caspian and in Siberia, which had barely been tapped. The reason for the falling extraction rates was that its oil infrastructure was old and technologically behind that used elsewhere in the world. After the enormous economic expansion in the early 20th century, the USSR under Brezhnev was entering a period of gradual economic decline that was affecting its entire economy, not just the energy sector.

However, advisers to Carter and his successor Ronald Reagan insisted that the invasion of Afghanistan was to be the first step in a Communist takeover of the Gulf oilfields. Using this argument, Reagan quickly secured funding from Congress to establish a permanent military presence in the Gulf.

At the same time as Reagan was building up US capacity in the Gulf, the CIA embarked on a large-scale covert operation in Afghanistan, where it supplied $1.2 billion worth of arms, including Stinger missiles, to the Afghan rebels. The mujahideen also received aid and weapons from China and Pakistan.

The CIA, working with the Pakistani intelligence services (ISI), is widely believed to have encouraged some 35,000 Muslim radicals from more than 40 countries to come to Afghanistan and join the fight against the Soviet army. CIA strategists also flooded into the country to help plan the mujahideen's military operations and train its soldiers. Mujahideen and volunteers – "Arab Afghans" – were fed a mixture of American military knowledge and Islamic law. The US, however, did not divulge that its real objective was the overthrow of the USSR, not just the liberation of Afghanistan from the Soviet army.

Among the recipients of US arms and training was Osama Bin Laden, the "black sheep" of one of Saudi Arabia's wealthiest families, who came to Afghanistan in 1979. By 1984 Bin Laden was the head of the Maktab al-Khidamar (MAK), an organization channelling money, arms and soldiers from outside Afghanistan into the war. The MAK received substantial help from the Pakistani ISI, through which the CIA carried out most of its covert operations in the country.

The "Arab Afghans" were, however, easier for the CIA to deal with than the unpredictable local warlords, who made up most of the mujahideen and were constantly switching sides and fighting among themselves. By contrast, the volunteers who came to Afghanistan from all over the Islamic world and further afield were single-minded about their mission to drive the Soviets out of Afghanistan.

The Soviet invasion, which sparked Afghan resistance, initially involved an estimated 30,000 troops, a force that ultimately grew to 100,000. The mujahideen were supported by aid from the US, China and Saudi Arabia, arriving via Pakistan and Iran. Although the USSR had superior weapons and complete air control, the rebels successfully eluded them.

The conflict largely settled into a stalemate, with Soviet and government forces controlling the urban areas, and the mujahideen operating fairly freely in mountainous rural regions. As the war progressed, the mujahideen improved their organization, and, with the imported arms from the US and elsewhere, the Soviet forces no longer had a technological advantage.

After the deaths of 15,000 Soviet soldiers, and the failure to put down the mujahideen, the new Soviet leader Mikhail Gorbachev finally withdrew from Afghanistan in February 1989, under a UN-mediated agreement. Although the USSR continued to send aid to the pro-Communist government of President Najibullah, his regime collapsed four months after the demise of the USSR itself in December 1991.

At the end of the war Afghanistan was in ruins. Over one million Afghans had died and a further five million were refugees in neighbouring countries. For those that remained, life expectancy had fallen to 40 years, among the lowest in the world. The country's economy too had been devastated, and with mines covering approximately 2 per cent of the entire country, even subsistence farming was dangerous. The only really profitable activity was growing opium poppies in the high mountain valleys.

After Soviet soldiers withdrew, the fighting continued; Afghanistan was still awash with arms from the USSR and the CIA. The line of conflict between Communists and mujahideen was redrawn after the Cold War ended, replaced by mainly ethnic conflict between Pashtuns and Tajiks.

The regional powers – Iran, Pakistan and China – continued to fund various factions and warlords. Things changed when Pakistan armed and funded the Taliban, a fundamentalist movement that had emerged towards the end of the war against the Soviets. The movement was created by Afghans who lived in exile and had trained in very conservative *madrasas* (Islamic seminaries) in Pakistan. After the Cold War, the Taliban movement took advantage of the Pashtun tribes' resentment of the corruption of other mujahideen leaders and the pre-eminence of non-Pashtuns within the government.

The Taliban advanced rapidly across Afghanistan, helped by the Pakistani army, capturing Kabul in September 1996. The US also backed the Taliban's advance to power, hoping it would find a way to stabilize Afghanistan. Among many Afghan villagers, too, their religious extremism seemed to promise a return to law and order and an end to the fighting, looting and rape.

Once the Taliban took the country, however, it immediately imposed an extreme version of Islam, similar to Wahhabism, the predominant creed in Saudi Arabia. The Taliban prevented women from working, denied them education and healthcare, and forbade them to go out unless completely covered. Ethnic minorities were repressed just as brutally.

The Iran-Iraq War

Less than a year after Soviet troops entered Afghanistan, another war began in neighbouring Iran. On September 22nd, 1980, ministers from the OPEC countries had arrived in Vienna to celebrate the organization's 20th anniversary, and the achievements of unity between the oil-producing countries. Then came the news of a devastating attack by one of its members on another: Iraqi planes had launched a surprise bombing raid on Iran, and its troops were pressing forward across the border.

Three days after the invasion, the Iraqi leader Saddam Hussein boasted that he would be in Tehran in ten days. In fact, the war was to last eight years, killing hundreds of thousands on both sides, destroying the two countries' oil infrastructure, and dragging foreign governments from both sides of the Cold War into the conflict.

The pretext given for the invasion was the attempted assassination of Iraqi Foreign Minister Tariq Aziz. In fact, there were many reasons for the war to break out between Iran and Iraq. Primarily, it was a struggle between the two largest regional powers for supremacy in the Persian Gulf. Both countries were bigger and richer than any other in the region except Saudi Arabia, which had a far smaller population and less developed army. If Iraq could successfully invade its neighbour, it would become the dominant country in the region and would be able to exert control over its valuable oil trade.

Saddam Hussein had chosen the moment well; Iranian defences along the border were meagre. After the Islamic revolution the previous year, Iran's army had been purged drastically, with the Sharia rulers removing senior and experienced officers from power. Most of the army was now made up of fervent but poorly armed and poorly trained militias, and the new religious rulers knew very little about military strategy. The arsenals of top of the range US hardware built up under the Shah were depleted by spare-part shortages.

The contentious Iran-Iraq border was yet another legacy of the treaties drawn up after World War I, when the defeated Ottoman Empire was divided up and new borders were drawn and nations created. There were three Iranian territories the Iraqi government particularly wanted: the lands around the Shatt-al-Arab river delta, the province of Khuzestan, and three islands in the Persian Gulf – Abu Masa, Greater Tumb and Lesser Tumb. Iraq also wanted better access to the sea: its coastline was only 26 miles long, compared to Iran's of more than 400 miles.

The Shatt-al-Arab marked 120 miles of the Iran-Iraq border, and its delta was of vital importance to both countries. Not only was it the route by which oil tankers and other shipping reached the sea, it was also the location of much of their key oil infrastructure. Iran's Abadan refinery, for example, was built on a mud flat in the delta. In 1975, Mohammad Reza Pahlavi, the Shah of Iran, had attacked Iraq over the waterway, which was under Iraqi control at the time. Soon afterwards both nations signed the Algiers Accord, in which Iraq made territorial concessions, including the waterway, in exchange for normalized relations. (Iraq had staged a battle against Iranian forces a year earlier in 1974, resulting in heavy casualties on both sides.)

The region Iraq targeted for invasion was the province of Khuzestan, which itself was extremely rich in oil. For centuries there had been rivalry between Iraq's predecessors, the kingdoms of Mesopotamia and the Persian kingdoms east of the Tigris and the Euphrates, over this territory. Khuzestan had been won and lost many times. Qasim, the previous ruler of Iraq, had protested at the loss of Khuzestan, allocated by the Ottomans to Iran and remaining an Iranian province ever since. However, attempts to have Iraq's territorial claims recognized by the Arab League, or to promote secessionist movements within the region, proved unsuccessful, and certainly contributed to the deteriorating relations between the two countries. Under Saddam Hussein's regime, Iraqi radio stations were set up to broadcast into "Arabistan" to encourage Iranian Arabs and Baluchis to turn against Tehran. In retaliation, Iran armed and funded Kurdish rebels to rise up against the Ba'athists.

A few months before war broke out, Iraqi terrorists attacked Iran's embassy in London.

There was also the complete incompatibility between secular, socialist Iraq, ruled by the "infidel Ba'ath party" as the Ayatollah described it (Michael E. Dobe, US Diplomacy, October 31st, 1986), and the conservative religious regime in Iran. Saddam Hussein and the Ayatollah personally disliked each other, and in 1978 Saddam had expelled the Ayatollah from Iraq at the Shah's request. The Ayatollah was threatening to spread the Islamic revolution to the rest of the Middle East, to Saudi Arabia, Kuwait and especially Iraq.

Alarmed by the revolution in Iran, Saudi Arabia and Kuwait had supplied substantial financial support for Iraq's invasion, and the surprise attack cut through the disorganized Iranian army. Iraq forces advanced further into Iran, striking towards the heart of the country and to the city of Ahvaz in Khuzestan.

However, the Iraqis soon found that the reports they had been receiving from Iranian exiles about the ineffectiveness of the Iranian army were incorrect and exaggerated. In June 1982, Iran mounted a counter-offensive that recovered the territory it had lost in the early weeks of the war, and advanced into Iraq. Although Iraq then offered a ceasefire, the Iranians fought on, determined to destroy Saddam Hussein's government. For the next six years, most of the fighting took place within Iraq, though it has been suggested that this was a deliberate tactical ploy by the Iraqis, who would be fighting from their own well-equipped defensive positions.

This was an extremely brutal war. Both sides, especially Iran, used "human wave" attacks, in which wave after wave of untrained soldiers were thrown forward into battle. Iran is reported to have sent groups of young children forward into minefields, to clear the way for tanks and infantry, though this has not been proved. Iraq, with its supplies of sophisticated weaponry purchased from the Soviet bloc, the UK, US and Europe, had less need to rely on human wave attacks.

Iraq made frequent use of the nerve agent tabun and other chemical weapons, killing 20,000 Iranians in a single attack. The US warned Iraq several times against using chemical weapons, but State Department documents reveal more concern over its effect on Iraq's public image rather than the human cost. A November 1983 State Department document refers to Iraq's "almost daily use of CW" (chemical weapons). (Michael Dobbs, *Washington Post*, December 30th, 2002) Another recommends that the US should approach the Iraqi government on this issue as soon as possible to avoid "unpleasantly surprising" them with "public positions we may have to take on this issue." This was shortly before the US made an official statement condemning the use of chemical weapons.

The use of chemical weapons by the Iraqis was widely known, but there was no serious international condemnation. The Islamic revolution in Iran, and the subsequent creation of a state based on Sharia law and intent on spreading this beyond Iran's borders, was at that time as shocking to politicians in Moscow as in Washington and London. As well as the US, UK and western European countries, the USSR also sought an Iraqi victory, though without any real enthusiasm about Saddam Hussein's regime.

"I hope they kill each other," said Henry Kissinger, the former

Secretary of State. (Mike Whitney, *Al-Jazeerah*, February 17th, 2004)

But the US appears to have come to the conclusion that Saddam Hussein was the lesser of two evils. The relationship between Washington and Baghdad was an ambiguous one. The CIA had helped to propel Saddam and the Ba'ath party to power and encouraged them to wipe out the Iraqi Communist party, but once in power, they had nationalized the country's oil industry and moved closer to the USSR. The US had retaliated by adding Iraq to its blacklist of "terrorist states" and by funding right-wing Kurdish separatists in the north of the country.

Iraq continued buying billions of dollars worth of military hardware, chiefly from France and the USSR, but also from China, Egypt, Germany and other sources, including European companies that manufactured chemical weapons. The US provided financial aid, weapons and intelligence (including satellite pictures of targets within Iran) to Iraq, and it increased its support after 1982 when the war was carried inside Iraqi territory. This was despite an official discouragement of any arms sales to the belligerents.

Towards the end of the war, in 1987 and 1988, US ships engaged in naval battles with Iran. On July 3rd, 1988, the US cruiser USS *Vincennes* tragically shot down an Iranian passenger plane, Iran Air Flight 655, killing all 290 passengers and crew. The American government said the aim had been to shoot down an Iranian F-14 Tomcat, which had been in the same area as the passenger plane.

Perhaps the most important US support for Iraq was in allowing the neutral oil tankers heading to Iraqi ports to fly the American flag, and thus be safe from Iranian attack, guaranteeing Iraq's revenue stream for the duration of the war.

Despite the ban on exporting weapons to either Iran or Iraq, many companies in the US and UK exported arms and "dual use" technology, which could be used for either military or civilian purposes – materials such as sophisticated computer equipment, metals and chemicals, helicopters and armoured vehicles. This emerged during the early 1990s in a series of scandals that became known as "Iraqgate". The secret trade continued right up until the Iraqi invasion of Kuwait in August 1990.

From 1982, when Iran carried the war into Iraqi territory, the US started to provide direct support for Iraq, supplying it with intelligence and economic aid, and resuming diplomatic relations with Baghdad. The same year, US President Ronald Reagan signed a secret National Security Decision Directive setting out a US policy of preventing Iraq from losing the war against Iran. (Michael Dobbs, *Washington Post*, December 30th, 2002) This was done despite the official US policy of neutrality, which technically stopped it from arming either of the belligerents.

The Reagan administration removed Iraq from the US State Department's list of countries regarded as supporters of international terrorism in 1982, which allowed Iraq to receive credit guarantees from the Export-Import Bank (Eximbank), so that it could buy American products and technology on credit. Iraq's industrialization programmes and its intensive military spending ate up most of the cash from its oil exports, which made obtaining credit for technical purchases from the US important. Iraq was eager to obtain more technology from US companies. However, the US government was fully aware that Iraq had active chemical and biological weapons programmes, and was therefore concerned about providing technology; the US's export control system was intended to prevent countries like Iraq from obtaining technology that could be used in chemical, biological or nuclear weapons programmes.

Iraqgate investigations also revealed that exports were to military organizations, including the Iraqi Air Force, Iraq's Ministry of Defence and the al-Qaqaa State Establishment, which carried out research and production of explosives. When UN teams inspected Iraqi nuclear research sites after the first Gulf War, they found dual-use technology from the US and other Western countries.

In 1989, the FBI raided the Atlanta branch of Italy's largest bank, Banca Nazionale del Lavoro (BNL). They discovered that BNL had channelled $5 billion into Iraq between 1985 and 1989. The Atlanta branch manager, Christopher Drogoul, was charged with making illegal loans to Iraq, some of which were used to purchase military technology. Drogoul claimed that he was merely one of the players in a large-scale effort, known of by the US government, to supply arms to Iraq. The US Justice Department did not pursue this claim.

BNL was a subsidiary of BCCI, the Bank of Credit and Commerce International, majority-owned by the royal family of Abu Dhabi, which had folded in July the same year. BCCI was found to have been heavily involved in money laundering for organized criminals and drug traffickers, as well as handling financial transactions for terrorist organizations. Osama Bin Laden had an account with BCCI. During the Afghanistan war, the CIA used BCCI to channel funds to the anti-Soviet resistance. After the bank collapsed, with the loss of $11 billion in assets, the first Bush administration in the US, as well as the British government, are alleged to have fought against lawsuits brought by people who had lost money, to prevent details of the bank's activities emerging.

Other companies discovered to be shipping dual-use technology to Iraq included Matrix Churchill, a leading British tool maker, Hewlett-Packard and Tektronix. In 1987, Matrix Churchill (then named TI Machine Tools of Coventry) was acquired by TMG Engineering Ltd. TDG, a company chaired by Safa al Habobi, the Iraqi official responsible for procurement, owned 89 per cent of TMG Engineering.

After the acquisition, Matrix Churchill's business with Iraq increased significantly. While the British directors on the Matrix Churchill board presented TDG as a group of European and Middle Eastern businesspeople aiming to restructure the company, it later emerged that they knew the company was controlled by Iraq, and that Habobi himself was heading a secret procurement drive for the Iraqi military. Two senior company officials informed British intelligence about what was really going on, but the British government decided to allow most of the sales to go ahead.

After the first Gulf War in the early 1990s, the government's case against Matrix Churchill for illegal sales to Iraq collapsed when the defence revealed that the government had known about the true purpose of the exports.

The investigation into arms sales to Iraq, which was headed by Sir Richard Scott uncovered evidence that the British government had on numerous occasions failed to stop illegal exports to Iraq, even though they knew that company officials were lying about their end use.

The American government had, at the same time, also been secretly selling weapons to Iran; first indirectly (possibly through Israel) and then directly, in what became known as the Iran Contra affair.

The Iran Contra Affair

In 1979, the Republican presidential candidate Ronald Reagan is alleged to have sent three of his associates, George Bush, Richard Allen and Donald Greg, to two meetings with arms dealers Manchari Gorbanifar and Albert Hakim, and senior Iranian diplomats. Reagan's team promised on his behalf that the US government would sell more than $1 billion of arms to Iran if hostages being held by a militant Islamic group in Lebanon were not released until after the presidential election. Reagan expected that people would be less likely to vote for the incumbent president, Carter, if he failed to secure the release of the hostages. He also wanted a strongly armed Iran because of his fear, based on the CIA report published three years before, that the USSR was planning to invade Iran and Iraq to replenish its declining stocks of oil. Protecting Iran would keep the major oil companies, important donors to the Republican party, happy, and ensure their continued support.

On April 25th the following year, the then President Jimmy Carter made a last-ditch attempt, Operation Desert Claw, to rescue the 53 hostages. The mission, already doomed to failure due to mechanical problems and adverse weather, turned to disaster when a helicopter collided with a transport plane at the rendezvous point, Desert One. Carter went on to lose the election, making it possible for the plan hatched by Reagan and the Iranians to go ahead.

Relations between the US and Iran since the 1979 revolution had not been good, and the Iranian government was known to have links to militant Islamic groups who were carrying out bombings in western Europe, as well as the group holding the hostages in Lebanon. Since Reagan had no authority to make the deal – in fact it was directly contrary to the Democratic-dominated Congress's opposition to selling arms to Iran – he had to hide evidence of his deal with the Iranians. The men appointed to deal with it set up an elaborate network of dummy companies to conceal the fact that arms from the US government were being sold to Iran. Profits from the arms sales were sent to the Contras, a right-wing military organization set up to stamp out land reform in Central America.

The arms trading began on March 9th, 1981, seven months after the Iran-Iraq war began. Two dummy corporations were set up under the aegis of Iranian sympathizers. The first corporation bought weapons from the US government, which sold them to the second, with a small mark-up. Profits from the first company were transferred, via the CIA, to the Contras. Gorbanifar, branded a "liar" by the CIA in the 1980s, is now known to have acted as intermediary. (Dana Priest, *Washington Post*, June 9th, 2005)

The other player in the Iran Contra deception was Israel. In August 1985, the Israeli government proposed to Reagan that they could act as an intermediary. Israel would export 508 of its American-made TOW anti-tank missiles to Iran. In return, Iran would persuade the terrorists in Lebanon to release the Reverend Benjamin Weir, an American still being held by them. The US would then send replacement missiles to Israel. The deal was masterminded in the US by Robert McFarlane, the Assistant to the President for National Security Affairs, and the US Secretary of Defense Caspar Weinberger.

The next round of negotiations, in November, was less successful. The Israelis offered to ship 500 HAWK anti-aircraft missiles to Iran in exchange for the release of the remaining American hostages. This time the value of the deal was over $14 million, and would therefore require Congressional notification. McFarlane told General Colin Powell that the president had decided to go ahead with the sale anyway. The deal then fell through because the Iranians decided the missiles shipped from Israel were substandard.

Negotiations between Washington and Tehran continued, and in January 1986 the Reagan administration approved a new plan under which an American intermediary would sell arms to Iran in exchange for the release of the hostages. The proceeds would again go to the Contras. After some haggling over the mark-up allowed to the intermediaries, 1,000 TOW missiles were shipped to Iran. Meanwhile, the terrorists were capturing new hostages as fast as they released the old ones. There were no more arms-for-hostages deals, but shipments of weapons and spare parts to Iran were not stopped until November.

Aside from releasing the hostages, the benefit to the Reagan administration was the funds available for the Contras, who were trying to force the left-wing Sandinista government out of power in Nicaragua. The Democratic Congress was opposed to giving help to the Contras, which was banned under the 1982–3 Boland Amendment. Through the Iran Contra agreements, the Contras received weapons and training from the CIA, with the aim of preventing the spread of Communism.

Details of the arms-for-hostages deals first emerged in an article in *Ash-Shiraa*, a Lebanese magazine, published on November 3rd, 1986, after a consignment of guns was shot down over Nicaragua. There was a brief attempt to conceal the evidence: National Security Adviser Oliver North and his secretary Fawn Hall shredded some incriminating documents on November 21st, but four days later Attorney General Edwin Meese admitted that profits from arms sales to Iran were being used to support the Contras in Nicaragua.

Under pressure from Congress and the press, Reagan announced that an investigation would be launched under former Senator John Tower, which became known as the Tower Commission. Reagan also said he had not been informed of the arms-for-hostages operation. The Tower Commission implicated senior Reagan officials, including North, Poindexter and Weinberger, but did not determine whether the President had been involved. Its only criticism of Reagan was that he had "ultimate responsibility, and should have controlled his National Security staff better."

The US was ordered to pay a fine to Nicaragua after the International Court of Justice ruled in favour of Nicaragua in the Nicaragua v. United States case. Despite UN pressure, the US refused to pay.

The Sandinista government continued in power until February 1990. After several years in power, their initial lustre had worn off, and their popularity declined because of government corruption and economic difficulties. With the end of the Cold War and the decline of the USSR, the government also lost its main subsidiser.

The decade after the Cold War would see new alliances and global divisions, and new agendas on the parts of the oil companies and world governments. The wars in the Middle East had left unresolved problems. Afghanistan, now under the yoke of the Taliban, had been a breeding ground for fundamentalism and terrorists just as much opposed to the West as they had been to the USSR. When the alliances against Communism were no longer needed, the tenuous links between the US and the oil-producing countries of the Middle East were broken. And the Cold War had left another legacy in the region: it was now awash with arms from both sides in the conflict.

Chapter Seven: Burning Down the House that Saddam Built

The Cold War that had divided the West and the Communist bloc came to an end more suddenly than anyone could have imagined. In 1989, the Berlin Wall came down and East and West Germany were reunified. Communist regimes across Eastern Europe fell one after another.

The threat of nuclear armageddon had been lifted. But only a year later, in August 1990, Iraqi tanks rolled across the border into Kuwait, raising fears of an Iraqi domination of the world's oil resources. This was the first strike in a new polarizing of the world, with America and its allies pitted against the Islamic Middle East.

After the first Gulf War, when the Iraqi occupiers were driven out of Kuwait, sanctions were imposed against the defeated Iraq and an "oil for food" programme introduced. It is now estimated that Saddam's regime stole well over $10 billion from the UN-administered programme between 1996 and 2003 (recent estimates put the amount as high as $21 billion), with some of the money siphoned off being used to buy international support and undermine the UN itself. Several senior UN officials, as well as politicians in France, Russia and other countries, have been implicated.

The US Senate, currently dominated by the Republican party, has launched an investigation into "oil for food", and there is considerable pressure from the US for the UN Secretary General Kofi Annan to resign. However, a report released in May 2005 by Democratic senators includes evidence that the US military and State Department were aware of the illegal oil sales but did nothing to stop them, and even on occasion facilitated such sales. This emerged during the investigation of whether two US oil companies, Bayoil and Odin Marine, broke the UN sanctions.

The election of George W. Bush, a Texan oilman with many oil executives among his staff, as the new American president in January 2001 saw an immediate change in US foreign policy. The US had long been concerned about how to secure its oil supplies. Now, not only did the Bush administration reject environmental legislation, it actively sought to promote the interests of US oil companies abroad.

The bombing of the World Trade Center on September 11th, 2001, prompted the Bush administration to declare "war on terror" and invade Afghanistan, and, according to some conspiracy theorists, provided an excuse to invade Iraq, a policy that had allegedly been developed before the 9/11 conspiracy. The lucrative contracts for running post-war Iraq's oilfields – many of which have gone to Vice President Dick Cheney's former company Halliburton, despite the company being involved in various corruption scandals – are believed to have been earmarked for key Bush associates before the war even began.

The First Gulf War

Moving at dawn on August 2nd, 1990, the Iraqi troops that had been massed on the Kuwaiti border crossed into Kuwait and within hours had occupied strategic posts throughout the country. Kuwait's army, which numbered 20,300 men compared to Iraq's one million, was rapidly overwhelmed. Iraqi soldiers took all government buildings in the capital Kuwait City, including the Emir's palace, on the day of the invasion.

Fighting in the capital was "short and fierce" according to reports from the Soviet Embassy in the city centre. The Emir fled to Saudi Arabia along with the Kuwaiti air force, while his brother and most of the palace guard were killed defending the palace.

The following day, with Kuwait City already under their control, Iraqi soldiers took control of the oilfields in the south of the country, including the Great Bagram field, one of the largest in the Middle East. Iraq set up a puppet government in Kuwait City, while taking Western visitors and oil workers hostage.

Oil was the primary reason for Iraq's invasion of Kuwait. Originally, the tension between Iraq and its neighbour dated back to the Anglo-Ottoman Convention of 1913, in which Kuwait was treated as an autonomous region within Ottoman Iraq. After World War I, Kuwait was under a British mandate, and later became an independent monarchy. Since Kuwait had previously been part of Iraq, the Iraqi government did not accept Kuwaiti independence, considering it an illegitimate legacy of colonial rule. In the 1960s, British troops had been deployed in Kuwait to deter an Iraqi invasion.

After the Iran-Iraq war in the 1980s, there was a more compelling reason for the invasion: Iraq was heavily in debt to several Arab countries, owing $14 billion to Kuwait alone. Baghdad wanted to raise the price of oil through OPEC to pay off its debts.

After the initial militancy of the oil producers in the 1970s, the oil price had gradually inched downwards as OPEC states increased production. In the years between 1970 and 1990, the price of oil had increased far more slowly than inflation (a rise in line with inflation would have seen oil prices of $75 a barrel). In 1990, oil was at $17 per barrel.

Iraq claimed that it was protecting the entire Arab world by acting as a buffer against Iran, and that Kuwait and Saudi Arabia should therefore reduce or cancel its war debts. Saddam Hussein also presented himself as the only Middle Eastern leader willing to stand up to the US and Israel. Kuwait, however, had increased oil production, which had the effect of lowering prices.

Baghdad also claimed that during the Iran-Iraq war, Kuwait had drilled for oil and built military outposts on the Iraqi side of the border.

Two weeks before the invasion, Iraq had accused its neighbour of stealing oil from the disputed border region and of exceeding its OPEC production quotas and thereby driving down oil prices. Saddam Hussein's immediate goal on invading Kuwait was to increase oil prices to $25 per barrel.

In late July, as Iraqi troops were already gathering on the border with Kuwait, American ambassador in Baghdad April Glaspie met with Saddam Hussein.

Ambassador Glaspie was later interpreted as giving tacit support for the invasion, telling Saddam that the US has "no opinion on the Arab-Arab conflicts, like your border disagreement with Kuwait." (New York Times, September 23rd, 1990)

Later in the meeting (according to the official Iraqi transcription), she added that "[US Secretary of State] James Baker has directed our official spokesmen to emphasize this instruction."

US officials point out that Glaspie expressed concern over the build-up of forces on the Kuwaiti border, and did everything "by the book". Shortly after the invasion, Ambassador Glaspie left the US foreign service, which raised speculation that she had, in fact, given tacit encouragement to Saddam's invasion.

However, there is no apparent motivation for the US to encourage Saddam's territorial ambitions; on the contrary, the US had a lot to lose.

Positions on Iraq within the US government were divided. Relations between the two countries had warmed during the Iran-Iraq war, despite the country's use of chemical weapons against Iran. After the war there were attempts within Congress to isolate Iraq over its hostility to Israel, its human rights violations, especially against the Kurdish and Shiite minorities, and its military build-up. Opposition to Iraq therefore came both from neo-conservatives, such as National Security Adviser Paul Wolfowitz, and from those on the left in Congress.

After the war the Iraqi government claimed to have evidence of a joint CIA-Kuwaiti plot to destabilize Iraq, initially by bringing down oil prices. This was intended to take advantage of Iraq's weakened economy after the eight-year war with Iran, to put pressure on Baghdad in the ongoing border delimitation negotiations. Both the CIA and Kuwait describe the meeting as routine and deny allegations of a conspiracy.

The real fear of the US administration, however, was not the invasion of Kuwait, but the danger of an Iraqi invasion of Saudi Arabia.

Immediately after the invasion, in fact only hours after Iraqi troops entered Kuwait, delegations from Kuwait and the US requested a meeting of the UN Security Council. The Security Council passed Resolution 660, which condemned the invasion and demanded that Baghdad withdraw its troops. The following day, the Arab League passed a similar resolution, but called for the conflict to be resolved within the Arab League without foreign intervention.

The UN Security Council followed up its initial resolution with Resolution 661 that imposed economic sanctions on Iraq. There was at that stage no real consideration of military action to liberate Kuwait, partly because it was assumed that Iraq would bow to international pressure.

However, there was another factor at work. Invading Kuwait had put Iraq in possession of Kuwait's oil reserves. It had also brought Iraqi forces closer to Saudi Arabia's vast Hama oilfields. If Iraq took Saudi Arabia as well as Kuwait it would control 65 per cent of the world's oil supply, and would be able to set world prices. This would put Iraq among the world's major powers, able to provide or withhold oil as it chose. No government, even the US, the world's one remaining super-power, would be able to make a foreign policy move without taking Baghdad's reaction into consideration.

"Our jobs, our way of life, our freedom and the freedom of friendly countries around the world would all suffer if the world's great oil reserves fell into the hands of Saddam Hussein," said George Bush soon after the invasion. (Roff Smith, *Sunday Age*, January 27th, 1991)

The situation was most worrying for the US. After the first oil price shock, most European governments had made an effort to become less dependent on oil. During the 1980s, France became 35 per cent less oil reliant, Germany 31 per cent less, and the UK 37 per cent less, according to data from the consultancy Cambridge Energy Research Associates. The US, meanwhile, was importing approximately the same amount of oil per capita as Europe but consuming an equal amount of its own oil reserves.

The price hike following Iraq's invasion of Kuwait was expected to slow growth and increase inflation in western Europe, but the US was heading for a severe recession if the rise was allowed to stand.

As well as its enormous oil reserves, there were other reasons to suppose that Saddam was interested in taking Saudi Arabia, with its relatively weak army and long, ill-defined border running through the desert. Iraq's war debt to Kuwait was dwarfed by the $26 billion it owed to Saudi Arabia.

Soon after the invasion, Saddam Hussein began making verbal attacks on Saudi Arabia, drawing attention to its close links to the US and claiming that the Saudi monarchy had no right to possess the holy cities of Mecca and Medina. The secular Ba'ath regime took on a notably more religious hue as Saddam added the words "Allahu Akbar" to the national flag and broadcast images of himself praying in Kuwait. In response, US President George Bush launched the defensive Operation Desert Shield to prevent Iraq from invading Saudi Arabia. The first US troops arrived in Saudi Arabia on August 7th.

After the initial deployment of American soldiers, the military build-up in the Gulf continued until 500,000 troops were stationed in Saudi Arabia. By October, American military forces in the area were calculated to be sufficient to stop an invasion of Saudi Arabia. Oil prices, meanwhile, had reached $40 per barrel.

Both the UN Security Council and the Arab League passed a series of resolutions in the months leading up to the first Gulf War. UN Resolution 678, passed on November 29th, gave Iraq a withdrawal deadline of January 15th, 1991. It authorized "all necessary means to uphold and implement Resolution 660" (which had ordered Iraq to withdraw from Kuwait), effectively endorsing the use of force.

By late 1990 it was apparent that Saddam Hussein was unlikely to back down, and the US was seeking domestic and international support for war. This was justified, said the government, by the importance of oil to the national economy, and the longstanding friendship between the US and Saudi Arabia (it was almost 50 years since Roosevelt's visit to Ibn Saud).

When the protests of "No blood for oil!" became too intense, the government added arguments about Iraq's human rights situation, the unprovoked aggression against Kuwait, and indications that Saddam was building up an arsenal of non-conventional weapons (chemical and biological) and aiming for nuclear capacity. Opposition to the war in Iraq was never as strong as that against the Vietnam War.

Although 74 per cent of the 660,000 troops facing Iraq in the Gulf by early 1991 were American, a coalition of 34 countries had been persuaded to join in opposing Iraq, including the Muslim nations of Bahrain, Morocco, Oman, Pakistan, Qatar, Saudi Arabia and the United Arab Emirates. (A number of the US's smaller allies were persuaded to join the war by promises of financial aid or debt forgiveness.) France, formerly Iraq's largest supplier of weapons, was also persuaded to join the coalition.

Despite several peace deals being proposed, the US insisted that war could only be averted by Iraq's unconditional withdrawal from Kuwait. Iraq wanted its withdrawal from Kuwait to be accompanied by a simultaneous withdrawal of Syrian troops from Lebanon and Israeli troops from the West Bank and other occupied territories.

On January 12th, 1991, the US Congress authorized the use of military force in the Gulf, and this was followed by decisions from the other coalition members. The day after the January 15th deadline, Operation Desert Storm was launched. This was a massive air campaign with over 1,000 sorties every day. Iraq was bombarded with the full force of the US's military arsenal, with smart bombs, cluster bombs, cruise missiles and the rest of its state-of-the art equipment, that enormously outgunned Iraq's arsenal, the largest in the Middle East. The coalition first targeted Iraq's air force and anti-aircraft guns, using stealth bombers to knock out the Iraqi air defences. Only one coalition plane was lost on the first day of the war. After the first week, the Iraqi air force started deserting to Iran.

Iraq's initial retaliation had been to fire eight Scud missiles into Israel, hoping to provoke Tel Aviv into joining the war, which would encourage Arab nations to leave the coalition. It followed by dumping up to one million tons of Kuwait's crude oil into the Persian Gulf, the largest oil spill in history. Iraqi Scud missiles also attacked coalition bases in Saudi Arabia.

Coalition bombing targeted command centres within Iraq and Kuwait, followed by military targets, first Scud missile launchers, then weapons of mass destruction sites, weapons research facilities and naval forces. Other facilities needed by military forces as well as civilians – electricity production facilities, telecommunications equipment, port facilities, oil refineries, railroads bridges, dams and even sewage works – were targeted. Two live nuclear reactors were bombed, despite the UN resolution banning attacks on live reactors.

Although the coalition forces tried to avoid civilian targets, on February 13th, 1991, two smart bombs destroyed an air raid shelter in Baghdad, killing hundreds of Iraqis.

The US had hoped that air war would be sufficient to drive the Iraqi occupiers out of Kuwait. But on February 24th, the ground campaign, Operation Desert Sabre, began. Only three days later, Iraqi troops, demoralized by the air bombardment, were deserting in thousands and the remnants of the Iraqi army were leaving Kuwait.

The war ended with the liberation of Kuwait. Unlike in the second Gulf War, which was to take place 13 years later, discussions of removing Saddam from power came to nothing.

The US had hoped that the Iraqi people would rise up against Saddam, or that he would be overthrown in an internal coup. After the invasion, Washington used CIA agents within Iraq to ferment revolt against the regime. However, both policy changes within the US and the opposition of fellow coalition members prevented the war from being carried inside Iraq. Even when a popular rebellion began in the south of the country, the coalition held back. The rebellion, unsupported by the outside world, was brutally suppressed.

Later, a Kurdish rebellion in the north was similarly crushed, with thousands of Kurdish refugees fleeing across the border to Turkey.

Regime change was something that US President George Bush discussed in his 1998 book, *A World Transformed*, co-written with Brent Scowcroft. They pointed out that had coalition forces continued into Iraq, turning the ground war into an occupation, they would have "been forced to occupy Baghdad and, in effect, rule Iraq. The coalition would instantly have collapsed, the Arabs deserting in anger and other allies pulling out as well. Under those circumstances, there was no viable 'exit strategy' we could see ... Had we gone the invasion route, the United States could conceivably still be an occupying power in a bitterly hostile land." Interestingly, this is very similar to the situation that exists in Iraq today.

The precise number of casualties during the first Gulf War are not known. On the coalition side, there were around 378 deaths, including 295 US deaths, 47 UK deaths, 40 Arab deaths, and 2 French deaths.

According to a report commissioned by the US air force, there were an estimated 10–12,000 Iraqi combat deaths in the air campaign and around 10,000 casualties in the ground war. Many Iraqi soldiers were killed in the "bulldozer assault" on the fortified "Saddam Line", where ploughs mounted on tanks were used to bulldoze the line, burying hundreds of Iraqi solders alive. The number of troops killed in the assault is not known.

In the years after the war, Iraqi civilians and soldiers from both sides discovered increased rates of cancer, leukaemia and birth defects. The incidence of "Gulf War Syndrome", as it came to be called, is blamed on the use of depleted uranium in US shells.

Financially, the Gulf War cost the US between $60 and $70 billion, though the US received $36 billion from Kuwait, and financial help from Saudi Arabia and other oil-producing Gulf States, as well as $16 billion from Germany and Japan.

Kuwait also faced the huge cost of repairing its destroyed infrastructure, in particular the oilwells either blown up or ignited by the departing Iraqi forces. Most of the country's 1,080 operational oilwells had been packed with C-4 explosives within a week of the invasion. When Operation Desert Sabre began and it became clear that Iraq would be defeated, between 500 and 600 of the wells were ignited; in some the entire wellheads were blown off and orange flames were burning furiously above ground, while wells that failed to ignite were shooting out geysers of oil at the rate of 40,000 barrels a day. These wells were surrounded by oil lakes over a metre deep.

A *Washington Post* reporter described the scene in Kuwait: "The burning wells pour acrid black smoke into the sky that blots out the sun during the day for miles around, depending on the wind's direction, at night, the fires light the horizon with an orange glow that is at once ghastly and strangely beautiful." (Lee Hockstader, *Washington Post*, April 1st, 1991)

Saddam had understood that the destruction of the oilwells was what would hurt Kuwait and the US the most. Oil from Kuwait's oilfields was being lost at a rate of six million barrels a day, an estimated $100 million in lost revenues, to be added to the clean-up cost incurred paying Texan oil fire-fighters over $1,000 a day. The environmental consequences of the spillage into the Gulf and the burning oilwells in Kuwait were estimated by the UN to be on a par with the Chernobyl disaster.

No Fly Zones: The Undeclared War

After Iraqi troops had left Kuwait, the UN Security Council agreed on a resolution to end the war. The resolution demanded that Iraq destroy its chemical, biological and nuclear arms under UN supervision before a permanent ceasefire would be allowed.

The UN trade embargo on non-conventional weapons would continue, while some conventional weapons purchases might be permitted at a later date, depending on need. Economic sanctions would also continue, until the Security Council set up a mechanism for compensating Kuwait and other victims of Iraqi aggression, and until Iraq completed the required destruction of its weapons and agreed not to allow any terrorist organizations to operate from its territory.

The "oil for food" programme was later introduced in response to the human cost of the economic sanctions. (In 1998, two years after the "oil for food" programme began, a UN study estimated that 90,000 Iraqis had died as an indirect consequence of the sanctions in the early 1990s.)

After the uprisings in the north and south of the country, "No Fly Zones" were created to protect the Kurdish and Shiite minorities from Iraqi air attacks. These were set up to the north of the 36th parallel and south of the 32nd. In the decade after the first Gulf War, the US and UK, who were monitoring the zones, flew more sorties than during Operation Desert Storm and dropped bombs several times a week. It was a continuing war that went almost unreported outside Iraq.

The No Fly Zones were being enforced by the US and UK, but the legality of this action was dubious. The first Gulf War had ended with a vague ceasefire agreement. But there was no UN resolution to legitimize the US and UK flights and bombings within the No Fly Zones.

"Iraq does not recognize the no-fly zone because it was not a UN job. It was imposed by the Western powers," said Iraqi Foreign Minister Tariq Aziz in 1993. (Robert Dreyfuss, *The American Prospect*, December 30th, 2002)

Within the UN there was a stalemate, since the Security Council would not support the No Fly Zones, but with the US and UK both wielding veto power, neither could they condemn it.

Although the original intention of the No Fly Zones was to protect the Kurdish and Shiite minorities from attack, increasingly the bombings became a means for the US and its allies to pressure Iraq to comply with weapons inspections and other UN and coalition demands.

This undeclared war also included two sustained bombing campaigns: Operation Desert Strike in September 1996 and Operation Desert Fox in December 1998.

In 1998, President Clinton was facing impeachment. The US Senate had approved two articles of impeachment, alleging that he had committed perjury in the testimony he gave to the grand jury in a case of sexual misconduct brought by a former Arkansas state employee Paula Jones, and in lying about his relationship with White House intern Monica Lewinsky. Many observers assumed that Operation Desert Fox was a cynical ploy to divert attention from the scandal.

The bombing campaign as well as the economic sanctions prevented Iraq from getting back on its feet again; civilian infrastructure such as electricity generators, and water and sewage treatment plants were destroyed and could not be repaired. This added to the increasing opposition to the US within the Arab and Muslim worlds. The continuing presence of US troops stationed in Saudi Arabia was undermining the Saudi regime and encouraging extremist Islamic groups to emerge. In response, the Saudi government became more hard line, and started trying to prove itself by funding distribution of religious materials to Islamist groups in the Middle East, Afghanistan and the newly independent states of Central Asia.

As part of the conditions for a full ceasefire in Iraq were restrictions on its weapons of mass destruction, and a United Nations Special Commission (UNSCOM) on weapons was set up to monitor compliance. The inspection team found some evidence of biological weapons programmes as well as other signs of non-compliance, but in many cases the Iraqi government placed restrictions on who would be allowed to monitor their weapons sites, and in 1997 expelled all US inspectors, claiming that they were spying on Iraq.

The US later admitted this was true, and in 1998 Scott Ritter, a weapons inspector and US marine, resigned from the team claiming that the US was blocking investigations to avoid a confrontation with Iraq, and also alleged that the CIA was using the inspections as a cover for covert operations in Iraq.

The inspection team continued until 1999, when they were replaced by a new team that restarted inspections in 2002, but by this time Iraq was heading inevitably for war with the US and its allies.

Under Clinton's presidency, the bombing raids within the No Fly Zones had been kept relatively quiet. After George W. Bush was inaugurated in January 2001, these routine raids were suddenly given a much higher profile. They also intensified in frequency and violence after September 11th, and in the run up to the second Gulf War, which began in March 2003.

The "Oil for Food" Scandal

The UN had imposed sanctions on Iraq after its invasion of Kuwait, but after the first Gulf War it became evident that without access to foreign currency, food and medical supplies, ordinary Iraqi people were facing a humanitarian catastrophe. In 1995, the UN Security Council passed a resolution allowing Iraq to sell limited amounts of oil to buy food and other essential supplies. However, this opened the way for Saddam Hussein to siphon off billions of dollars from the scheme, and create one of the world's largest ever systems of corruption.

Some reports on the scandal estimate the amount siphoned off from the "oil for food" sales as up to $21 billion. The money was used to fund Saddam's weapons programmes, his regime and his taste for luxurious living, as well as to buy off government officials and other important contacts abroad with the aim of undermining the UN sanctions. Those implicated in the scandal went as high as Benon Sevan, the head of the programme in Iraq, as well as the son of the UN Secretary General Kofi Annan.

The "oil for food" idea was first broached in 1991, when the UN Secretary General sent an interagency mission to assess the humanitarian situation in Iraq and Kuwait immediately after the war. The UN mission reported that "the Iraqi people may soon face a further imminent catastrophe, which could include epidemic and famine, if massive life-supporting needs are not rapidly met." Despite this concern, in 1991 the Iraqi government several times turned down offers by the UN to allow limited oil sales for humanitarian supplies.

Four years later, on April 14th, 1995, the UN Security Council adopted Resolution 986, setting up the "oil for food" programme. Iraq was allowed to sell $2 billion worth of oil every six months, two-thirds of it to be used to buy food and medicines and to meet Iraq's other humanitarian needs. This was intended as a temporary measure to avert a humanitarian crisis in Iraq, until the country complied with Security Council resolutions, including the requirement to allow inspections of its weapons sites. The first Iraqi oil was exported under the "oil for food" programme in December 1996, and the first shipments of food arrived in Iraq in March 1997.

In 1998, the limit on Iraqi oil exports was raised to $5.26 billion every six months, again with two-thirds of the proceeds to be spent on the humanitarian needs of the Iraqi people. The ceiling on Iraqi oil exports was finally removed in December 1999.

It is now clear that during the 13 years of UN sanctions, the Iraqi government siphoned off billions of dollars from the scheme. Not only that, but profits gained by Saddam Hussein's administration were used to buy influence to try and undermine the UN sanctions system itself.

The full scale of the corruption is still being unearthed. Who was involved and by how much they benefited remains to be proved – and may never be proved. A report from the US Senate committee investigating the scandal says that Saddam's regime siphoned off at least $21.3 billion from the programme, a far higher figure than previously estimated. This includes almost $4 billion from oil smuggling during the immediate post-war years.

After the "oil for food" programme was introduced, the Senate committee estimates that the Iraqi government took $9.7 billion from smuggling under the programme, $4.4 billion in kickbacks on aid contracts, and $2.1 billion from the sale of substandard imports of medicines and other products at inflated prices to the Iraqi people.

One of the worst scams was the sale to Iraqi hospitals of out of date or otherwise useless medicines, which the doctors contemptuously termed "chalk". It was not that the hospitals had no drugs as Iraqi propaganda claimed, but that the drugs they had were completely ineffective. The Iraqi administration and the foreign pharmaceutical companies involved split the profits from offloading these useless medicines under the "oil for food" programme. (David Blair, *The Daily Telegraph*, April 23rd, 2004)

How did the Iraqi government get away with it? First, the monitoring by companies contracted by the UN to oversee the programme was inadequate; either due to inefficiency or corruption. An independent inquiry by the UN's Office of International Oversight Services finds persistent lapses in supervision in the programme, though not corruption of UN staff. Its contractors are also accused of overcharging the programme by hundreds of thousands of dollars for hours they did not work. The investigation also found that auditors did not properly check oil purchase and humanitarian aid contracts, and that had they done so they would have uncovered a large part of the corruption.

US officials have claimed that UN officials repeatedly turned a blind eye to rampant corruption within the "oil for food" programme, though this has not been proved.

The majority of the money that flowed into Baghdad was from illegal bilateral trade deals between Iraq and its neighbours. The US and UK are alleged to have turned a blind eye to deals with their allies Jordan and Turkey, as an unofficial form of compensation for the losses they had suffered due to the trade embargo on Iraq. Jordan was initially the most important trading partner for Iraq, until 2000 when Iraq started supplying Syria with oil under the pretext of "testing" the oil pipeline between the two countries.

Often the contractors fulfilled the letter of the law, but even when their intentions were good, they did not do enough to prevent breaches of the sanctions. For example, the general counsel of the inspection firm Saybolt told the Senate inquiry that Iraq never put in place functioning meters at Mina al-Bakr, which meant that Saybolt could not measure the flow of oil into individual tankers. Instead, the inspectors had to use an alternative method of measurement, which, while compliant with international commercial standards, was not as foolproof or as accurate as a meter.

There were also two incidents in 2001 when oil tankers leaving Iraq were "topped up" with over 200,000 barrels of oil after inspectors had formally certified a lower amount. Saybolt has suspended one of its employees following allegations that he had accepted a $105,000 bribe from Iraqi officials.

As well as supporting himself and his cronies, Saddam used much of the money to buy friends abroad, especially those who would help to undermine the UN sanctions and bring them to an end. He personally approved the recipients of what the regime termed "special allocations" or "gifts" from Somo, the State Oil Marketing Organization. Deputy Prime Minister Tariq Aziz handled the contacts with high-profile foreigners. "Russian traders were the chief beneficiaries, receiving 30 per cent of oil export contracts, followed by the French with 15 per cent and the Chinese with 10 per cent, though recipients also included American and British nationals. The money was paid into a complex network of secret bank accounts, and sent to Iraqi embassies abroad in diplomatic bags." (Anton la Guardia, *The Daily Telegraph*, October 8th, 2004) Russia, France and China were the three permanent members of the UN Security Council that were trying to lift sanctions on Iraq.

Benon Sevan, the UN official responsible for supervising the programme, was also implicated. He is alleged to have been allocated contracts, known as "vouchers", to sell 7.3 million barrels of Iraqi oil through the Panamanian-registered African Middle East Petroleum Co. and other front companies. As well as Sevan, other high-profile names have emerged on top-secret lists maintained by the Iraqi Vice President Taha Yassin Ramadan and Oil Minister Amir Rashid, though it has not been proved whether these are lists of beneficiaries, or simply "wish lists" of people to approach. The lists include former French interior minister Charles Pasqua, the far-right Russian leader Vladimir Zhirinovsky and his Russian Liberal Democratic party, former president Megawati Sukarnoputri of Indonesia, and the son of Lebanese President Emile Lahoud.

The UN has been criticized for allowing Saddam Hussein and his government to decide who would get the contracts, when it must have been obvious this would lead to corruption. The US ambassador to the UN, Ambassador Negroponte, testified in Congress that many states in the Security Council insisted on keeping Saddam Hussein in charge of this. The US has questioned why they allowed this and whether some kind of corruption was at work.

Meanwhile, the US and UK have also been criticized for making exceptions for their friends in the Middle East, Turkey and Jordan. The report from Democratic senators to the US Senate investigation into "oil for food" said that officials from the US State Department and the US military turned a blind eye to illegal shipments of almost eight million barrels of oil to Jordan that completely bypassed the "oil for food" programme. (Julian Borger & Jamie Wilson, *The Guardian*, May 17th, 2005) The report presented further evidence that the Bush administration was aware of illegal oil sales under the "oil for food" programme, and that oil sales to the US were responsible for 52 per cent of the total illegal sales of oil from Iraq, more than the rest of the world put together. It states that: "The United States was not only aware of Iraqi oil sales which violated UN sanctions and provided the bulk of the illicit money Saddam Hussein obtained from circumventing UN sanctions. On occasion, the United States actually facilitated the illicit oil sales."

Investigations into the sales found that a US company, Odin Marine, transported the oil to Jordan from the port of Khor al-Amaya in seven huge tankers. The port was operating without UN approval and was not being monitored by UN officials.

According to the *Guardian* article, the Senate report contains evidence that Odin Marine "repeatedly sought and received approval from US military and civilian officials that the ships would not be confiscated by US Navy vessels in the Maritime Interdiction Force (MIF) enforcing the embargo."

An official from the US State Department allegedly reassured Odin that the US was "aware of the shipments and has determined not to take action."

The Senate report also alleges that the US Treasury knew that Bayoil, a Texas oil company, had facilitated payment of at least $37 million to Saddam Hussein's regime, but took no action to prevent the payments, and stood in the way of UN efforts to obtain information about Bayoil's actions.

The 2000 Presidential Election in the US

After George W. Bush became president, it became clear that the sanctions, however debilitating for the Iraqi people, would never be lifted until there was a change of regime in Iraq.

Republican George W. Bush, son of the former President George Bush, secured his place as US president after over a month of recounts and political wrangling that had polarized the country. Bush's rival, former Vice President Al Gore, conceded defeat despite winning a majority of the popular vote.

Before the election, Bush had only been in politics for six years. Prior to being elected Governor of Texas in 1994 he was a part owner of the Texas Rangers baseball team. He had also started various ventures (generally unsuccessful) in the oil industry.

Bush's election was a sharp shift to the right in American politics. The majority of his Cabinet were millionaires (some multimillionaires). While this is not uncommon in US politics, it was unusual that almost all members of the Cabinet got rich in the same industry: oil.

Among the new Cabinet were Vice President Dick Cheney, former chief executive of Halliburton oil company, which had earned him over $50 million; Condoleeza Rice (who has now replaced Colin Powell as Secretary of State), who was a Chevron director from 1991 until 2001, when she was appointed National Security Adviser to George W. Bush; and Commerce Secretary Donald Evans, the former head of oil at gas exploration company Tom Brown Inc., who still held stocks worth at least $5 million in the company. Many of the new administration had worked under Bush's father, also a former Texas oilman.

George W. Bush's career had been less successful, and questions of conflict of interest had been raised during his father's presidency. After his failing company Spectrum 7 was taken over by Harken Energy, Harken was given exclusive drilling rights by the government of Bahrain. This was despite the fact that Harken had never drilled a well outside the US. The SEC later carried out an investigation into suspicious trades involving Harken stock, but decided not to take action against Bush.

After 2000, US policy became notably more pro-industry, and environmental legislation was reversed. Bush "unsigned" the Kyoto Protocol on Climate Change that Clinton had committed the US to during his presidency.

An investigation by the *Observer* newspaper revealed in 2003 that White House officials were undermining US government scientists in an attempt to play down fears about global warming. According to the *Observer*, members of the Bush administration were working with right-wing lobby groups funded by the oil industry to discredit scientists who claimed that pollution was a growing problem.

A leaked email sent from Myron Ebell, a director of the right-wing lobby group Competitive Enterprise Institute (CEI), to Phil Cooney, chief of staff at the White House Council on Environmental Quality, in June 2003, reveals that White House officials asked CEI to play down a report from the US Environmental Protection Agency which admitted for the first time that humans are contributing to global warming. It also discussed tactics for getting rid of certain EPA officials, notably Christine Whitman, head of the agency.

"It seems to me that the folks at the EPA are the obvious fall guys and we would only hope that the fall guy (or gal) should be as high up as possible. Perhaps tomorrow we will call for Whitman to be fired," Ebell wrote in the email.

Between 1998 and 2003, the CEI received over $1 million from Exxon.

September 11th, 2001

The newly elected president seemed more at home on his ranch in Texas than in Washington running the country. On the morning of September 11th, 2001, he was visiting a primary school when an aide walked in to give him an urgent message. Bush remained seated in the classroom for the rest of the lesson, despite the fact that the aide had just brought news that a hijacked plane had crashed into one of the World Trade Center's twin towers in New York.

This was just the first of four terrorist hijackings by members of al-Qaeda, a militant Islamist organization led by Osama Bin Laden.

The second plane plunged into the other tower of the World Trade Center, and shortly afterwards both towers came crashing down to the ground.

The third aircraft targeted the Pentagon, the headquarters of the US Department of Defence, and the fourth plane, which was believed to be heading for either the White House or the president's country retreat Camp David, crashed into a field near Shanksville, Pennsylvania, after passengers rebelled against the hijackers. No one on any of the aircraft survived. Passengers and crew members who managed to make mobile phone calls from the doomed aeroplanes reported that the hijackers had taken control by using hand knives to kill one or more flight staff or passengers and threaten the rest.

Altogether, 2,986 people were killed on September 11th, making it the deadliest ever attack on US soil. As well as the airline passengers, 2,595 people in the World Trade Center, including 343 firemen, and 125 workers at the Pentagon died as a direct result of the attacks.

Five days after the attacks, al-Qaeda leader Osama Bin Laden denied responsibility, saying in a public statement broadcast on Al-Jazeera: "I stress that I have not carried out this act, which appears to have been carried out by individuals with their own motivation."

However, in another speech sent to Al-Jazeera on October 29th, 2001, he appeared to take responsibility: "I say to you, Allah knows that it had never occurred to us to strike the towers. But after it became unbearable and we witnessed the oppression and tyranny of the American/Israeli coalition against our people in Palestine and Lebanon, it came to my mind," he said on the videoed speech.

"And as I looked at those demolished towers in Lebanon, it entered my mind that we should punish the oppressor in kind and that we should destroy towers in America in order that they taste some of what we tasted and so that they be deterred from killing our women and children."

Soon after the attacks, the US government declared that al-Qaeda and Osama Bin Laden were the main suspects and that they must be hunted down at all costs and brought to account for their actions.

Al-Qaeda had already been involved in attacks on American targets, the most serious being the bombing of the American embassies in Kenya and Tanzania. Despite the cooperation between Bin Laden and the CIA in Afghanistan some 15 years earlier, al-Qaeda saw the US as one of its main enemies because of the American support for Israel, and for the (undemocratic) regimes in Saudi Arabia, Egypt, Tunisia, Yemen and Jordan, which al-Qaeda also opposed.

This was the first time America had been the victim of such an attack, and it led to immediate changes in the country. The US and many other countries introduced tough new anti-terrorist legislation, freezing the assets of suspected terrorists and introducing new checks at public buildings, airports and other potential targets. After the rather inactive initial few months of George W. Bush's presidency, the "War on Terror" was launched after September 11th.

This was a major change in US foreign policy, under which the US government would put both economic and political pressure on regimes believed to be supporting terrorists, as well as intensifying efforts against the suspected terrorists themselves, and take military action if other efforts were unsuccessful. Whether this was in fact a "war", and how legal it was, is still in question.

In addition, the planned attacks on terrorists often happened to occur in countries in oil-producing regions. This led many outside the US, despite their sympathy after September 11th, and their condemnation of the attacks on the World Trade Center and the Pentagon, to claim that the war on terror was a pretext for Bush and his administration – with its many links to the US oil industry – to secure oil for America and in particular for his own cronies.

There have been hundreds if not thousands of different conspiracy theories about what really happened on September 11th. Some concern the attacks themselves; for example, it is claimed that the US air force shot down the fourth plane to stop the planned attack being carried out. And many South American newspapers and TV broadcasters have suggested that a missile, and not a plane, plunged into the Pentagon, since there is no picture of the plane entering the building and the hole made was "too small" to have been caused by an aeroplane.

One of the most common theories blames the US government for the attacks, claiming it was a deliberate ploy to unite the country behind George W. Bush and create a pretext for going to war in Iraq and Afghanistan. It is suggested that the Bush administration knew about the plan to attack before it was carried out but avoided taking action. In fact there is evidence that Bush was relatively inactive when it came to national security, especially compared to his predecessor Clinton, who reviewed the situation daily, and also that he ignored reports of suspicious activities. A daily briefing paper titled "Bin Laden Determined to Strike in US" was given to President Bush on August 8th, 2001, and contained a warning about "patterns of suspicious activity" detected in the US that were "consistent with preparations for hijackings." (Julian Borger, *The Guardian*, April 12th, 2004) However, this is usually put down to mismanagement rather than sinister intent.

Theories that the US government either planned or knew about the attacks beforehand are often linked to theories that the motive was to gain control of Iraq's oil reserves, take Iraq as a US base in the Middle East, and secure Afghanistan as a new pipeline route from the Caspian.

Another significant theory concerns the actions of the US government immediately after the attacks. Michael Moore's film *Fahrenheit 9/11* offers evidence that after the attacks, when all flights in the US were grounded, a special plane was authorized by the government to fly the members of Bin Laden's family from the US to Saudi Arabia. He points to links between Bush's previous business ventures and the Bin Laden business empire.

Even now, four years after the September 11th attacks, some key questions remain unanswered. For every one of the hijacked planes, there was a lengthy delay between the discovery that the plane had been hijacked, the notification of NORAD, the North American Aerospace Defence command, and the deployment of fighter jets.

The first plane, American Airlines Flight 11, had lost contact with ground control by 8.20 am. Flight attendants had called the FAA to report a hijacking, but NORAD was not contacted until 8.40 am and fighter jets were not deployed until 8.52 am. The same pattern was repeated with the next three flights, even though by that time a plane had already hit the World Trade Center. The fighter jets were not sent from the closest air force bases, and did not fly at their maximum speed. Had they done so, they would have reached the hijacked planes in time to intercept them before they hit their targets. Relatives of those who died in the attacks are still trying to find out what happened.

Operation Enduring Freedom

One month after the September 11th attacks, the US and its allies went to war in Afghanistan. The ruling Taliban had been given a choice: either give up Osama Bin Laden, who CIA intelligence reported was hiding in the remote Tora Bora caves, or the US would invade.

This was the first large-scale act in the war on terror. Operation Enduring Freedom started with a massive bombing campaign, even more sophisticated than that used in the Gulf War ten years before.

Was finding Bin Laden the only motive for the attack? Ever since the Russian invasion in 1979, and even before that, Afghanistan had been in a state of civil war. The regime under the hard-line, fundamentalist Taliban was relatively stable, except that the war continued in the north, where ethnic Tajiks, Uzbeks and Hazaras continued their fight against the mainly Pashtun Taliban forces.

Now that the five Central Asian republics just to the north of Afghanistan, formerly part of the USSR, had gained their independence, the region was suddenly of great interest. Beneath the Caspian Sea were some of the world's greatest oil reserves, especially Kazakhstan's massive Tenghiz field with around 30 billion barrels.

Both the Western oil companies and the oil-producing countries themselves – Azerbaijan, Kazakhstan, Turkmenistan and Uzbekistan – were interested in a route to take their oil to the outside world that did not go through Russia. The Baku-Tiblisi-Ceyhan pipeline from the Caspian across the Caucasus to Turkey's Mediterranean coast is almost complete. Another proposed route was south through Afghanistan and Pakistan to the Indian Ocean. However, the continued fighting and instability in the country (as well as the mountainous terrain) made it impossible to go ahead with this project.

In 1998, the US oil company Unocal had been keen to create a gas pipeline from the Dauletabad-Donmez basin in Turkmenistan via Afghanistan to Pakistan. Unocal had also proposed a one million barrel per day capacity oil pipeline between the Chardzou refinery in

Turkmenistan through Afghanistan and Pakistan to the Arabian Sea. This would be doubly valuable as the Chardzou refinery is already linked to Russia's western Siberian oilfields. Again, this pipeline was not built.

Unocal pulled out of the area after the US missile attack on Afghanistan in retaliation for the al-Qaeda embassy bombings in Kenya and Tanzania, and more intensive fighting between the Taliban and rebel groups in the north. The company said it would not commit to building a pipeline until a stable and internationally recognized government was in place. (Only three countries – Saudi Arabia, Pakistan and the UAE – recognized the Taliban.)

Operation Enduring Freedom might open the way for just such a government.

As in Iraq, the campaign started with air attacks and the newest generation of guided bombs. For the first time, the US set up bases in the formerly Communist Central Asian states of Uzbekistan, Kyrgyzstan and Tajikistan. The Taliban, faced by the enormous fire-power of the Americans, fled to their strongholds in the inaccessible high mountain areas on the border with Pakistan, and across the border in the remote and lawless Baluchistan province.

Somewhat to Bush's and his advisers' surprise, the Taliban did not surrender to air attacks alone. But after ground forces went in, there was only one full-scale battle – at a strategic road junction outside Mazar-e-Sharif. This appeared to be the Taliban's last stand, where they held out until American B-52s carpet-bombed the area. After that, the Taliban abandoned Mazar-e-Sharif and later Kabul.

It had taken the US merely a few days to drive the Taliban out of power in Afghanistan, with the loss of only 52 men, despite fears that the country would prove to be unconquerable after the experience of the British in the mid-19th century and the USSR in the 1980s.

Then came the matter of forming a new regime, which proved to be a far more difficult task. United against the Taliban, when their common enemy had fallen the Tajiks, Uzbeks and Hazaras of the Northern Alliance started to fight among themselves. They were also reluctant to pursue and defeat the remnants of the Taliban army who were gathering outside the cities.

The US urged the Northern Alliance leaders to finish off the Taliban in the Tora Bora area and other mountain hideouts, but they refused, even when bribed with millions of US dollars from CIA operatives. The Americans attempted to deal with the Taliban themselves, but after a team was ambushed and seven Americans killed, that plan was rapidly abandoned. Apart from bombing raids, the Taliban were left in their caves.

Four years after the war, little has changed in Afghanistan. Although President Hamid Kharzai (a Pashtun with a Northern Alliance Cabinet) was elected in the fairer than expected September 2004 elections, his government has no power to impose its rule outside the capital. Individual warlords hold sway in most regions of the country. For want of other ways to earn money, Afghan peasants are growing opium, which makes its way across Asia to the streets of Europe, despite the American pledge to end the trade. Apart from professionals in Kabul, women in most of Afghanistan are as much at risk as they were under the Taliban.

Neither Osama Bin Laden nor Mullah Mohammed Omar, the one-eyed cleric who led the Taliban, have been found. Taliban fighters are stealthily regrouping in parts of the country. There is no prospect of an oil or gas pipeline across Afghanistan in the foreseeable future.

The Second Gulf War

After Afghanistan, the Bush administration's next target was Iraq. The overthrow of Saddam Hussein had never been demanded in any UN resolution. It was, however, a major policy goal of George W. Bush (and to a lesser extent the Clinton regime). After September 11th, it was only a matter of time before Iraq was targeted.

The Republican party's campaign in the 2000 presidential election had called for a full implementation of the UN resolutions ending the war, as well as the removal of Saddam Hussein. The US under Bush stepped up support for Iraqi opposition groups, in particular the exiled pro-democracy group, the Iraqi National Congress.

The influential, mainly Republican think tank, Project for the New American Century, called in September 2000 for the US to use ground forces to contain Saddam. This view was also advocated by many within the Bush administration.

The war on terror launched after September 11th also advocated pre-emptive military action against potential terrorists. There was a small amount of evidence linking Saddam's regime to al-Qaeda, and certainly to other Islamic terrorist groups. After September 11th, the Russian President Vladimir Putin (who was fighting Islamic insurgents in Chechnya) warned the US that Iraq was planning terrorist attacks in the US.

This also fitted neatly with Bush's personal animosity towards Saddam Hussein (who had tried to have his father, the former president, assassinated), as well as with his possible ambitions concerning Middle Eastern oil. By 2002, removing Saddam Hussein from office was a major US policy goal, explicitly stated (though Washington was willing, it said, to accept major changes to Iraqi military and foreign policy instead).

Under international law, the US required explicit Security Council approval for an invasion unless an attack by Iraq was "imminent". However, US attempts to convince fellow Security Council members that a "growing" or "gathering" threat was equally dangerous were successful. A new joint resolution was agreed, allowing the US to, "defend the national security of the United States against the continuing threat posed by Iraq; and enforce all relevant United Nations Security Council Resolutions regarding Iraq."

The US set about creating a coalition of countries willing to support a war in Iraq. It also had to convince the world that Iraq posed a threat – in effect, by proving that Iraq had weapons of mass destruction.

In November 2002, the UN Security Council unanimously passed the resolution and agreed to resume weapons inspections. At the same time, the US was preparing militarily for an invasion of Iraq.

Among the US Secretary of Defense Donald Rumsfeld's stated goals for the invasion, along with the transition to democratic self-rule, eliminating weapons of mass destruction and Iraqi support for terrorists, and delivering humanitarian support, was the goal of securing Iraq's oilfields and resources. Some members of the Bush administration also speculated that if Saddam was toppled in Iraq, this would have a domino effect, spreading democracy among the dictatorships of the Middle East. (This was played down to avoid alienating friendly dictatorships like Saudi Arabia.)

Opposition to the planned war in Iraq was fierce, not only in the US but also in the UK and among other coalition members such as

Spain and Italy. Opponents argued that the claims of Iraqi military build-up, weapons of mass destruction and support for terrorism were either insufficient to justify going to war, or simply untrue – a fabrication to create popular support for what they believed was a war for oil.

Opponents of the war argued that the aim of the war was for the US to take control of Iraq's oil reserves (the second largest of any country after Saudi Arabia). The US could thereby have secure access to oil and no longer have to worry about its own diminishing reserves, while also exerting control over other countries that needed Iraqi oil. George W. Bush's many friends among the US oil and construction industries would benefit from the contracts for rebuilding and running Iraq's oil industry. His contacts among the armaments industry would also benefit. In addition, the events of September 11th had united a majority of the American people behind Bush for the first time. A quick victory over Saddam Hussein would keep his popularity high and distract attention from the faltering economy.

Abroad, Bush's allies were also seeking to convince their sceptical populations that there was a case for war. In the UK, British Prime Minister Tony Blair had based his argument on the weapons of mass destruction he believed Saddam Hussein to be stockpiling. A report published in September 2002, "Iraq's Weapons of Mass Destruction – The assessment of the British Government," claimed that Iraq possessed a large stock of chemical and biological weapons, some of which could be deployed in 45 minutes. It also claimed that Iraq was seeking to build up its nuclear capacity.

Yet there was still no agreement within the Security Council on an invasion of Iraq. Although Resolution 144, accepted unanimously in 2002, threatened "serious consequences" for Iraq should it fail to comply with UN conditions, it did not explicitly authorize the use of force. The US and UK wanted war, but the remaining three members of the security council – France, Russia and China – were opposed to war, and made a joint statement saying that a new resolution would be needed to authorize an invasion.

A new resolution could not be agreed with the Security Council divided. Kofi Annan, the UN Secretary General, made it clear that in his view the invasion was illegal under international law: "I have indicated it was not in conformity with the UN charter from our point of view, from the charter point of view, it was illegal," he said. (Kofi Annan, BBC World Service, September 16th, 2004)

Troops from the US and other coalition countries were already stationed in the Gulf in early 2003, because of the ongoing low-level conflict with Iraq. This allowed a gradual military build-up to take place from mid-2002 onwards, although this was not widely publicized. US military forces had abandoned the search for weapons of mass destruction in Iraq in January, since they had found nothing. However, in March 2003 the US gave Iraq an ultimatum: allow inspectors back in or risk invasion.

At 5.30 am (Baghdad time) on March 23rd, 2003, only 90 minutes after the deadline had passed, a massive bombing raid hit Baghdad. The US attack did not go precisely as planned, mainly due to the growing enmity to the war in Turkey, which refused to allow coalition troops to use its territory. Instead of starting with a lengthy air campaign, Bush had wanted to "Shock and Awe" the Iraqis with a simultaneous air and ground attack. This was intended to crush the Iraqi army as quickly as possible and attack the heart of the command structure, in order to minimize civilian casualties and damage to infrastructure – especially oil infrastructure.

Due to Turkey's objections, plans for a simultaneous ground attack from the north and south had to be abandoned. Divisions in the north had to relocate, delaying their participation in the war, while others attacked from bases in Kuwait. Among the criticisms levelled at the invasion was that there were insufficient US troops to control the country after key positions had been taken; this meant widespread insurgency and resistance in areas such as Fallujah, as well as ongoing problems of looting.

However, the objective of taking the country was achieved within about three weeks, with damage to the oil infrastructure kept to a minimum – one of the main objectives of the troops. This had led to what the US termed some "hard choices" being made. For example, the National Museum of Iraq, containing unique artefacts dating back several millennia, was looted; US forces in the area were busy guarding the nearby Ministry of Oil.

The US 3rd Infantry Division struck west then north through the desert towards Baghdad, while the US 1st Marine Expeditionary Force and a UK expeditionary force headed north through the marsh areas.

UK forces entered Basra, Iraq's second city and its main seaport, two weeks into the war, but it took a long time to take control of the city, even with the help of the local Iraqi police force. US forces were halted around Hillah and Karbala, where they encountered severe dust storms and the strongest resistance so far from Iraqis, but continued to press on towards Baghdad, entering the capital city three weeks after the invasion began.

A "Thunder Run" of US tanks encountered heavy resistance from Iraqis, including suicide attacks, but two days later a successful attack was launched towards the palaces of Saddam Hussein, which were secured by the American forces. As news of the conquest was broadcast through the country by television and radio, Iraqi resistance started to crumble, and people burnt posters of their leader and tore down his statues. Iraqi ministers were fleeing the city, or surrendering to the Americans. Baghdad was taken on April 9th, and Saddam's regime was at an end. Saddam himself had disappeared, it was assumed to his home region around the northern town of Tikrit. He was eventually captured nine months later, on December 13th, by US soldiers.

During the war, it emerged that the US had started allocating contracts for rebuilding Iraq before the war had even started. News reports in early March 2003 revealed that the US Agency for International Development (USAID) had secretly asked six American companies to bid for a $900 million government contract for rebuilding Iraq. These companies were Bechtel Group Inc., Fluor Corp., Halliburton Co. subsidiary Kellogg, Brown & Root, Louis Berger Group Inc., Parsons Corp. and Washington Group International Inc.

The six companies made total campaign contributions of $3.6 million to US political groups between 1999 and 2003, of which 66 per cent went to Republican groups or individual candidates; Halliburton was headed for five years by Vice President Dick Cheney; while former Secretary of State George Shultz is also the former president of Bechtel, and still serves on the company board.

At the same time, the US revealed that companies from countries that opposed the war in Iraq would not be allowed to bid for contracts.

George W. Bush's old enemy had been defeated. But the military campaign in the Gulf had created a region increasingly hostile to what was viewed as "American imperialism" and a lust for the region's oil.

The case for war looks increasingly thin as chaos continues in Iraq, and no weapons of mass destruction have ever been found. Arab and Muslim populations across the world have turned against the West, provoked by US actions in the Middle East. Iraq has gone through months of turmoil after the war, and even after the election of a new government, attacks on coalition forces and Iraqi government targets continue almost daily. Most of the country's oil infrastructure emerged from the war unscathed, but it took a long time before pipelines taking it to foreign markets became operational, and even now they need to be continually guarded.

Chapter Eight: Bribing the Brigands

As the US and other Western countries exhaust oil reserves close to home, they have to look further afield, and often to countries in which civil war, terrorism or the threat of unrest can make oil production a risky investment.

It has often been in the interests of major oil companies and foreign governments to back a regime that offers stability, however harsh or undemocratic it may be. For the US, energy has been an important factor in foreign policy ever since the 1940s, and Washington's energy policy has been increasingly backed by military force abroad. The US interventions in Iraq and Afghanistan have changed the political landscape of the Middle East. Washington is also providing military and financial aid to regimes that can provide a stable environment for oil companies to operate in.

In looking for alternatives to Middle Eastern oil, the US has targeted three areas: Latin America, West African countries around the Gulf of Guinea (particularly Nigeria), and Azerbaijan and Kazakhstan in the Caspian basin. Some of the more controversial recipients of military aid include Colombia, Uzbekistan, and a slew of oil-producing African countries around the Gulf of Guinea. The US navy is guarding sensitive points along the world's main oil routes, from the African coastline to the South China Sea. France, China and other countries are also stepping up their aid efforts to compete with the US and win new oil sources. "The problem is that the good Lord didn't see fit to put oil and gas reserves where there are democratic governments," said US Vice President Dick Cheney, then CEO of Halliburton, at an energy conference in 1996. (Brian Whitaker, The Guardian, April 5th, 2004)

Among the US's top ten suppliers of crude oil, only three, Canada,

Norway and the UK, are stable democracies. Other top suppliers include three Middle Eastern countries (Saudi Arabia, Iraq and Kuwait), two African countries (Nigeria and Angola), and two countries in Latin America (Mexico and Venezuela).

In recent years, the US and other large importers of oil have been offering growing amounts of financial and military aid to the governments of these oil-producing countries. Human rights abuses by the governments offering access to oil have frequently been underplayed, and stability has been prized over democracy.

Two methods by which Western nations set out to gain or buy influence in these countries are through sending military or financial aid. As the French oil company Elf's "Angolagate" scandal revealed, foreign aid is often politically motivated, and facilitates the creation of cosy relationships between government officials and businesspeople in the donor and recipient company. Backhanders to officials from both countries in return for business concessions are commonplace. Military aid may be offered with the intention of helping the government to defeat internal opposition, or specifically to secure oil infrastructure, which has become a prime target for sabotage. Military aid usually also involves the payment of lucrative "commissions" to senior figures in the producing countries. Rebel or anti-American groups understand that to hit the US where it will hurt the most, they only need to target their country's oil infrastructure, a relatively "soft" target compared to mounting an attack in the US.

In Saudi Arabia, for example, two-thirds of oil produced is processed at the Abqaiq refinery, then exported through just two terminals, Ras Tanura and Ras al-Ju'aymah. Every day one-tenth of the world's oil supply flows through Ras Tanura. Destroying any one of these terminals would take 50 per cent of Saudi Arabia's oil off the market for at least six months, causing oil prices to soar and potentially plunging the oil-importing nations into recession. According to Robert Baer, a former CIA Middle East field officer and author of *Sleeping with the Devil: How Washington Sold Our Soul for Saudi Crude*, "Such an attack would be more economically damaging than a dirty nuclear bomb set off in midtown Manhattan or across from the White House in Lafayette Square." Oilwells, pipelines, tankers and other infrastructure have been targeted by the Iraqi resistance, and by rebel groups in Saudi Arabia, Angola and Colombia.

Between 2000, when President George W. Bush came to power, and the end of 2003, military aid to the top 25 countries exporting oil to the US increased by 1,800 per cent (from $52.6 million in 1999 to $1.02 billion in 2004). During the same period, the overall increase in military aid to all world countries rose by only 150 per cent, from $4.76 billion in 1999 to $11.68 billion in 2004. Most of the increase was accounted for by spending in Iraq, Colombia, Russia and Oman.

As well as sending military and financial aid, the US is increasingly risking its own soldiers in protecting global oil routes. In Iraq, two years after the invasion, US soldiers are still risking their lives to protect the country's oilfields and the pipelines to Turkey and other countries. This is also the case in Colombia, Saudi Arabia and Georgia, where a pipeline taking Caspian oil to the Mediterranean was officially opened on May 25th, 2005.

Dick Cheney's comment also ignored the destabilizing effects of oil itself. The presence of government instability or internal unrest in oil-rich countries is not purely coincidence. The discovery of oil and the resultant influx of cash to a relatively small economy can itself be dangerously destabilizing, especially in countries in which a single region or ethnic group is the beneficiary. The combination of historical rivalries and a sudden rich-poor divide (often along ethnic lines) has often proved to be explosive.

As we have seen, for example in the Biafra war, the discovery of oil is often a trigger for conflict. The Ibo people of the oil-rich Biafra region were culturally and religiously distinct from the ruling groups in Nigeria. After a military coup in the capital Lagos, the Ibo leadership no longer had a voice within the government and could not influence how the revenues from "their" oil were used. The Biafrans declared their independence from Nigeria after it appeared that the oil proceeds would benefit only the federal government in Lagos and people of other regions.

The billions of dollars in play mean that ruling elites in countries from Saudi Arabia to Gabon to Azerbaijan seek to hold onto power by whatever means necessary. The oil wealth available is a further incentive to prevent free and fair elections and to suppress the freedom of the media, in order to crush opposition to their rule and prevent evidence of government corruption and the theft of oil money being published. In the long term, this can lead to armed rebellion. In countries in which elections are rigged and peaceful means of expressing dissent are crushed, opposition forces may see no alternative but to resort to revolution or terrorism.

Aid, Drugs and Oil in Latin America

Proven reserves of oil in Latin America total 102.2 billion barrels, a small amount compared to the 726.6 billion in the Middle East. The continent is, however, one of the US's main suppliers, due to its proximity and the mature oil industries of Mexico and Venezuela, both of which have been extracting oil on a large scale since the early 20th century.

The lion's share of the continent's proven resources are located in Venezuela (78 billion barrels), followed by Mexico (16 billion barrels) and Brazil (10.6 billion barrels). There are considerable reserves in the Amazon basin, which are being exploited by international oil companies. Argentina, Colombia, Ecuador and Peru are also producing oil. Colombia, though its proven reserves are only 1.5 billion barrels, is estimated to have huge and relatively untapped oil and gas reserves that could in theory be almost as large as Venezuela's.

Colombia has become increasingly important in US energy calculations. Between 1980 and 1999, the country's oil production increased from 100,000 barrels per day to around 844,000 barrels per day. However, conditions in the country, and access to its oilfields, are far less stable than in Venezuela or Mexico. During decades of civil war, guerrilla warfare and drug trafficking, Colombia's oil infrastructure itself has often been targeted. FARC (the Revolutionary Armed Forces of Colombia – People's Army) and other left-wing guerrilla movements have been engaged in a many-decades-long battle with government security forces and illegal right-wing paramilitary groups like the AUC. The ongoing violence has prevented economic development and reforms from getting underway, and as a result the drug trade has boomed, providing a means for farmers and other citizens to earn a living and funding many of the guerrilla and paramilitary groups. US policy in the country has been an uneasy mix of Cold War strategy, the fight against drug trafficking, and the politics of oil.

The US first became involved in Colombia under President Kennedy in 1962, with a CIA and US Special Forces programme to train the Colombian police and paramilitary groups in counter-insurgency techniques. These included sabotage and terror. In 1976, the right-wing military dictatorships that ruled six Latin American states – Argentina, Bolivia, Brazil, Chile, Paraguay and Uruguay – formed "Operation Condor", a system to share intelligence in order to locate and assassinate political dissidents. Members of their security services exchanged notes on counter-insurgency and torture techniques. Operation Condor is alleged to have had at least the tacit backing of the US. Since then, US involvement in the country has escalated. From counter-insurgency actions during the Cold War, the US later became involved in the "war on drugs" – which had many parallels with today's war on terror. In April 1986, a new National Security Decision Directive for the first time defined drug trafficking as a matter of national security. Five years later, US troops started operating in Colombia alongside CIA agents. Part of their work was in protecting the country's oil infrastructure from sabotage. (This policy was introduced three years after US oil company Occidental Petroleum discovered the vast Caño Limón oilfield in Colombia.)

In 1998, the Colombian government launched "Plan Colombia", a multistranded government initiative intended to revive the shrinking economy, strengthen government institutions and central control over areas effectively lawless or under the control of guerrilla groups, and stamp out the drug trade, as a means to producing a lasting peace in the war torn country. In support of Plan Colombia, in 2000 US Congress approved a $1.3 billion emergency military aid package for the country. This made Colombia the third largest recipient of US assistance in the world (after Israel and Egypt). Bill Clinton, then the US president, justified this by arguing that the Colombian government needed US support to defeat the guerrilla armies and paramilitary groups protecting Colombia's drug trade.

The US has stressed that Plan Colombia is not merely a military exercise, but has played an active role in armed attacks on cocaine laboratories and the controversial aerial spraying of suspected coca crops. The original domestic programme took a four-part approach: peace, economic and social development, political reform and security. However, the US funding for Plan Colombia was 90 per cent military. Originally, the US contribution was intended to complement economic aid from the European Union. The EU later withdrew its funding after 37 Colombian human rights groups and other non-governmental organizations appealed to Brussels not to support the plan.

In April 2001, the new US President George W. Bush announced the new $731 million "Andean Counterdrug Initiative" (ACI), which at first was essentially a continuation of Clinton's support for Plan Colombia. Although it stresses a pan-Andean approach, with support for the whole region, the lion's share of aid goes to Colombia, where 90 per cent of the cocaine and up to 70 per cent of the heroin entering the US is produced. Again, the programme focuses on training for the police and military forces, and supplies of weapons.

After September 11th, 2001, the "war on drugs" in Colombia became a counterpart to the new "war on terror", and US-initiated programmes to stamp out drug trafficking were extended to groups defined as terrorist.

Aid allocated under the ACI was to be used in a unified campaign against drugs and terrorist groups, as FARC, the ELN and the right-wing AUC are now defined. Aid from anti-drug programmes is now also used for counter-insurgency operations, which considerably expands the scope of the US involvement in Colombia.

As well as its contribution to preventing drug trafficking, Robert B. Charles, Assistant Secretary for International Narcotics and Law Enforcement Affairs, told a Senate subcommittee in March 2004 that the ACI "is also a bulwark against the threat of terrorism in Colombia, Bolivia, Peru, Brazil, Venezuela, Ecuador, and Panama. In short, it is a regional hemispheric and national security programme, with direct implications, for homeland security and for our well being here in the continental United States ... In Colombia, and elsewhere in the hemisphere, the link between drug money and terrorism is incontrovertible."

In 2004, Bush's foreign aid bill included $731 million for the ACI. A further $110 million was earmarked for Colombia under the Foreign Military Financing programme, the US's main military aid programme that does not target drug trafficking. In 2003, part of the US's Foreign Military Financing for Colombia was undertaken to fund a new programme to protect the Caño Limón-Coveñas oil pipeline. The only amendment made by Congress was a request that $17 million of this sum be used to provide aircraft and related assistance for the Colombian police force.

Despite the US commitment, the efficacy of military aid in stamping out the cocaine trade has also been questioned. After more than a decade of substantial US military aid and active involvement in the country, both drug production within Colombia, and Colombian drug imports into the US have increased. This is partially due to successful efforts in neighbouring Bolivia and Peru to reduce their drugs trade, which has caused Colombian producers to increase their exports to meet the demand.

Drug trade and trafficking increase in times of conflict, when earning an income legally is difficult, and drugs can bring in the quick cash needed to keep the war going. During times of war, when normal policing may break down, and the high risk of drug trafficking may be seen as a risk worth taking, traffic increases. This has been the case with the heroin trade in Afghanistan and South East Asia, and it has also happened in Colombia.

Fighting drug traffic is the official reason given for US involvement in Colombia. However, there are strong indications that the US is equally interested in protecting its oil interests in Colombia, and in paving the way for future exploration. The supply of oil from Colombia and development of the country's oil industry would contribute to US efforts to reduce dependence on imports from the Middle East, especially since relations between the US and Venezuela have worsened.

FARC and the Army of National Liberation (ELN), the two main opposition guerrilla groups, have consistently targeted Colombia's oil industry, especially targets associated with foreign oil companies, chiefly the US company Occidental Petroleum and the British BP. Since oil is Colombia's main source of income (at least its main legal export), the oil industry is an important target for rebel groups. Attacks on oil infrastructure are intended to slow economic growth, and thereby undermine support for the government and cut off its sources of revenue. Colombia's oil industry is especially vulnerable, since the main oil-producing regions are both situated in remote parts of the country. The Caño Limón field, managed by Occidental Petroleum, is in the far north east of the country, and the Cusiana/Cupiagua field (managed mainly by BP) in north-central Colombia is also far from government centres. Oil has to be transported through long pipelines run through the Colombian jungle and areas controlled by guerrilla forces.

From 1982 to 1999, the ELN attacked the oil pipeline from Caño

Limón to the coast 586 times, spilling more than 1.6 million barrels of oil. In 1999 alone, there were a record number of pipeline bombings, 79 during one year. As well as costing the Colombian government and the foreign oil companies millions of dollars, these attacks have also discouraged other oil companies from operating in the country. As a result, exploration and development of new fields has not been carried out, holding back development of the industry. The guerrilla groups portray Occidental Petroleum, BP and other foreign oil companies as foreign exploiters, draining Colombia of its natural resources.

The Colombian government has stepped up its efforts to protect the oil industry, even though this, combined with the guerrilla war and the efforts to stop drug trafficking, has put a considerable strain on its resources. Government forces are deployed along the main pipelines and in the oil-producing regions.

US officials insisted that US-backed military efforts would primarily target the south east, the region where most of the coca plantations and cocaine laboratories are believed to be. However, the equipment from the US has improved the government's ability to fight the insurgents all over the country. (The most recent package included 30 Black Hawk helicopters, 33 refurbished UH-1N "Huey" helicopters and several P-3 spy planes.) The Colombian army has made it clear that it will use the aid and arms it receives from the US to fight all guerrilla groups, whether or not they are involved in drug production and trafficking. The US has presumably also calculated that if it funds the war against drugs in the south, the government will be able to devote more of its own resources to defending the oil infrastructure in the north east.

During its involvement in Colombia, the US has focused its efforts against the guerrilla organizations that pose the greatest threat to the oil industry, not those most heavily involved in the drugs trade. If the US government was sincere in its efforts to stamp out the drugs trade, it would perhaps look at the national army and right-wing paramilitary groups such as the AUC, rather than just FARC and other left-wing groups.

Until recently, FARC guerrillas have only taxed the drugs trade; they have not been involved in it themselves. Both AUC and the Colombian military have been actively involved in drug trafficking. In

November 1998, this was demonstrated by the arrival of a Colombian air force plane at Fort Lauderdale-Hollywood International Airport in the US. The plane, which had been in the hands of the Colombian air force throughout its journey, was carrying over 700 kilos of cocaine.

FARC is estimated to be responsible for 2.5 per cent of Colombia's coca production, while the AUC is responsible for 40 per cent. However, the AUC was only placed on the US's list of foreign terrorist organizations in September 2001, despite the fact that it is just as violent and illegal as FARC.

US efforts within the country are still concentrated on FARC; its only sanctions against the AUC are to suspend visas for AUC members and put people connected with the organization on a visa watch list. US corporations in Colombia continue to work with the AUC to secure their operations in the country, and the US government has made no move to ban this.

Is this because while FARC and other revolutionary groups attack the country's oil infrastructure, the AUC tries to defend it?

As well as the hundreds of millions of dollars committed to Colombia, the US government has also deployed its own troops to protect the oil-producing areas and oil pipelines.

Part of the 2003 allocation under the Foreign Military Financing Act was used to fund training by US Army Special Forces personnel from Fort Bragg, North Carolina. The US trained, and then armed, a new military force to defend the Caño Limón-Coveñas pipeline. Their task would be to guard the pipeline along its entire 580-mile route.

The oil companies are also believed to be supporting the military efforts in their areas. BP denied having links with paramilitaries, but acknowledged that it had used local private security contractors who were also training the Colombian police in counter-insurgency (Murillo, p.134) and has subsidized new military units in Colombia. All the oil companies pay a "war tax" of $1 per barrel. (Michael Klare, *Alternet*, May 4th, 2000) Most also employ private security firms to battle the insurgents. In June 2001, witnesses told a Colombian court that three American airmen providing protection for Occidental Petroleum had directed a military operation that mistakenly killed 18 civilians, including 9 children, in an attack on the village of San Domingo near the Caño Limón oilfield.

The airmen, operating from a US-built Skymaster plane, were

employed by a small US air surveillance firm AirScan that had previously been employed by Occidental to provide security along the Caño Limón pipeline.

The attack took place a day after the US airmen and Colombian intelligence reported FARC activity in the area. Colombian helicopter gunships bombarded San Domingo with air-to-surface rockets and cluster bombs, and strafed civilians with machine-guns. No rebels were killed.

Testifying in a military court, Colombia air force pilot Cesar Romero, who had been involved in the attack, said: "The coordination was done directly with the armoured helicopters that were supporting us and with the (Cessna 337) Skymaster plane flown by US pilots. The Skymaster and gunship crews talked directly to the ground troops." (Karl Penhaul, *San Francisco Chronicle*, June 15th, 2001) Both the Colombian air force and US officials said that the aircraft and almost all the arms used had been supplied under a 1989 US military aid package.

A spokesman for Occidental Petroleum denied claims by the Colombian air force pilots that they had contracted the Skymaster. However, in an anonymous interview with the *San Francisco Chronicle* in 2001, a senior official for the Colombian national oil company Ecopetrol said that the plane had always been funded by Occidental Petroleum, but that at the time of the attack payments from Occidental to AirScan were channelled through the Colombian Ministry of Defence rather than being made directly. (Karl Penhaul, *San Francisco Chronicle*, June 15th, 2001)

Occidental Petroleum has been one of the strongest supporters of the US funding for the government, even though that US funding is supposedly targeting only the coca growing areas in the south, far from its own operations. A *Newsweek* report revealed that under Clinton's presidency, Occidental and several major US arms manufacturers had been lobbying in favour of the $1.3 billion aid package for Plan Colombia.

US oil companies are alleged not only to have used terrorist counter-revolutionaries to defend their infrastructure, but also to prevent their Colombian workforces from setting up unions or going on strike to protest about pay or conditions. (Murillo, pp.133-4)

Since the early days of US involvement in Colombia, foreign

companies have consistently lobbied for greater involvement to defend their interests in the country. Hunt Oil and Kellogg, Brown and Root, a subsidiary of Halliburton, two companies with very close links to the Bush administration, both stood to benefit from the ACI, for example. It also provided a market for the manufacturers of armaments, helicopters, military vehicles and the herbicides used to spray suspected coca crops and opium poppies in the Andes.

Since Plan Colombia was introduced, new US bases, such as Manta in Ecuador, have been set up. The ACI is also enabling the US to establish a long-term presence in Latin America, where it is in a position to intervene should other conflicts break out in the oil-rich region.

"Oil For Doctors"

The US is not the only country offering aid to Latin American countries and receiving oil in return. In March 2003, Hugo Chávez, the left-wing president of Venezuela (Latin America's largest oil producer), and Cuban president Fidel Castro launched the "Barrio Adentro" programme, that in effect exchanged Cuban doctors for Venezuelan oil. Since then, 15,000 Cuban medics have set up 300 clinics in Venezuela's poorest and least accessible areas, while every day at least 53,000 barrels of Venezuelan oil are exported to Cuba.

Cuba receives a heavy subsidy on its oil: up to 25 per cent financing from Venezuela, payable over 15 years at 2 per cent interest after a two-year grace period. Cuba's debt to Venezuela, which will amount to around a billion dollars, may well remain unpaid.

The "oil for doctors" arrangement also benefits Hugo Chávez in Venezuela, where despite owning the world's fifth largest oil reserves, the difference between rich and poor remains acute. Cuban doctors working in the country report that they have dealt with many diseases now eradicated in Cuba, as well as illnesses that proper sanitation and knowledge about diet would make easily preventable.

The programme has added considerably to Chávez's personal popularity, especially among the poor, who make up 70 per cent of the population. After coming to power in 1999 on a platform that promised a mix of socialism and militarism, he was deposed by a military coup in April 2002. Although he was reinstated within two days, by 2003 his government's popularity had sunk to 35 per cent. Since then, however, his popularity has increased considerably; in August 2004 (after some 17 million Venezuelans had been treated by the Cuban doctors), Chávez won 59 per cent of the vote in a referendum on his presidency.

Despite criticisms from some quarters that the doctors are also political agitators, the programme has received widespread support. Although the president of the Venezuelan Medical Federation obtained a court order banning the Cuban doctors from working in Venezuela, the programme was allowed to continue pending a court decision after a government appeal.

It is not since Angola in the 1970s – another oil-rich country – that so many Cuban professionals have been deployed abroad. Since Venezuela is also one of the US's primary suppliers of oil, the situation in the country is being closely watched.

Buying Influence in Africa

Since George W. Bush came to power in 2000, US aid policy towards Africa has also become increasingly militarized. The war on terror has provided a justification for supplying military aid to the governments of oil-rich countries in the name of promoting stability and fighting terrorism, even when these rulers are corrupt or undemocratic and use the aid against their own people. Soon after the Bush administration was installed in the White House, Colin Powell, then Secretary of State, emphasized the importance of improving relations with Nigeria, Angola and other oil-producing countries. The report from Vice President Dick Cheney's Energy Task Force also pointed to the growing importance of African oil.

In June 2003, the Pentagon announced it was removing some 70,000 soldiers from Germany, where they were no longer required after the end of the Cold War, and relocating them to Africa and the Caspian. Their role is to combat terrorism as well as protect oil infrastructure. According to the *Wall Street Journal*, US officials said that a key part of their mission would be to ensure that Nigeria's oilfields are kept secure. (Gregg Jaffe, *Wall Street Journal*, June 10th, 2003)

The need to obtain oil has encouraged George W. Bush and his predecessors to turn a blind eye to corruption and human rights abuses in the oil-producing countries. The governments of Nigeria and Algeria, for example, have successfully masked domestic repression under the respectable cloak of the war on terror.

The increase in military aid to Africa has coincided with the continent's growing importance as a supplier of oil to the US. Africa now accounts for 16 per cent of US oil imports, chiefly from the Gulf of Guinea, which stretches from Liberia in the west to Angola in the south. The Gulf of Guinea contains over 10 per cent of the world's known oil reserves, and the US National Intelligence Council predicts that by 2015 Africa will account for 25 per cent of its oil imports.

US military officials frequently draw attention to the "growing terrorist threat" in north and sub-Saharan Africa as a way to justify their military engagement in the region.

In 2003, the *New York Times* quoted General James Jones, head of the US European command, as recommending the building of a "family of bases" throughout Africa, in addition to large existing bases such as those in Djibouti. (Eric Schmitt, *New York Times*, July 5th, 2003) In the meantime, US military exercises and training missions in Africa are being increased. The *New York Times* also revealed in July 2003 that the US was seeking to set up more bases in Algeria, Djibouti, Morocco, Senegal, Tunisia and Uganda, and was facilitating this process with offers of military aid.

The US Congressional Budget Justification for FY05 Foreign Operations, issued by the State Department in February 2004, reveals some of the influence that oil interests have had on decision making within the Bush administration. The large oil and gas reserves in Nigeria, Angola and other countries are mentioned in some detail. In the section on Angola, the report highlights the need to "ensure US private-sector oil access to a source of seven percent of US petroleum imports, a figure likely to rise in the coming years."

It also notes that during the previous five years US companies invested around $5 billion in the oil industry in Equatorial Guinea. Looking to the future in the small island state of Principe and Sao Tome, the report says that "In the coming decade, US companies are expected to participate in the development of petroleum resources in Sao Tome's territorial waters."

The US has also presented investment in oil production as a tool for development. In fact, in many cases corruption and mismanagement have caused oil to be more of a curse than a blessing. Rather than promoting development, it has undermined efforts to grow the economy as a whole by removing incentives for other forms of development. Nigeria, Africa's largest oil producer, has 100 million people below the poverty line. In terms of democratization, oil has again had a discouraging effect. The temptations to skim off some of the country's oil revenues have proved irresistible for many leaders and government officials, and the access to such riches has made leaders doubly inclined to hang onto power by whatever means.

Shell has been the dominant oil company in Nigeria since the colonial era, when British authorities gave it an effective monopoly on Nigerian oil. Since then, other oil multinationals have entered the country. Gulf Oil, now part of ChevronTexaco, entered the market in 1968. ExxonMobil, TotalFinaElf and other major companies are also operating there, as is BP, whose Nigerian holdings were nationalized in the 1980s because of Margaret Thatcher's position on Zimbabwe.

With just over 100 billion barrels of proven reserves in total, over two-thirds of Africa's proven reserves are located in Libya (36 billion barrels) and Nigeria (34.3 billion barrels). Algeria (11.3 billion barrels), Angola (8.9 billion barrels), Egypt (3.5 billion barrels), Gabon (2.4 billion barrels) and the Republic of Congo (1.5 billion barrels) are also significant producers.

US aid to Africa has increased significantly in recent years. Under the Foreign Military Financing programme, military aid to sub-Saharan Africa is set to double within six years, from $12 million in fiscal year 2000 to $24 million in 2006. From only one recipient in 2000, nine sub-Saharan African countries are now receiving aid under this programme. Meanwhile, IMET, the Pentagon's International Military Education and Training programme, has increased by 35 per cent, from $8.1 million to $11 million, over the same period. It now operates in 47 countries compared to 36. Between 2000 and 2003, funding under the Foreign Military Sales programme, the US's largest arms transfer programme, was expanded from $9.8 million to $40.3 million.

Other US military initiatives in Africa include the Pan-Sahel Initiative, which carries out training and exercises in Chad, Mali, Mauritania, Niger and other nations in the region, though the US is alleged also to have been involved in combat under the cover of the programme. A $100 million programme has been proposed for military and anti-terrorist training in East Africa.

The US military presence in oil-producing areas of Africa is growing rapidly. The war on terror is frequently cited as the reason for this involvement, but the oil-rich countries around the Gulf of Guinea tend to be the largest beneficiaries, with increasing arms deliveries to Angola and Nigeria from the US Department of Defense.

The US navy is increasingly being used to protect routes used for oil shipments. While key areas are the Persian Gulf and the South China Sea, African waters are also seeing a greater naval presence. "To increase the US naval presence in waters adjoining Nigeria and other key producers, carrier battle groups assigned to the European Command (which controls the South Atlantic) will shorten their future visits to the Mediterranean ... and spend half the time going down the west coast of Africa," said US General James Jones in May 2003. US strategic interest in Nigeria, a former British colony, increased after the discovery of new deep-water oil reserves right off the coast.

Since the death of the former Nigerian leader General Sani Abacha in 1999, military aid has increased rapidly, from $90,000 in 1999 to over $4 million in 2003. In 1999, Nigeria bought arms worth $74,000 from the US. Only two years later, the US exported $3.1 million worth of arms in 2001 alone.

This assistance is needed in part to protect Nigeria's oil industry. Organized gangs of thieves steal up to 20 per cent of total output and sell it abroad. Part of the money from these illegal sales is then used to buy more sophisticated weapons to use against the police and private security forces protecting the oil infrastructure. Several oil company employees have been taken hostage, and two oil workers from the US were killed when a ChevronTexaco boat was attacked.

In the drive to find new sources of oil, the human rights aspect seems to be sidelined. The US State Department's Human Rights report reveals extra judicial killings by the Nigerian police and army, but the US continues to supply the country with arms and military aid. There is no way to monitor whether the arms supplied are used for regional peacekeeping or, for example, to quash dissent in the oil-rich Niger Delta region. In return for military aid, and for technical assistance to African navies and anti-piracy efforts, the US is hoping to have access to bases in Nigeria for training and, potentially, military operations.

The US is not the only country interested in links with oil-rich regions of Africa. France, China, India and Japan are all working to create new ties with the continent, and heavily targeting the oil-producing countries. Africa was included on the Indian government's Hydrocarbon Vision 2005 report, as an alternative to Middle Eastern sources already dominated by the Seven Sisters oil companies. At the same time, India is increasing aid to African countries, particularly in the form of medicines, and in 2003 New Delhi offered to provide security services along the African coast.

France, which once colonized large parts of Africa, is striving to counter US diplomatic advances, especially in Algeria. Currently, 20 per cent of France's oil comes from West Africa, and after its former colonies gained their independence France has maintained a close relationship with many of these countries. Successive French presidents from General de Gaulle onwards have forged personal links with African heads of state. The majority of France's foreign aid is targeted at Africa. France's Department of Cooperation has an African aid budget that is five times larger than the UK's.

This aid bought France the right to maintain a heavy military presence in Africa. In 1990, there were over 12,000 French troops in Africa, plus military advisers in 16 countries.

While France has been moving away from a direct policing role in the decades since independence, it has continued to maintain a significant presence in the oil-producing countries. In Gabon, Elf-Aquitaine controls the oil industry almost entirely, while France supplies 44 per cent of Gabon's imports, 75 per cent of its foreign investment and 80 per cent of its foreign aid. In 1964, French troops intervened in Gabon to return the first post-independence president Leon M'Ba to power, and later continued its presence in the country to support the next president, Omar Bongo, turning a blind eye to his excesses of corruption and oppression. Back in 1987, the French government had been annoyed by President Bongo's visit to US President Ronald Reagan. Paris immediately set out to reassert its superior claims to Gabon's oil. French Interior Minister Charles Pasqua was dispatched to Libreville, the Gabonese capital, to discuss with President Bongo the traditional ties between Gabon and France.

This resentment is now re-emerging as the US seeks to create new links with Algeria, formerly a French colony, and plans to build a Nigeria-Algeria pipeline (via Niger) are developed. It was the Algerian war of independence that sparked the 1968 riots in Paris, and the end of France's colonial era. Located just south of the Mediterranean, and with proven oil reserves of over 9.2 billion barrels, Algeria is important to Paris. Algeria's potential oil reserves are even higher; since the country was embroiled in a civil war for many years, the oil industry is relatively small, and foreign companies are now keen to enter this new location.

In 2003, Jacques Chirac became the first French president to visit Algeria since independence. His aim was to build a coalition against the war in Iraq, as well as to improve relations with Algeria, a major exporter of oil and gas to southern Europe.

In July 2004, the French government announced a new military pact with Algeria, covering weapons and technology transfer, training, and intelligence sharing. Finance Minister Nicolas Sarkozy later approved a $2.5 billion aid package. Other diplomatic overtures included an invitation for Algerian President Abdelaziz Bouteflika to attend a commemoration of the liberation of Vichy France from Nazi occupation.

The growing warmth between Algeria and the US is therefore ringing alarm bells in Paris. President Bouteflika has twice visited the White House, and a proposal for a US military base in Algeria is under discussion. This has in part been prompted by the war on terror. The Salafist Group, an Algerian rebel group with links to al-Qaeda, refused to disarm after the civil war. Another group, the GSPC, also linked to al-Qaeda and with a mission to create an Islamic state in Algeria, took 32 European hostages in 2003. President Bouteflika was the first leader from the Arab world to condemn the September 11th attacks. Algerian generals are now pushing the US to allow them access to combat aircraft and other military technologies previously denied to them.

China too is an increasingly active player in Africa, and has good relations with many African states. Some of these date back to the 1950s, when Maoist China first forged links with newly independent African states, competing with the West and the USSR for influence. Now Beijing has friendly relations with almost all of Africa's 54 states.

China's ambitions in Africa are two-fold. As a rising superpower, it is increasing its geopolitical clout and its position as "leader of the third world". But Africa also represents a valuable source of oil and other raw materials, and unlike the Middle East it has not yet been shared out among the big Western oil companies.

Since the early 1960s, China has been promoting itself as the "leader of the third world", and as a former colony itself can identify with post-colonial Africa. China has consistently built up goodwill among its African friends through grants, low interest loans, technical assistance and educational exchanges. In 2000, China forgave debts amounting to $1.2 billion from African countries. By 2003, a total of 15,000 Chinese doctors had worked in Africa, treating almost 180 million cases of HIV/AIDS, as well as other diseases. Recently, 10,000 African students were offered scholarships to universities in China.

As well as gaining political support (for example for its "One China" policy), China has used its African policy to gain new trade contracts for the supply of African raw materials, especially oil. Chinese demand for oil is growing at approximately six times the global average, and its domestic supply is running short.

The China National Petroleum Corporation (CNPC) has an advantage over Western oil companies in that unlike them it is not held back from cooperating with governments such as the Sudan's by fears of negative publicity or legal challenges from human rights groups.

In the Sudan, China has become the largest foreign investor and the largest supplier of arms, while the Sudan is now responsible for 5 per cent of China's oil imports. CNPC is the largest investor in the Sudan's oil sector (with investments totalling $15 billion), helping the country to become a net exporter of oil. Recently, the CNPC employed 10,000 mainly Sudanese workers to build a pipeline transporting oil the 900 miles from the Kordofan field to Port Sudan on the Red Sea. CNPC also owns 40 per cent of the Greater Nile Petroleum Operating Company, which runs much of the country's oil industry.

As well as funding social programmes to encourage stability within the country, Beijing has encouraged the Sudanese government to take action to stop the violence in Darfur, a key oil-producing region, but has opposed plans for UN action to stop the killing in Darfur, and threatened a veto when this was proposed. (The actions of foreign oil companies in Darfur will be discussed in more detail in Chapter 9.) Chinese companies supply the Sudanese military with arms, tanks and helicopters to clear civilians from the oilfields, as well as fighting anti-government rebels.

In Nigeria, China is rebuilding the rail network. In 2004, China proposed to take over the Nigerian government's share in the oil refineries at Port Harcourt and Kaduna. In October 2004, Lagos set up a technical committee to investigate these proposals, as well as the Chinese offer for extensive investment in the upstream oil industry and other energy sources.

After the war against Eritrea caused US businesspeople and charity volunteers to pull out of Ethiopia in the late 1990s, China took the opportunity to establish itself there. Aid packages, businesspeople and teachers were rapidly dispatched to Ethiopia, and China is now planning to build a military base there, as well as starting an oil exploration programme. China is also seeking a closer relationship with Gabon. In 2004, President Bongo made a one-week visit to China, culminating in the signing of an agreement for technical and economic cooperation, and a $5 million aid package for Gabon. Earlier that year, China had signed an oil supply agreement with Gabon.

Aid For Future Oil Suppliers: US Bases in the Caspian Region

The discovery of the 40-billion-barrel Tenghiz field off the Kazakhstan coast caused great excitement among the US's energy policy-makers. The initial hype that the Caspian could replace the Middle East as the primary source of world oil had been deflated, but as with other areas with potential to become oil exporters, US military aid to the Caspian is increasing. The newly independent states of the Caucasus and Central Asia received around $40 million in military aid in 2004. In 2002, the US Congress also agreed a "Special Supplement" for the Caucasus amounting to $70 million.

The Caspian basin has proven oil reserves of between 17 and 33 billion barrels, of which 12.5 billion barrels are in Azerbaijan and 17.6 billion barrels in Kazakhstan. The region is relatively unexploited, and potential reserves are estimated at up to 32 billion barrels in Azerbaijan, 92 billion barrels in Kazakhstan, and 38 billion barrels in Turkmenistan.

Since independence from the USSR in 1991, the Caspian countries have started to exploit their oil commercially. According to the US Energy Information Administration, in 2002 regional oil production was around 1.6 million barrels per day. By 2010 this is expected to rise as high as 5 million barrels per day. The discovery of Kazakhstan's vast Tenghiz field is already boosting production.

The great problem facing the countries in the region, and the oil companies that want to operate there, is how to extract the oil and transport it to world markets. Until 1991, a distribution network only existed for transporting the oil to nearby countries and to Russia, which used to get much of its oil from the area in the Soviet era.

Central Asia and the Caspian also have great geostrategic significance. A modern version of the "Great Game" played out between the British and Russian empires in the 19th century is now developing in Central Asia and the Caucasus. All the regional powers – Russia, the US, Turkey, China, Europe, and even India and Pakistan – are seeking influence in the region, offering aid and technical assistance.

New bases in Uzbekistan and Kyrgyzstan were set up by the US and their allies and used for bombing raids and sorties over Afghanistan during Operation Enduring Freedom. Washington also reached agreement to use airfields in Tajikistan, and a fly-over agreement with Kazakhstan. In return, the Central Asian countries received tens of millions of dollars in military and economic aid. With the conflict now over, the bases have achieved semi-permanent status. (Russia, meanwhile, is strengthening its ties with the Kazakh government in Astana, and opened its own base near the Kyrgyz capital Bishkek, making Kyrgyzstan the first country to host both US and Russian military bases.)

The growing US presence in Central Asia is in part a component of the "war on terror". Central Asia is situated on the fault line between Europe and western Asia. Tajikistan is only just recovering from a bloody civil war between Muslim opposition forces and the post-Communist government. The newly independent states, with their largely Muslim populations, have been targeted by fundamentalist groups such as the IMU (Islamic Movement of Uzbekistan) and Hizb-ut-Tahrir whose aim is to set up an Islamic Caliphate in Central Asia.

The determinedly secular governments of Tajikistan, Uzbekistan and Kyrgyzstan have therefore ranged themselves alongside the US in the "war on terror", and their diplomatic and practical support has won them significant financial benefits. Also, particularly in Uzbekistan, this allowed the national governments to repress any opposition to their rule, under the guise of fighting terror. In fact, there is some question over whether the IMU or Hizb-ut-Tahrir would have received much support in the first place had the Uzbek government not been so repressive.

The Uzbek President Islam Karimov allowed the US to set up Camp Stronghold Freedom, a military base at Khanabad near the Afghan frontier. Karimov, whose security forces are alleged routinely to lock up dissidents on spurious terror charges, is a strong supporter of the "war on terror". (For information on the human rights situation in Uzbekistan, see Freedom House's *Nations in Transit 2004* and *The Human Rights Context of the Andijan Events*, Human Rights Watch 2005.)

Until the May 2004 riots in the Uzbek town of Andizhan, resulting in the deaths of around 500 people at the hands of the Uzbek security forces, the US, UK and other countries largely ignored human rights abuses in Uzbekistan. Tashkent received $45.1 million in US military aid in 2002, and $13.6 million in 2003. When the British ambassador in Tashkent, Craig Murray, started making outspoken criticisms of the country's human rights record in 2003, he was recalled to London "for medical treatment". He was later reinstated after a Foreign Office investigation cleared him of most of the charges against him, but has now left the foreign service.

Oil is a large part of the reason behind the importance of this region, and, just as with Saudi Arabia or its African oil suppliers, why the US is inclined to turn a blind eye to issues such as press censorship, untransparent elections and human rights abuses. Even the countries with very little oil – Kyrgyzstan, Tajikistan and Georgia – have a great strategic value due to their location and the need to preserve regional stability. Oil is explicitly mentioned in a State Department request to Congress to fund a "rapid-reaction brigade" in Kazakhstan. The State Department argues it is needed to help Kazakhstan "respond to major terrorist threats to oil platforms."

Before the Caspian region could become a major oil supplier, a way had to be found to transport its oil to world markets. Pipelines from Kazakhstan to China, from Turkmenistan through Afghanistan to Pakistan, and through the Caucasus to the Mediterranean, have all been considered. Fearing the leverage Russia could wield if oil could only reach Europe via its territory, a consortium of major oil companies with the support of the US and European governments, as well as those in the region, have recently completed building a new pipeline to carry Caspian oil across the Caucasus.

The 1,000-mile pipeline takes oil from the city of Baku, through the Georgian capital Tiblisi to the Turkish port of Ceyhan on the Mediterranean coast. It is designed to carry one million barrels per day.

As well as the oil revenues the pipeline would bring, the governments in Baku and Tiblisi welcomed the pipeline for a different reason; they assumed it would mean a US commitment to their territorial integrity. If, as they feared, Russia might harbour ambitions to once again rule its "near abroad", the US would most probably commit its troops to keeping the pipeline – and by extension the Caucasian countries – out of Russian control.

The pipeline, built by a consortium of 11 major oil companies led by BP, is already camouflaged and closely guarded along much of its length to prevent the constant threat of sabotage. It runs close to Chechnya and Ngorno-Karabakh. In Georgia there are frequent clashes between the government in Tiblisi and separatists in Abkhazia and South Ossetia. Finally, it runs through parts of eastern Turkey where the army is engaged in an ongoing guerrilla campaign against Kurdish separatists.

The US has provided millions of dollars worth of arms and equipment to the Georgian military, to equip them to protect the pipeline. It has also sent military specialists to train the Georgian units responsible for guarding the pipeline.

Whether the influx of arms and oil money will have the same impact in the Caspian as it has had in the Middle East, Colombia and West Africa remains to be seen. Petrodollars have rarely, if ever, helped countries to reduce poverty or inequality. In many cases, oil has actually held back economic development – as has been the case in Africa and South America – and rising income differentials have led to unrest and sometimes civil war. Whether in Colombia, Nigeria or Kazakhstan, the majority of the populations of the oil-rich states are not benefiting from their oil. Within donor countries, development aims come into conflict with the need to secure sources of oil.

The world economy today is helplessly dependent not just upon oil, but on cheap oil, and very little has been done to counter this. Transport, agriculture, the chemicals and plastics industries – not to mention the current fashion for gas-guzzling SUVs – are all based on cheap and abundant oil. Instead of reducing our dependence on oil as we approach the point at which oil production will peak and start to decline, the populations of the US, Europe, Japan and other developed and industrializing countries are increasing their oil imports. The demonstrations in the UK when petrol prices went up in September 2000 gave a small indication of how consumers will react to a permanent hike in oil prices when we reach that point. As oil supplies start to dwindle, we can expect ever more oil-related conflict in the 21st century.

Chapter Nine: Killing for Oil

Oil is located in some of the world's more turbulent regions, such as the war-torn southern Sudan, Colombia and Angola, as well as in countries like Indonesia and Myanmar that have been under the control of repressive and brutal dictators. Oil companies still do business in these areas and deal with these dictatorships. This has led to accusations that oil companies have ignored, tolerated, or even encouraged human rights violations, provided they were able to continue extracting oil and making a profit.

Oil companies are also alleged to have intervened in their host countries' destinies, funding (or bribing) politicians, backing attempted coups and supporting one or – as in the case of Elf in Angola and the Congo – both sides in civil wars.

Human rights and environmental groups are trying to bring the world's major oil companies to account for what they say are cases of complicity in human rights violations and massive environmental damage. Unocal has agreed to compensate villagers in Myanmar who were forced at gunpoint by the Burmese army to work without pay on the pipeline from the offshore Yadana gasfield. A case is pending against Mobil for its alleged complicity in massacres in the Aceh province of Indonesia. In Ecuador, ChevronTexaco is being sued for the environmental damage that local people claim it caused by tipping millions of tons of industrial waste into the Amazon rainforest.

Total and Unocal in Myanmar

Work on a pipeline from the Yadana gasfield in the Andaman Sea, 38 miles off the coast of Myanmar (formerly Burma), to Thailand began in 1995, and was completed three years later. A four-company consortium, comprising California-based Unocal, the French company Total, in partnership with the state-owned Myanmar Oil and Gas Enterprise (MOGE) and the Petroleum Authority of Thailand Exploration & Production (PTT-EP), carried out the pipeline project.

The pipeline runs under the sea for 218 miles, then a 41-mile section cuts across the Tenasserim region of southern Myanmar to the Thai border. Although it is only a small proportion of the total length of the pipeline, the Burmese section has been highly controversial.

Since 1962, Myanmar has been ruled by a military dictatorship. The regime was introduced after a military coup led by General Ne Win, who ruled the country for 26 years. Under Ne Win, the people of Myanmar were plunged into poverty, while government officials and foreign business operating in the country grew rich. In 1990, the party of opposition leader Aung San Suu Kyi won a landslide victory in the first free elections in almost 30 years. However, the military refused to relinquish power, and Aung San Suu Kyi has been under house arrest for much of the time since then.

Pressure from human rights groups caused a number of world governments to cut diplomatic relations with Myanmar. In the US, Congress outlawed all US investment in Myanmar. Although this did not ban existing investments, most US companies responded to Aung San Suu Kyi's call for them to pull out of the country. Unocal remained.

Another major player in the oil industry to remain in Myanmar was the French/Belgian company Total Oil, the world's fourth largest oil company. Total has been operating in Myanmar since 1992, and it provides annual revenues estimated at up to $450 million to the military government. Natural gas has become Myanmar's largest source of export revenues, accounting for around 30 per cent of exports in the year 2002–3.

Another consequence of Total's continuing involvement in Myanmar is its impact on French policy towards the country. France has opposed all moves to strengthen the EU's common position on Myanmar, in order to protect Total's investment. In October 2004, oil and gas were exempted from EU economic sanctions, under pressure from France.

Before Total and Unocal started construction of the pipeline, the farmers and fishermen of the villages among the jungle on the southern coast of Myanmar lived in relative isolation, generally ignored by both the government in Yangon and rebel groups waging a guerrilla campaign against the regime. When construction started and the Burmese military entered the area to provide security for the pipeline, their lives changed immediately for the worse.

According to the case brought against Unocal, after the plan to build the pipeline was agreed, four military battalions, each with 600 men, were formed in the area, even though it was at least 150 miles from any significant rebel activity. Their real purpose was to force the villagers at gunpoint to build infrastructure for the pipeline project, such as roads and army camps, without pay. Those that could fled into the jungle, while others were beaten and abused, forced to carry building materials through the jungle for weeks on end.

"The government calls us volunteers," said one middle-aged rice farmer. "But the truth is, we were slaves." (Adam Zagorin, *Time*, November 24th, 2003)

In February 1996, American human rights groups filed a lawsuit against Unocal in a Los Angeles court on behalf of 15 Burmese villagers. They alleged that Unocal knew, or should have known, that the army was committing human rights abuses while providing security for its operations and clearing a path through the jungle for its pipeline. They also planned to sue Total, but could not establish sufficient grounds to try the French oil company in California. Total is, however, fighting off a legal challenge in the French and Belgian courts.

The case was brought under the US's Alien Tort Claims Act (ACTA), an arcane piece of legislation originally passed in 1789 to prevent piracy. The ACTA enables foreigners to sue US companies or individuals in the US for alleged violations of international norms on crimes such as genocide, slavery and torture, if they cannot obtain a fair trial in their home country.

Unocal has always denied it knew of the abuses. However, as early as 1992 a consultant to the oil company warned that "throughout Burma, the government habitually makes use of forced labour ... in such circumstances Unocal and its partners will have little freedom of manoeuvre." Once the project had started, another adviser, former US military attaché John Haseman, told Unocal that the Burmese army was committing "egregious human rights violations" that were directly related to the project. (US Court of Appeal for the

Ninth Circuit, John Roe v. Unocal Corporation and Union Oil Company of California)

Hasseman's report to Unocal, quoted at the trial, stated "The most common [rights violations] are forced relocation without compensation of families from land near/along the pipeline route, forced labour to work on infrastructure projects supporting the pipeline and imprisonment and/or execution by the army of those opposing such actions."

In February 2005, after an eight-year legal battle, Unocal lawyers announced they had reached an out of court settlement. The oil company agreed to pay compensation to the villagers, now in hiding under assumed names to avoid reprisals from the military. Details of the settlement have not yet been released.

The case potentially has great significance for other groups that have been the victims of human rights violations by authoritarian governments working with multinational companies in other countries. Over 30 similar cases are currently being considered in the US courts, including those brought by Indonesian villagers against ExxonMobil, and the people of the Ecuadorian Amazon region against ChevronTexaco. The Unocal case could set a precedent that will make it easier to hold multinational corporations accountable for their involvement in human rights abuses.

However, the possibility of bringing multinationals to account in the US may depend on whether the ACTA continues to exist. During the eight-year legal battle between Unocal and lawyers representing the Burmese villagers, the White House under George W. Bush campaigned for the court not to apply the ACTA. The National Foreign Trade Council (NFTC) and the International Chamber of Commerce (ICC), both of which represent multinational companies, are lobbying US lawmakers to repeal it.

Mobil in Indonesia

There is a similar situation in Indonesia, where the extent of Mobil's complicity in massacres carried out by the Indonesian military in the oil-producing Aceh region is still unproved. Aceh is on the northern tip of Sumatra, one of the main islands in the Indonesian archipelago. The Indonesian capital, Jakarta, is on the island of Java, to the south east of Sumatra.

After three centuries of Dutch rule (interrupted by a brief period under the British), Indonesia was occupied by Japan during World War II. Many of the Indonesian elite and intelligentsia, led by the future president Sukarno, cooperated with the Japanese, and toward the end of the war Japan backed their plans for an independent Indonesia. Once allied forces started driving the Japanese out of their captured territory, the Dutch army, with backing from the allies, tried to retake its former colonies, and in particular the oil-rich 'Dutch East Indies' as it was then known.

Indonesia declared its independence on August 17th, 1945, but this was not recognized by the Netherlands until December 29th, 1949, after a four-year war of independence. Sukarno was ousted from power in 1967 by General Sukharto, who took power with US backing on the pretext of preventing a Communist coup, and set up a military dictatorship in the country.

The strongly Muslim Aceh people of northern Sumatra had attempted to win their independence in 1945. But Aceh was well endowed with oil and gas – in 1971, Mobil Oil had discovered an onshore field with an estimated 14 trillion cubic feet of gas – and just as with East Timor (annexed by Indonesia in 1975), Jakarta had no intention of giving it up. Instead, a lengthy war of skirmishes, killings and military intimidation began in Aceh.

The region, despite having one of the world's largest onshore gasfields, is now wretchedly poor; 90 per cent of oil and gas revenue is taken from the province, and almost all the contracts and management jobs go to ethnic Javanese. Oil and gas extraction is carried out by a joint venture between Mobil and PT Arun (a company majority-owned by the Indonesian state oil monopoly Pertamina, in which Mobil had a 35 per cent stake).

The Free Aceh Movement declared the province's independence soon after the Mobil/PT Arun venture began operations in 1976, causing an immediate escalation in violence. In 1990, Javanese troops flooded into Aceh. Human rights groups estimate that over 5,000 Acehnese have been killed by the Indonesian military since 1989. In 1998, the bloodiest year of the conflict, 2,000 Acehnese were killed in a military push.

Like other foreign companies in the country, Mobil and PT Arun had been paying the cash-strapped Indonesian military to protect its operations against sabotage. The exact sum they paid is not known. (Although it is known that the US mining company Freeport McMoRan paid $5.6 million in "security fees" to local commanders in 2002.)

According to the International Labour Rights Fund (ILRF), which in 2001 filed a lawsuit against ExxonMobil on behalf of 11 Acehnese victims of human rights abuses, members of the military units employed to provide security for Mobil's gas extraction and liquefaction project "regularly have perpetrated ongoing and severe human rights abuses against local villagers, including murder, rape, torture, destruction of property and other acts of terror." ("ExxonMobil: How the Company is Linked with Indonesian Military Killings, Torture and other Severe Abuse in Aceh, Indonesia," International Labor Rights Fund)

The ILRF further states that "ExxonMobil apparently has taken no action to stop this violence, and instead, reportedly has continued to finance the military and to provide company equipment and facilities that have been used by the Indonesian military to perpetrate and literally cover up (in the form of mass graves) these criminal acts."

On December 28th, 1998, following a statement from a coalition of 17 human rights groups, *Business Week* magazine ran a devastating exposé about army massacres around Mobil's oil refinery and Indonesian state company Pertamina's gas plant at Lhokseumawe. The piece, titled "What did Mobil know?", documents some of the atrocities uncovered around Lhokseumawe, and examines whether these happened with Mobil's knowledge and the oil company's tacit consent.

Mobil Oil Indonesia, Mobil's wholly owned subsidiary, is alleged to have provided support to the army, including lending the military excavating equipment that was used to dig mass graves. One grave was discovered on Pertamina-owned land, only three miles from a Mobil plant. Another allegation is that a former Mobil employee "disappeared" after being seized by security forces on Mobil property.

Both Mobil and Pertamina deny that they knew of any human rights abuses in the area where they were operating. Mobil also points out that it was operating on land and from buildings owned by Pertamina, and that almost all its equipment was either leased from contractors or owned by Pertamina.

In 1998, *Business Week* carried out a five-week investigation in

Indonesia, interviewing over a dozen sources that either witnessed atrocities or discovered their consequences. Among them were two Mobil contractors who found human body parts near company sites.

While it has not yet been established whether Mobil's managers knew what was going on, people living in the area say it would have been impossible to be unaware of the massacres. "There wasn't a single person in Aceh that didn't know that massacres were taking place. From the children to the elderly to the mentally ill, everybody was afraid," H. Sayed Mudhahar, a former top government official in Aceh, said in an interview with *Business Week*.

Another of *Business Week*'s interviewees, a damage claims inspector working for a Mobil contractor, described an incident in late 1990. Travelling along a road leading to one of Mobil's oilwells, he arrived at a vacant sugar plantation, where pigs were feeding in what looked like a bulldozed pit with earth pushed over it.

"They were obviously human bones ... The pigs were rooting down there on a hip bone, around the white knobbly part," he said, adding that he informed a Mobil manager, who did not make a record of the incident. Mobil claims to have no knowledge of the incident.

An area of land acquired by Pertamina for Mobil to develop, crossed by "deep, wide crevices created by seismic activity" became notorious as "Skull Hill". Witnesses told *Business Week* that "the stench of rotting human flesh on Skull Hill could be smelled half a mile away." Mobil employees travelled to work along a road that passed Skull Hill on a daily basis during 1990 and 1991.

In the early 1990s, rumours also spread about massacres in Bukit Sentang, a village about 15 miles from Skull Hill. In 1991, Mobil widened a road that passed through the village. A former Mobil employee, who frequently used the road to reach a Mobil-operated gasfield, told *Business Week* that "every time I drove out there, the subcontractors stopped my car. They said, 'No, don't go out there. Don't you know the army is killing people and burying them in mass graves with Mobil equipment?'" He added that the use of Mobil equipment to dig mass graves became a topic of lunchtime conversation at the company's "Bachelor Camp" mess hall.

At the ExxonMobil shareholders' meeting in Dallas in May 2002, Cut Zahara Hamzah, a former Acehnese resident and board member of the International Forum for Aceh, described what she had witnessed growing up in Lhokseumawe, near Mobil's LNG plant:

> My husband used to work for ExxonMobil for six years. He related that he and several of his friends were often ordered to repair equipment and vehicles used by TNI soldiers in their military operations. They often found blood splashed all over the equipment and vehicles. When in the end he and his friends were arrested and tortured by the TNI soldiers who were based within the ExxonMobil complex, the Company did not lift a finger to try to help them...
>
> My brother, Jafar Siddiq Hamzah, was a human rights activist and a permanent resident of the US who used to live in New York. He went back to Aceh in July 2000 to investigate cases of human rights violations that include the involvement of Mobil Oil in giving facilities to the perpetrators of gross human rights violations in Aceh. He was kidnapped in broad daylight in August of that year and a month later his mutilated body was found wrapped in barbed wire.

In 2003, General Endriartono Sutarto, Indonesia's military commander, said that he wanted to withdraw his troops from large mining and energy projects, and for the police and the companies themselves to take over that responsibility. This would affect ExxonMobil and BP as well as several international mining companies. However, this has not yet happened.

ExxonMobil, despite closing down its operations briefly in 2001, when sabotage against the company (including attacks on vehicles and shots at company planes) became too intense, is still operating in Aceh, making approximately $2 billion per year. Human rights organizations are trying to force the company to disclose how much it is paying to the Indonesian military for security.

Its alleged complicity in military actions is not the only harm Mobil may have done to the people of Aceh. Its mining and processing operations have devastated local communities by poisoning rivers and seas with oil and other industrial spills, forced relocations and constant noise pollution over a period of several decades. ("Exxon Mobil: probably the worst oil company in the world?," Friends of the Earth briefing, 1999) In December 1997, 1,600 people were forced out of their homes after three gaswells erupted near the villages of Tanjungkarang and Dalam.

Cut Zahara Hamzah also told ExxonMobil shareholders about the harm that roads built by the company (presented by Mobil as a contribution to development) had caused to farming communities: "The roads cause the closing of the water source to some parts of the fields and destroy the existing irrigational system, with the end result being the loss of livelihood for most villagers who depend on their rice farming."

No verdict has yet been reached on the case brought against ExxonMobil by the International Labour Rights Fund. While fighting the lawsuit, ExxonMobil appealed to the White House for support. In a letter dated July 29th, 2002 (leaked document published by the ILRF), the State Department wrote to a federal judge, stating that "... the Department of State believes that adjudication of this lawsuit at this time would in fact risk a potentially serious adverse impact on significant interests of the United States, including interests related directly to the on-going struggle against international terrorism."

It adds that: "To the extent that this litigation contributes to a worsening of the economic conditions in Indonesia that breed instability, it would adversely affect US interests ... This litigation is likely to further discourage foreign investment, particularly in extractive industries in remote or unstable areas that require security protection."

Elf in Africa

A trial that ended in November 2003 spectacularly exposed former French state oil company Elf's corrupt and anti-competitive activities in Africa, as well as France's entire post-colonial Africa policy. Thirty former Elf senior executives were convicted of misusing company assets, siphoning off around €350 million (£237 million) into secret bank accounts, and spending company assets on – among other things – mansions, expensive jewellery and alimony fees.

Even more seriously, the case revealed that the company had for decades been paying kickbacks to government officials in Africa. When governments ran into financial difficulties, or wanted to raise cash to fund military expansion or other programmes, Elf officials encouraged their ruling elites to enter oil-for-debt agreements that effectively mortgaged their country's future to Elf. Elf was also revealed to have been actively involved in funding both sides of the civil war in Congo Brazzaville, and indirectly doing the same in neighbouring Angola.

Overall, €10 million (£6.7 million) had been paid to Gabon's President Omar Bongo, with similar large sums going to the leaders of Angola, Cameroon and Congo Brazzaville, to ensure these countries remained loyal to France, as well as favouring Elf over British and American oil companies.

Among those convicted were three top executives. Former Elf chairman Loik Le Floch-Prigent and former director Alfred Sirven were both sentenced to five years in jail. Le Floch-Prigent was fined €375,000 and Sirven €2 million. André Tarallo, Elf's former director for Africa and Hydrocarbons, known within the company as "Mr Africa" was fined €2 million and sentenced to four years in jail.

Le Floch-Prigent admitted he had paid €3.5 million of Elf funds to his former wife Fatima Belaid on their divorce, to buy her silence about the dealings within the company.

Created by the then French President Charles de Gaulle in 1965, Elf has always been closely linked to the French government, and the SDCE, the French intelligence service. With operations in Cameroon, Gabon, Equatorial Guinea, Congo Brazzaville, Nigeria and Angola, its actions have also been connected to France's post-colonial Africa policy known as "Francafrique", under which Paris maintained relations and influence with French-speaking Africa.

Elf has been deeply penetrated by French political parties, first the Gaullists, and later the socialists after François Mitterrand became president and allegedly asked the newly appointed Le Floch-Prigent to "even things out". The company was used as a source of funds for both top company executives and the entire French political class. Throughout the trial, Le Floch-Prigent claimed that he was in "daily contact" with the Elysée palace, and that "all the presidents of France" had known of, and condoned, Elf's illegal dealings. He also claimed that Elf transferred at least €5 million per year to each of France's main political parties.

Even though Elf was privatized in 1994, the company's character did not really change until its merger with the Franco-Belgian company TotalFina in 1999.

ELF IN CONGO BRAZZAVILLE

Congo Brazzaville (also known as the Republic of the Congo) was one of the states in which Elf had the most devastating influence. The oil company not only treated the African state as a colony, buying off its ruling elite and encouraging it into debt, it also funded both sides in the civil war that started in 1997.

Testifying in Paris, Tarallo said that the company's official policy was always to support the existing government, which in Congo Brazzaville was President Denis Sassou-Nguesso, leader of the formerly Marxist Congolese Labour Party (PCT). Under Sassou-Nguesso, the PCT moved further away from the Soviet sphere of influence and developed new ties with France, China and the US. Tarallo himself acted for many years as an unofficial adviser to Sassou-Nguesso.

After a quarter century of one-party rule, the country started to democratize in the early 1990s. Pascal Lissouba won the multiparty elections in 1992.

The transition to democratic rule was a fairly turbulent one; later that year (after an attempted coup partly funded by Elf), Lissouba dissolved parliament and called new elections for 2003. The results of the 2003 elections were disputed, sparking civil unrest in June and again five months later.

Just before the mid-2003 elections, Lissouba had asked Elf for a loan, mainly to pay the salary arrears for the country's civil servants. This was denied. Le Floch-Prigent claimed this was for reasons of "political stability". He apparently believed that if Lissouba won an outright victory in the elections, this could lead to ethnic violence. The only person capable of uniting the country, in his opinion, was Sassou-Nguesso.

Instead, the Congolese government raised oil taxes and royalties from 17 per cent to 33 per cent. It also agreed an oil-backed loan for $150 million with the US oil company Occidental Petroleum. In the long term, the terms of the loan were ruinous for Congo Brazzaville; it committed the country to selling oil for $3 per barrel. However, the infusion of cash into the economy did help Lissouba to win the 1993 election, much to Elf's consternation.

Le Floch-Prigent later testified that he had advised the French government to delay payment of the loan through the Congolese central bank, itself controlled by France. Although this advice was not acted upon, both Elf and the French government were furious at the incursion of an American oil company into oil-producing Francophone Africa.

Lissouba held onto power until just before the July 1997 elections. With tension mounting between his supporters and those of Sassou-Nguesso, he ordered government forces to surround his rival's compound in the capital Brazzaville. In the following four months of conflict, much of Brazzaville was destroyed. In October, Angolan troops joined the war on Sassou-Nguesso's side, rapidly returning him to power. Fighting broke out twice during 1998, but Sassou-Nguesso managed to hold onto power, and was re-elected to the presidency in the 2002 election.

The former Congolese finance minister, Nguila Moungounga, has alleged that Elf financed several attempts to replace Lissouba with Sassou-Nguesso. Once Sassou-Nguesso started openly seeking power in 1996, Elf was in an awkward position due to its official policy of supporting the leader in office. Testimony given at the Elf trial indicates that Elf resolved this conflict by supporting both sides so it could be sure to have backed the winner.

Paris also appeared to be hedging its bets. After civil war broke out in 1997, the French Foreign Ministry stopped referring to Lissouba as "President". Rather than distinguishing between the government and the rebels, they also referred to Lissouba and Sassou-Nguesso's forces as "the sides".

There is some evidence to suggest that Tarallo and his former colleague Jack Sigolet helped to arrange arms purchases for Lissouba, from the Belgian arms-trafficker and money-launderer known as "Jacques Monsieur". These arms were paid for with money siphoned off from national oil revenues.

French newspaper reports allege that Elf also provided more substantial help to Sassou-Nguesso's forces. *Le Monde* documents financing from "the secret financing networks of oil companies." (*Le Monde*, October 17th, 1997) A report from *Le Canard Enchaîné* in 1997 claimed that boats owned by Elf had been used to transport Angolan troops to Pointe-Noire, the town at the heart of Congo Brazzaville's oil region. (*Le Canard Enchaîné*, October 22nd, 1997) When the Angolan troops took and pillaged Pointe-Noire, Elf vehicles and infrastructure were not touched.

Lissouba himself, speaking in 1997, said that he planned to sue Elf for its role in returning Sassou-Nguesso to power, accusing the company's leaders of "complicity in acts of terrorism, voluntary destruction and homicide" and "criminal association" with the leaders of the rebellion. (*Dow Jones Energy Service*, November 28th, 1997) He added that a lawsuit might help Elf "to rid itself of certain habits," but that he did not want to fundamentally damage the company.

"I live off Elf," he said. "Why would I want to destabilize it?"

"ANGOLAGATE"

Elf was also indirectly involved in the 27-year civil war in neighbouring Angola, which lasted from 1975 to 2002, where again company officials have been charged with supporting both sides in the civil war. The trial exposed a similar system – known as the "Elf System" – of bribery, influence peddling, and the use of oil-backed loans to extend its power within the country.

While its official policy was to support the elected MPLA government in Luanda, Elf also appointed a company representative to handle relations with the opposing UNITA party, embroiled in a 30-year civil war against the MPLA. Tarallo handled relations with President Eduard dos Santos of the MPLA, while another senior executive, Alfred Sirven, was assigned to UNITA.

Yves Verwaerde, a former member of the European parliament and a supporter of UNITA, testified that UNITA leader Jonas Savimbi had complained that Elf was supplying the MPLA with helicopters and other military equipment, and financing its military operations against UNITA. Savimbi made the same threat to Elf as he did to the American oil companies in Angola: he would sabotage their oil infrastructure if they continued to do business with the government in Luanda.

However, there is evidence that UNITA was also receiving payments from Elf. Accused of preparing a $2.5 million slush fund for candidates in the 1992 elections in Congo Brazzaville, Alfred Sirven claimed that the money was in fact intended for UNITA. (Global Witness, p.25) In the run up to the 1992 elections, UNITA received over $16 million from the French company, and Elf was discovered to have signed a secret deal with Savimbi under which it would become the country's foremost oil company if UNITA won the election. (Le Floch-Prigent's testimony at Elf indictment, March 2003) While the money was officially earmarked for the political campaign, UNITA was rearming during the run-up to the election and is likely to have spent at least part of the money on arms. After UNITA lost the election, the civil war resumed.

By funding both sides, Elf is therefore likely to have contributed to prolonging the civil war in Angola, during which 1.5 million people were killed.

In 1992, UNITA managed to make significant inroads into MPLA territory for the first time. With the demise of the USSR, the government in Luanda had lost its greatest ally and its chief supplier of arms. Dos Santos turned instead to France for help, but here again, sympathies were divided between the MPLA and UNITA. Dos Santos' attempts to obtain help through Jean-Bernard Curial, the head of a food aid company, were initially unsuccessful. Mitterrand's presidency was inclined to help dos Santos, but at that time the socialist French presidency was cohabiting with a centre-right parliament. The Defence Ministry, through which military assistance would normally be channelled, was headed by François Leotard, a supporter of UNITA.

Instead, the president's son, Jean-Christophe Mitterrand, a former adviser to his father on African affairs, introduced Curial to Pierre Falcone, adviser to the Sofremi security company, which was under the control of Charles Pasqua's Interior Ministry.

Falcone then contacted Russian émigré and businessman Arkadi Gaidamak. According to the human rights organization Global Witness, which interviewed Gaidamak, the two men travelled to Angola, "where they were provided with Angolan diplomatic passports, after which they operated as *de facto* Angolan officials." (Global Witness, p.44) Gaidamak later admitted that arms had been supplied to the government in Luanda.

According to *Le Monde*, Curial testified that under the first contract, signed in November 1993, $47 million worth of mostly Russian arms were provided to Angola. This was later amended to cover $463 million worth of arms. (Global Witness, p.44)

In June 1989, Jean-Christophe Mitterand was arrested on suspicion of having helped Angola to obtain $500 million worth of weapons from French arms manufacturer Brenco International, but the government never pressed charges.

Shell in Nigeria

Other oil companies are alleged to have been involved in human rights abuses in Nigeria and the Sudan, where they have worked with government forces driving people off their land to clear it for oil, or employed soldiers who have killed and intimidated local people on their behalf.

Shell has been at the centre of the controversy in Nigeria, where it is the largest foreign player. Its joint venture with the Nigerian National Petroleum Corporation (NNPC), the state oil company, is responsible for almost half the country's total production. Other major companies including ExxonMobil, ChevronTexaco, Elf and the Italian company Agip also have joint venture agreements with the CNPC.

During the half-century of oil exploitation in Nigeria, the industry has had a very damaging effect on the local environment in the oil-producing regions. The Niger Delta, where most of the oil is located, is one of the world's largest wetlands, with around 3,750 square miles of mangrove forest, and unique species of plants and animals.

Despite decades of oil production, there is surprisingly little good-quality independent scientific data on the overall or long-term effects of hydrocarbon pollution on the Delta, yet oil-led development has clearly seriously damaged the environment and the livelihood of many of those living in local communities. Within the oil regions, local people have experienced oil spills that kill the fish and agricultural crops they live on, and pollute their water supplies. The nature of the territory means that oil spills on land or freshwater swamps are particularly damaging, since the spill is concentrated in a small area and unable to dissipate.

The oil companies have altered the landscape, digging often poorly designed causeways and drainage canals that, according to a report from the NGO Human Rights Watch, have damaged the hydrology of the sea-flooded freshwater swamps and mangrove forests, again killing off crops, destroying fishing grounds and damaging drinking water supplies.

Although the oil companies say that they are meeting the highest environmental standards in their Nigerian operations, environmental laws are relatively poorly enforced in Nigeria compared to many other countries. While compensation has been paid to some local people whose livelihoods have been damaged by oil companies' activities, both local people and human rights groups claim that the payments are inadequate. Since the country does not have a fully functioning court system, residents do not have recourse to an independent arbiter, and local judges base their decisions about compensation on the oil companies' own assessments of the damage. The oil companies also claim that many of the spills are caused by sabotage and refuse to pay compensation in these cases. (Again, it is the oil companies who decide whether a particular spill has been due to sabotage or their own negligence.)

Communities in the Niger Delta have had to contend with the environmental damage of oil production while receiving little or none of the revenues. While oil production and related activities have helped to expand the local economy, this has tended to benefit only a skilled minority. Protests against the oil companies, initially localized and disorganized, began to gain momentum in the early 1990s. The Movement for the Survival of the Ogoni People (MOSOP), led by the famous Nigerian author Ken Saro-Wiwa, managed to mobilize tens of thousands of Ogonis (one of the smaller ethnic groups in the oil-producing region). MOSOP's mass protests at Shell facilities in Ogoni and intimidation of Shell staff caused the company to close down production in 1993. (The flowstations in Ogoni are still closed, although Shell operates pipelines across the region.)

The government in Lagos responded violently to MOSOP, viewing the threat to oil production as an attack on the country's entire political system. According to a report from Human Rights Watch, "thousands of Ogonis were detained or beaten by the Rivers State Internal Security Task Force, a military body specifically created to suppress the protests organized by MOSOP, and hundreds were summarily executed over a period of several years." ("The Price of Oil: Corporate Responsibility and Human Rights Violations in Nigeria's Oil Producing Communities," Human Rights Watch, 1999)

The movement's leader, Ken Saro-Wiwa, was arrested along with several of his colleagues on a charge of murdering four traditional leaders in the region. On November 10th, Saro-Wiwa and eight other MOSOP activists were hanged by the military government. Saro-Wiwa's body was dumped in an unmarked grave and acid was poured over it. The tribunal, according to human rights groups, "blatantly violated international standards of due process and produced no credible evidence that he or the others were involved in the killings for which they were convicted." ("The Price of Oil: Corporate Responsibility and Human Rights Violations in Nigeria's Oil Producing Communities," Human Rights Watch, 1999)

Although MOSOP was the largest and most effective of the movements in the oil regions, since 1995 protests by communities demanding compensation or development projects for their villages have continued. Some protests have deliberately targeted oil infrastructure, since given the political climate in Nigeria and the overwhelming reliance on oil this is the only way to guarantee media attention. There have been cases of sabotage of oil pipelines and damage to oil companies' property, and more recently some incidents of hostage taking.

The Nigerian government continues to hit back through special security task forces. The Rivers State Internal Security Task Force is the largest and most notorious of these, but added to it is Nigeria's paramilitary Military Police and regional forces such as Operation Flush in Rivers State and Operation Salvage in Bayelsa State.

The oil companies also hire their own police forces, which are recruited and trained by the Nigerian police force, but paid for by the oil companies. These forces, known as "supernumerary police" are supposed to operate only on the oil companies' properties. The oil companies also employ private security firms for security at the entrances to their properties and for other duties, while individual landowners are paid to protect the oil pipelines running across their properties.

After the death of Nigerian leader General Sani Abacha, security has been relaxed somewhat, and many political prisoners released, while the population have greater freedom of expression. The new government under General Abdulsalami Abubakar withdrew the Internal Security Task Force from Ogoni, and Ogoni exiles returned to their homeland.

However, under the new regime, security in the oil regions continues to be heavy. Almost every community can cite members who have been beaten, detained or killed by the army, the police or the Mobile Police, the paramilitary arm of the Nigerian police force, who have earned the nickname "kill and go". Often, these beatings are directed indiscriminately at members of a community (including children) that has peacefully protested against the role of the oil companies.

There have been numerous allegations that Shell cooperated with the Nigerian military, especially during the Ogoni crisis. According to Human Rights Watch's report, "The Price of Oil", a document alleged to be a leaked government memorandum from 1994 implicated Shell in planned "wasting operations" by the Rivers State Internal Security Task Force, stating that the oil companies should pay the costs of the operations. The head of the Task Force has publicly stated several times that the Task Force's objective was to enable Shell's oil production, stopped during the crisis, to resume.

Some former members of Shell's own security forces say that they were told to deliberately create conflicts between different groups in the region, as well as intimidating protestors during 1993 and 1994.

Shell has attempted to distance itself from the repressive policies of the government and Nigerian security forces, but it has admitted that it made direct payments to the Nigerian security forces in 1993. It claims that the payments were made under duress.

After newspaper investigations revealed in 1996 that Shell had negotiated arms imports for the Nigerian police, the oil company said it had imported small arms on behalf of the Nigerian police force, but that they were for use by the "supernumerary police" on attachment to Shell.

Although Shell's operations in Nigeria have been the most notorious, other companies, including Chevron (later merged with Texaco), have also been involved in similar controversies. In May 1998, around 200 protestors took over Chevron's Parabe platform, shutting down production. In the ensuing skirmish between the protestors, the navy and the Mobile Police, two unarmed protestors were shot dead. Chevron admitted that it had called on the navy for assistance, and had flown the navy and the Mobile Police to the platform.

Violence between rival gangs seeking control of "black oil" – illegally diverted oil supplies – has been a growing problem over the last decade. This now accounts for 10 per cent of Nigeria's total oil revenues.

Since late 2003, hundreds of people have been killed in battles between two gangs, the Niger Delta People's Volunteer Force (NDPVF), led by Asari, and the Niger Delta Vigilante (NDV), led by Ateke Tom.

Their battles for control of villages south east and south west of Port Harcourt have killed many fighters from both sides as well as innocent bystanders. The violence has had a devastating impact on the region, creating tens of thousands of refugees and causing schools and businesses to close down.

Killing For Oil in the Sudan

Sudan potentially has some of Africa's largest oil reserves, estimated at between 600 million and 1.2 billion barrels. As yet they have been relatively underexploited, due partly to the civil wars that have divided the country.

Petroleum exploration in the Sudan began in the 1950s, originally offshore in the Red Sea and the Sudanese continental shelf. Exploration stalled soon after, with the country's first civil war that broke out almost immediately after Sudan gained its independence. With the exception of a brief period of peace during the 1970s and early 1980s, Sudan has been at war internally ever since, with the mainly Arab and Muslim north pitted against the ethnically African groups of the south who practise Christianity or indigenous faiths.

It was not until 1974, two years after the peace accord, that Chevron obtained large concessions in the country. Chevron discovered the Muglad and Melut basins, and drilled for oil near the town of Bentiu in 1978; soon after, it discovered the Heglig field.

Overall, Chevron spent around $1 billion on exploration, but the company never recovered its costs. Chevron suspended its operations in the southern Sudan in 1984 after a rebel attack that killed three expatriate oil workers, as did Total, which had also obtained Sudanese oil concessions.

Civil war broke out again in the early 1980s, with the southern rebels seizing most of the rural areas in the south and besieging government forces in the cities. Both sides in the war, which has to date killed hundreds of thousands of people, have been guilty of violence against civilians.

However, it was the government that armed bands of tribal militias, who have since 1983 carried out a genocidal campaign against the Nuer, the Dinka and other people of the south. To clear the land for oil exploitation, the Sudanese military has been practising a scorched earth policy against people in the southern oil regions. Militias have ridden into southern villages, killing, raping and looting. The national army backs them up with helicopter gunships that bomb the villages and strafe anyone they see moving below with machine-guns. ("Sudan, Oil and Human Rights," Human Rights Watch, September 2003)

The southern Sudanese people are perceived by the government in Khartoum to be sympathetic to the rebel groups, and therefore a threat to oil production. The government, which is directly responsible for the displacements, has done this in order to create a secure environment in which the foreign oil companies can operate, and to transport the oil through pipelines to its supertanker port on the Red Sea. ("Sudan, Oil and Human Rights," Human Rights Watch, September 2003)

In the 1990s, the government started to stir up intraregional rivalries, especially between the two largest southern ethnic groups, the Dinka and the Nuer, and to buy off some of the southern rebel groups. Khartoum planned to get its southern allies to do its work for it. Nuer-dominated groups were encouraged to turn against the rebel Sudan People's Liberation Army, SPLA, with its mainly Dinka officers, resulting in a bloody war between the two southern factions in the oilfield areas. This cleared the way for Western and Asian oil corporations to develop oil infrastructure such as the north-south pipeline and the road being built by Sweden's Lundin Oil AB.

Although oil companies operating in the Sudan deny any connection between the war and the oil industry, the government has stirred up rivalry in precisely the areas along the pipeline route or those targeted for oil exploitation.

In 1999, when the pipeline route and the oilfields initially scheduled for development were cleared, fighting broke out in another oil-rich area. The SPLA has retaliated by attacking oil infrastructure and killing the soldiers and militias that guard it.

The Sudanese government has used revenues from oil production to build up its arsenal and provide arms to certain southern groups. Statistics from both the oil companies and the government reveal that in the year 2001, Sudan earned $580 million in oil revenues, of which 60 per cent was put to military uses, both arms imports and the building up of Sudan's own armaments industry.

"Sudan will be capable of producing all the weapons it needs thanks to the growing oil industry," Sudanese Minister of Justice General Ali Mohamed Yassin announced the year after the pipeline was opened. ("The Scorched Earth: oil and war in Sudan," Christian Aid, March 2001)

International oil companies operating in the Sudan have claimed to be ignorant of the link between the forced displacements and oil extraction. According to a report by Christian Aid, "Canadian company Talisman maintains that it found an 'empty landscape' when it joined [the consortium] GNPOC in 1998. It says the area was not depopulated by oil because it was never inhabited ... At best, Talisman is guilty of failing to do its homework; at worst, of deliberately turning a blind eye," says the report. ("The Scorched Earth: oil and war in Sudan," Christian Aid)

A study by the NGO Human Rights Watch revealed in 2003 that oil company executives had repeatedly been informed of the forced displacements as well as the attacks on civilian targets, including schools and hospitals, and their connection to the clearing of the land for the oil industry, both by their advisers and at public meetings. ("Sudan, Oil and Human Rights," Human Rights Watch, September 2003)

Since the early 1990s, some Western oil companies have pulled out of the Sudan, including Talisman and Lundin Oil. However, companies from elsewhere in the world have rapidly stepped in to take their place: the China National Petroleum Corp. (CNPC), Malaysia's state oil company Petronas and the Indian company ONGC Videsh Ltd are all now operating in the Sudan.

The Bush administration in the US has been keen to lift sanctions on Sudan, and to that end worked with the government in Khartoum and the SPLA to broker a peace deal.

In February 2003, however, rebellion erupted in the Darfur region in western Sudan on the border with Chad, leading to one of the world's worst humanitarian crises. State sponsored militias known as the "Janjaweed" have carried out a brutal campaign in Darfur. Helicopter raids are followed by brutal attacks by Janjaweed fighters who routinely kill all male inhabitants of a village, then rape or kidnap the women and burn the village to the ground. According to documents obtained by Human Rights Watch, "Sudan government documents incontrovertibly show that government officials directed recruitment, arming and other support to the ethnic militias known as the Janjaweed." ("Ties Between Government and Janjaweed Militias Confirmed," Human Rights Watch, July 2004) China, which has significant oil interests in the Sudan through the national oil company CNPC, has opposed a UN resolution for sanctions against the Sudan. The south of Darfur has sizeable oil reserves.

Destroying Lives and Livelihoods in Latin America

The major oil companies have acquired a bad reputation in Latin America for their damage to the environment – and consequently to the health and livelihoods of local people – as well as for their role in the ongoing conflict in Colombia.

COLOMBIA

As well as the aid sent by the US government, which has arguably been instrumental in intensifying the country's guerrilla war (see Chapter 8), forces employed by individual oil companies have allegedly been involved in extra judicial killings in Colombia.

A consortium operating in the Caño-Limón oilfield in the north east of the country, consisting of US company Occidental Petroleum, Royal Dutch Shell and the Colombian national oil company ECOPETROL, "took no action to address reports of extra judicial executions and a massacre committed by the state forces assigned to protect the consortium's facilities." ("Corporations and Human Rights", Human Rights Watch, 1999) The companies responded that human rights violations were the responsibility of governments, not of individual companies. The oil companies have not indicated that they will be taking any steps to ensure that forces operating on their behalf do not commit further human rights abuses, although Royal Dutch Shell (the only one of the companies with a human rights policy) is currently in the process of pulling out of Colombia.

Another consortium, this time in the Cusiana-Cupiagua oilfields, is also making payments to Colombian security forces. When contracts for the consortium comprising BP, ECOPETROL, Total and Triton came up for renewal, the payment structure was changed so that instead of paying money direct to state security forces, they would be channelled through ECOPETROL to the national Ministry of Defence.

However, the companies concerned have continued to make payments directly to the Colombian police.

According to BP (the only company in this consortium with a human rights policy), however, human rights clauses were included in the new contract and a committee has been set up to monitor the military units providing security for the companies.

In spite of these precautions, the BP-led consortium continued to be in the spotlight for its security activities. In 1997, allegations emerged that the private security firm Defence Systems Colombia (DSC), a subsidiary of the UK-based Defence Systems Limited employed by the consortium, had imported arms into Colombia and had trained the Colombian police force in counter-insurgency techniques. DSC refused to cooperate with the investigation, but renewed its contract with the security firm for another year. Later allegations stated that DSC had set up intelligence networks to monitor individuals opposed to BP.

ECUADOR

Texaco operated in the Ecuadorian Amazon for almost 30 years, from 1964 to 1992. Its activities in the Oriente region, a tropical rainforest rich in biodiversity and home to 95,000 indigenous people and many endangered species, left a legacy of environmental damage that is still affecting the region.

In 1993, 30,000 Ecuadorian people living in the Amazon basin filed a lawsuit against Texaco, arguing that the company should have to clear up the environmental damage it had left, at a cost of approximately $1 billion. The plaintiffs claimed that Texaco had dumped 4.3 million gallons of toxic oil waste a day into open toxic waste pits during the time it was operating in Ecuador, and that it left behind over 600 such open-pit toxic waste sites. Texaco, they alleged, dumped the waste into open pits and left it there instead of reinjecting it into the earth, as is done in the US and is common oil industry practice. The company saved on average $3–4 per barrel on each of the 1.4 billion barrels it extracted.

A decade after Texaco pulled out of Ecuador, local people claim that streams and rivers near Lago Agrio, the centre of Texaco's operations, are still covered in a film of oil. The incidence of cancer, throat and stomach problems and skin disease is unusually high in the area.

The case against Texaco was filed at the New York Federal District Court, and in 1996 the Court ruled that it did not have jurisdiction to try the case in New York, and that it should be tried in Ecuador. This ruling was reversed in 1998, but the case was again thrown out in 2001. In 2002, the US Court of Appeals for the Second Circuit dismissed the case, on the grounds that it should be tried in Ecuador.

Another case brought by five indigenous groups and eighty communities is now being tried in Lago Agrio.

After 30 years as an exporter of oil, Ecuador has suffered extensive environmental damage, and the country remains poor and indebted. In an attempt to raise cash for loan repayments to the World Bank and other international financial institutions, Ecuador has granted Occidental Petroleum, a US company also operating in Colombia, the right to do business there.

Another threat to local people is the OCP (Oleoducto de Crudos Pesados) pipeline to carry crude oil to the Pacific Coast. The pipeline will require Ecuador to double its oil production. Local activists claim that the construction work will cause further environmental damage, particularly deforestation, along its route, and there is a high risk of earthquakes, which could cause spills from the pipeline, damaging the fragile ecosystems in the area. Security guards employed by the oil companies have cracked down violently on peaceful protests against the pipeline.

Many of the world's longest established oil companies – the old Seven Sisters – have made a conscious effort to change their murky image. Under chairman Ron Oxborough, Shell was one of the first multinationals to issue a "triple bottom line" in its company reporting, and also introduced a section on how its activities affected society and the environment into its corporate reporting. BP also reports the environmental impact of its operations and its community investments around the world, and some other companies have followed suit.

But is this change only skin deep? Oil companies continue to do business with corrupt and repressive regimes, and they continue to operate in regions like Darfur and the Niger Delta, where local people oppose their presence and protests are brutally crushed by government security forces. Rather than dealing directly with security threats, oil companies may subsidize local militias or national armies, or employ security companies such as Defence Systems Ltd to protect their operations.

In addition, while the big Western oil companies occasionally bow to pressure from public opinion at home, new players like China's CNPC have no such limitations. As oil prices increase and competition for supplies becomes ever more intense, the world's consumers may become increasingly tempted to turn a blind eye to abuses in producing countries.

Chapter Ten: Conflicts of the Future

The oil wars of the 20th and early 21st centuries may be nothing compared to the battles of the future. Oil is a finite resource. The next two to three decades will see demand soar, driven up by booming populations and the new industrial societies of China, India and South East Asia, while supply peaks and starts its slow, terminal decline. At some point in the future, oil will become prohibitively expensive to extract. As supplies dwindle and prices rise, the current top consumers, the US, Europe and Japan, will be competing with China, India and other emerging nations for increasingly scarce reserves. Russia is the only major industrial nation that can and will continue to meet its own fuel needs. Importing countries will become more aggressive in finding new oil sources and shutting out their rivals, or else find alternative sources of energy, a course that most are at best pursuing half-heartedly.

The Middle East will remain the world's foremost oil producer, and probably the theatre for most of the future oil wars. Despite the much hyped new finds in the Caspian and the Arctic, Middle Eastern reserves (around 67 per cent of the global total) still dwarf those elsewhere in the world, and the region will become responsible for a higher proportion of world oil production as reserves elsewhere are used up. A "third world war" between the Western and Islamic worlds, spreading outwards from the Middle East, is not impossible. Certainly the resentments caused by the US's interference in the region have contributed to the decline in relations there, and the Bush administration shows no sign of softening its stance; Iran and Syria are the next Middle Eastern targets in the White House's sights. Other major oil-producing regions – and potential hotspots for war – are West Africa, the Caspian, Latin America and the South China Sea.

How Long Have We Got?

Within the next few years, or possibly decades, the world will reach "Peakoil", the point at which oil production reaches its highest level and begins to decline. The concept of Peakoil was first introduced in 1956 by the geophysicist M. King Hubbert. As early as 1949, Hubbert had predicted that the age of oil would be brief. He observed that extraction of a finite resource in any large region rises along a bell-shaped curve. The curve peaks when around half of the resource has been extracted.

Hubbert used the example of oil in the US (excluding Alaska), fitting a bell curve to US oil production statistics. His analysis projected that crude oil production would continue to increase for around 13 more years before peaking in 1969. His contemporaries scoffed, but 14 years later, actually in 1970, US oil production peaked, and since then has declined almost continuously. The US has made up the shortfall with imports from abroad. Oil production in several other world regions, such as the former USSR and Latin America, has also followed the Hubbert curve.

Already there are signs that global oil production and new oil discoveries are slowing down. (Heinberg, pp.84–117) Currently we consume six barrels of oil for every one barrel we discover. Most of the world's oil is produced from a handful of giant oilfields, but the last giant find was 40 years ago, in Iran in 1964. Since then, while there have been many new finds, these have tended to be relatively small fields. The only giant field to start production in the last decade is the 10-billion-barrel Tenghiz field in Kazakhstan. At current consumption rates, this field would sustain global oil consumption for four months.

The oil companies have attempted to play this down, but there are signs that they too are aware of the approach of Peakoil. In 2004, Shell was forced to drastically revise downwards its reserve estimates. The recent spate of mergers between the major oil companies is another sign that the oil industry is retrenching rather than competing, in preparation for the contraction of the industry.

Peakoil will mean the end of cheap oil. When Peakoil does occur, the shortages and soaring oil prices will have a devastating effect on the world's economies. The recessions in virtually all oil-importing countries after the OPEC oil price shocks will be tiny compared to the effect of Peakoil. The chaos in 2000, when motorists blockaded oil refineries and petrol stations across the UK to protest against rising fuel prices, is a small indication of how consumers may react to a significant and permanent price hike.

Demand for oil is currently increasing by approximately 2 per cent per year. By 2025, demand is expected to rise from the current 81 million barrels per day to 121 million barrels per day. Most of this increase in demand will come from the developing world (where energy demand is set to rise by 91 per cent) and the US. Overall demand in the developed world will rise by only 33 per cent.

According to UN data, world population is growing by about 80 million people per year, and this growth rate is expected to change very little during the next few decades. After 2015 the population growth rate will start to decline, but by 2050 world population will still be growing by about 50 million people every year. This will not only put pressure on oil, but on all natural resources: land, food, water and other types of fuel. Water could become a cause of war on a par with oil within the next half-century.

Economic growth in developing regions such as Latin America will drive up domestic oil consumption and mean that less is available for export. The buoyant economies in China and India have created growing middle classes whose conspicuous consumption matches that in Western nations. Statistics show soaring car sales in both countries, especially China, as well as energy-intensive manufacturing processes. Manufacturing one car consumes, on average, 25–30 barrels of oil, while the manufacture of a personal computer consumes 20 times its own weight in fuel.

The precise year in which we will reach Peakoil is not known. A report titled "The Mitigation of the Peaking of World Oil Production" prepared in March 2005 for the US Department of Energy shows that governments are taking the problem seriously. That report predicts that Peakoil will arrive in 2037. Other studies are less optimistic, with some anticipating that oil production will peak as early as 2008.

Fears about Peakoil are not publicized, but there is a growing consensus that a decline in oil production is no longer a question of "if" but "when", and of the devastating impact this will have on the US and other oil-consuming countries. The US Department of Energy report concludes: "… the world has never faced a problem like this.

Without massive mitigation more than a decade before the fact, the problem will be pervasive and will not be temporary. Previous energy transitions were gradual and evolutionary. Oil peaking will be abrupt and revolutionary."

The Consumers' Long-Term Plans

THE US

The US is the world's largest consumer of oil, using over 20 million barrels per day during 2003, of which 12.25 million were imported. It is also the world's second largest producer of oil, extracting 7.5 million barrels per day, mainly from oilfields in Alaska, California, Louisiana and Texas (including those under the Gulf of Mexico). However, it has only 2.2 per cent of the world's proven oil reserves, and these are being rapidly consumed. Between 1990 and 2000, the US's proven reserves were depleted by 20 per cent.

US President George W. Bush is keen to start developing the Alaskan oil reserves that lie under the Arctic National Wildlife Refuge (ANWR). Although Bush presented a bill in 2001 that sought to allow development of a small part of the ANWR, opposition from Democrats and environmental groups was so strong that Congress never voted on the issue.

Even if Bush, now with a larger Republican majority in Congress, manages to push through the bill, it will have little impact on the US's long-term energy situation. According to the US Energy Information Agency, production at the ANWR would not begin before 2013, by which time the US is expected to be consuming over 23 million barrels of oil per day. At its peak, the ANWR is expected to supply a mere 875,000 barrels per day.

The entire ANWR region is estimated to hold around 10.4 billion barrels, about US consumption in one year (although geologists admit it could be much more or much less). Exploitation of this reserve could partly make up the shortfall from other US oilfields whose production is expected to decline dramatically over the next two decades, but it will only reduce imports from 70 per cent to 66 per cent of total consumption.

Imports from those outside the Middle East could also begin to tail off. The UK's North Sea oil production peaked in 1999 and is set to halve within the next decade, while Norway's is starting to level off. Onshore oil production in Mexico, another big US importer, is also beginning its downward curve.

Canada supplies more oil to the US than any other country, and recently had its reserves estimate revised upwards to take into account the Alberta oil sands. This raised Canada's proven oil reserves from 4.9 billion barrels to 180 billion barrels, second only to Saudi Arabia. However, even with new technologies that make extraction of the oil from sedimentary rocks possible, the extraction process uses 5–10 times as much energy, land (the rocks are crushed in huge open cast mines) and water than normal oil mining.

Under the current US administration, energy policy focuses on getting access to more oil. There has been little or no exploration of how to conserve oil supplies by reducing consumption or becoming more energy efficient.

The overwhelming influence of the energy industry on the current administration was revealed in 2002 when (heavily censored) documents relating to the Energy Task Force led by Vice President Dick Cheney were supplied to the Natural Resource Defense Council (NRDC) under order from a US District Court judge. Officials working under Cheney had sought extensive advice from the energy industry, and inserted its advice – often word for word – into the government's energy plan.

All the recommendations from Chevron CEO David J. O'Reilly, for example, on steps the government could take to "eliminate federal barriers to increased energy supplies," were included in the report.

NRDC lawyers also report that an email sent from the American Petroleum Institute, the body that represents the US oil and gas industry, to an Energy Department official on March 20th, 2001, provided a draft Executive Order on energy. This was "nearly identical in structure and impact," the NRDC say, to Executive Order 13211 that Bush issued two months later.

Also in March 2001, a lobbyist for Southern Company, one of the country's largest electricity generators, emailed a Department of Energy official suggesting amendments to the Clean Air Act and related enforcement actions. This suggestion was incorporated into the energy plan, and resulted, according to the NRDC, in the government's attempt "to weaken the Clean Air Act and retreat from high-profile enforcement actions against the nation's largest polluters, including the Southern Company."

Two other NGOs, Judicial Watch and the Sierra Club, brought a case against Cheney in an attempt to force him to disclose details about the workings of the Energy Task Force. They argued that industry representatives had been treated as if they were members of the task force, while other interested parties were shut out of the policy process. On May 11th, 2005, the Court of Appeals for the District Colombia Circuit ruled against the plaintiffs.

Unless there is a radical change of direction within the next decade, the US could be set on a course towards future oil-related wars and crippling economic depression once the effects of Peakoil begin to set in.

Rather than seeking alternatives to oil dependence, the Bush administration is looking for ways to change the world to preserve the current "Pax Americana", and many believe by military dominance and regime change in "unfriendly" countries, to extend US control over world oil resources. The US military bases now established in the Middle East, the Caspian, South East Asia and Latin America are seen by many as a means to protect the flow of oil, and potentially to be used as a springboard for further invasions.

CHINA

The Chinese economic boom is already having a profound effect on the dynamics of the world oil market. As recently as 1993, China was a net exporter of oil. It is now the second largest consumer in the world, after the US, importing 7.5 million barrels per day.

Currently, Chinese oil consumption is only 7 per cent of the world's total, but China has the world's fastest growing demand. Consumption doubled between 1993 and 2003. China is responsible for one-third of the global 2.5-million-barrel increase in oil consumption every day.

With the discovery of the Daqing oilfield in 1959, China seemed to be on the verge of becoming a major oil producer, following the pattern set in the US or even Saudi Arabia. By 1978, it was producing 100 million tons a year. Soon after, production started to level off. Between 1980 and 2003, despite intensive exploration and production, annual oil production has remained around 3.2 billion barrels.

In January 2003, oil imports contributed to the country's first monthly trade deficit since 1996. According to China's National Development and Reform Commission, an estimated two-thirds of China's oil demand increase is from the transportation sector, and this demand will continue to grow. Government and industry are doing little to change current consumption patterns. Switching to a less energy-intensive method of industrialization, or using more renewable energy sources, will result in a slower development rate.

China has become increasingly aggressive in seeking out new sources of oil from abroad. Currently China is importing oil via a new pipeline from Kazakhstan, from Siberia, from several African countries (including the Sudan, where other oil companies have pulled out because of human rights abuses) and Latin America, where it has a new supply agreement with Venezuela.

China has also laid claim to areas of the South China Sea around the Spratly Islands where potential for oil exploitation is believed to be very high. There is a considerable likelihood of conflict within this area as China, Vietnam, the Philippines, Taiwan, Brunei and Malaysia all have territorial claims on the area.

INDIA

India consumes 2.4 million barrels of oil per day, ranking sixth in the world according to energy demand. Although per capita energy consumption in India is around five times lower than the global average, this is expected to rise rapidly as the economy expands. GDP is currently growing by 5–6 per cent per year. India's population reached one billion in 1999, and with a growth rate of 1.7 per cent per year, by some estimates India is expected to pass China as the most populous country on earth by 2050.

In recognition of the growing demand for energy, in 2001 the Indian government produced its long-term strategy for the energy sector, "India Hydrocarbon Vision 2025". Oil and gas currently account for 45 per cent of India's energy consumption.

Although it has large supplies of coal, India has relatively small oil reserves. Recent explorations have already led to the discovery of a major new gasfield off the east coast, and gas is expected to increase in importance as oil reserves decline.

India's oil reserves are concentrated both off the coast near Mumbai (formerly Bombay) and onshore in Assam, and they amount to 5.9 billion barrels, 0.5 per cent of global reserves. Imports make up 65 per cent of its oil consumption, a proportion that the US's IEA forecasts will rise to 91.6 per cent by 2020.

"India Hydrocarbon Vision 2025" recommends exploration of all India's sedimentary bases in a search for more oil, and for existing operations to be made more efficient.

Indian oil companies are also seeking new sources of oil imports, with support from the Indian government. ONGC Videsh Ltd (OVL), a subsidiary of India's Oil and Natural Gas Corporation Ltd, has signed a long-term agreement with the Russian company Roseneft for a 20 per cent participating interest in the Sakhalin field. OVL also has a 45 per cent stake in an offshore gasfield in Vietnam, as well as interests in oil- and gasfields in Australia, Egypt, Iran, Iraq, the Ivory Coast, Libya, Myanmar, Qatar, Russia, the Sudan and Syria.

Where Will the Oil Come From?

Planning for future energy consumption has to centre on the Middle East. Although new oil finds in areas like the Caspian, Siberia and the American Arctic are coming into production, the Middle East still has two-thirds of the world's oil resources. Its oil is also easy and cheap to extract. In future, the Middle East will become responsible for a larger share of total oil production as reserves in other locations start to dwindle.

The Middle East

IRAQ

Iraq has the world's third largest oil reserves after Saudi Arabia and Canada, and once Iraqi oil starts flowing again at full capacity it will be quick and extremely cheap to extract. Current proven reserves are 115 billion barrels, though the oil multinationals now operating in Iraq have said they expect that further exploration could lead to additional discoveries, bringing the country's oil reserves up to an estimated 200 to 300 billion barrels.

ExxonMobil, ChevronTexaco, BP and Royal Dutch Shell, the four leading US and British oil companies, are looking forward to making enormous profits from exploitation of Iraq's oil reserves; they are expected to make profits of tens of billions of dollars every year. Overall profits could be as high as $9 trillion, with estimated annual profits of $95 billion per year for 50 years.

However, the profitability of the oil companies will depend on whether the violence within Iraq subsides. Currently, despite the recent elections, armed resistance in Iraq has grown, with attacks on Iraqi government targets and occupying forces a regular occurrence. Iraq has not yet increased its output even to the 2.5 million barrels per day it was producing before the war.

As well as military resistance, corruption in the oil industry – by far the country's most lucrative sector – is also keeping revenues low. Recently, the Iraqi Oil Ministry sacked more than 450 employees it suspected of selling fuel on the black market. Oil industry employees tampered with fuel pump gauges and gave incorrect measurements of tankers' contents to create a surplus that could then be sold on the black market. In Basra, the country's second city, set among Iraq's southern oilfields, oil smuggling is carried out quite openly. More than 20 illegal taps were recently discovered on one of the country's southern pipelines. Only 60 per cent of trucks carrying oil from wells to ports or refineries reach their destinations; the rest are hijacked.

Violence between resistance fighters and government forces and the occupying armies continues. After pictures of US soldiers abusing Iraqi prisoners in the Abu Ghraib prison, it was hard to present coalition forces as "liberating" Iraq. Violence is likely to continue for as long as foreign armies remain in Iraq, yet without them it is hard to see how the foreign oil companies would be able to operate among a hostile population.

The latest estimates are that the Iraqi security forces will not be able to guard their country for another five years. And even if the occupiers were to leave then, there are still deep divisions between different sectors of the Iraqi population. The difficulty in deciding who would run the Oil Ministry after the general election is a sign of the difficulties in finding agreement between different Iraqi factions. After the general election on January 30th, 2005, a coalition was formed between the Shiite United Iraqi Alliance with 140 seats in the National Assembly, and the Kurdish party with 75 seats. The longest negotiations took place not over appointing the prime minister or president, but over deciding from which party the oil minister would be selected.

Overall, the invasion of Iraq has created a tide of resentment against the US, not just in Iraq, but throughout the Middle East, the Arab world, and among many other countries such as France, Russia and China, who resent the unilateral approach taken by Washington.

IRAN

Iran is the second country on US President George W. Bush's "axis of evil", along with Iraq and North Korea. There has been considerable speculation that with Saddam Hussein toppled, Washington will next turn its attention to the Islamic Republic of Iran, another of the world's top oil producers, with, as stated, proven reserves of over 130 billion barrels.

Part of the pretext for this is that Iran too is said to be a supporter of anti-US terrorism, and it is no secret that since before the 1979 revolution Iran has been seeking to build a nuclear weapons capacity.

While Iran and the EU are preparing for talks on the issue, US Secretary of State Condoleeza Rice said in a speech at the American Israel Public Affairs Committee: "The world must not tolerate any Iranian attempt to develop a nuclear weapon, nor can it tolerate Iran's effort to subvert democratic governments through terrorism." She also stressed that pursuit of democracy is a central element of Bush administration policy in the Middle East.

However, the threat of a US invasion has encouraged Tehran to speed up its nuclear programme. The government announced earlier this year that it should have nuclear capacity by the end of 2005. This makes a US attack look increasingly unlikely. If it was to try to depose the government in Tehran before Iran has its own nuclear bomb, it would have to attack within the next six months.

Iran is a much tougher target than Iraq, with a population of over 67 million, three times as large as its neighbour's. The US alone does not have sufficient fighter planes or missiles to destroy all of Iran's suspected nuclear sites. And with the army still trying to put down resistance in Iraq, it does not even approach having enough ground troops for an attack.

The European Union is considering sanctions to deter the development of Iran's nuclear capacity, but none of the US's major allies, even the UK, its closest supporter in Iraq, supports a war against Iran. In recent years, the political climate in Iran appears to have been softening considerably, and relations with European countries are relatively good. An attack by the US would only serve to unite the population behind the religious leadership and create an upsurge in anti-American feeling.

If Iran does develop nuclear arms within the near future, this could be worrying for the future security of the Middle East, given its hostility towards Israel, and to a lesser extent its rivalries with Iraq and Saudi Arabia.

SAUDI ARABIA

The government in Saudi Arabia, the world's top oil producer, is under increasing pressure from the US on one side and the forces of radical Islam on the other.

Members of the Wahhabi sect of Islam, which is very strong in Saudi Arabia (ironically, among the ruling classes), were behind the September 11th attacks and 15 of the terrorists were Saudi nationals. Osama Bin Laden, leader of al-Qaeda, is from one of the most powerful Saudi Arabian families. The Bin Laden family runs global enterprises with a turnover of $5 billion a year, including the largest construction company in the Islamic world.

This caused relations between Saudi Arabia and the US (previously long-term allies) to deteriorate, even though the Saudi government condemned the attacks. Treatment of Saudi nationals living in the US, as well as those imprisoned without trial at Guantanamo Bay, has caused a further coolness between the two countries.

At home, al-Qaeda has mounted numerous attacks on foreigners in Saudi Arabia as well as on government targets. The government in Riyadh, which initially thought that tensions would subside after American troops left the country, have been forced to accept that the terrorist group is seeking regime change.

Meanwhile, relations between the Saudi Arabian government and the US have worsened. Riyadh is increasingly suspicious that the "zero tolerance" for terrorism policy touted by the US government does not apply to actions by Israel, and that it will not be possible to achieve a peaceful solution to the situation in Palestine. A growing number of Saudis believe that the US is financially supporting the Likud Party in Israel, and that the so-called "war on terror" is either a Judeo-Christian war against Islam, or a ploy to take control of the world's oil resources.

Although Saddam Hussein had threatened Saudi Arabia with invasion during the first Gulf War, the invasion of Iraq in March 2003 turned many Saudi Arabians against the US, and consequently against their own government.

Meanwhile, Saudi Arabia has become a somewhat embarrassing ally for Washington, undermining its claims to be spreading democracy through the Middle East. For the last two years, Washington has been calling, both publicly and privately, on Riyadh to reform the country's political system.

However, even if the Saudi government wanted to liberalize and promote democracy, it would be difficult to do this without violating the principles of Sunni orthodoxy. There are some moves to make the country slightly more democratic, for example by electing some officials in the governing councils, but these could spark opposition from extreme Wahhabi groups. At the same time, these groups have been seeking reform to the privileged status of the enormous Saudi royal family, which numbers about 7,000, with another 13,000 extended family members.

When change does come, the question is whether it will be the kind promoted by al-Qaeda or by the US. The government is reforming only with reluctance and very slowly. The likelihood of a revolution in Saudi Arabia within the coming decades is fairly high. The government is highly authoritarian, yet also perceived as corrupt and ineffective. The maintenance of several thousand members of the royal family in luxury and top government positions has also served to alienate people.

The Far East

THE SOUTH CHINA SEA
Ownership of the oil and gas reserves that lie under the South China Sea is being hotly contested by six countries: China, Vietnam, Malaysia, Taiwan, Brunei and the Philippines. Proven reserves are estimated at 7.5 billion barrels. Daily oil production in the region has reached 1.3 million barrels.

The Spratly Islands (claimed by all six countries) and the Paracel Islands (occupied by China since 1974, but claimed by Taiwan and Vietnam) could have significant untapped oil deposits. Chinese estimates put the total potential offshore reserves of the South China Sea at over 200 billion barrels, while a more conservative report by the US Geological Survey estimates there are around 28 billion barrels. Even the most optimistic Western estimates are of 1–2 billion barrels of oil in the Spratly Islands.

Within the last 20 years there have been 13 military skirmishes between countries with competing claims. Although growing trade links between China and Vietnam have helped to improve relations between the two countries, there have been occasional clashes over the disputed islands. The most serious of these occurred in 1998, when Chinese forces sunk three Vietnamese ships, killing 78 people.

The area has been increasingly militarized. At least five nations are said to have established military bases on the disputed islands, in breach of a regional cooperation agreement signed in 2002. Several states have also set up supposed "bird-watching towers" and "weather stations", which are believed to be concealed surveillance units. In April 2004, Taiwan reported that it had sent coastguards to turn back a Chinese oil exploration vessel that had entered its part of the South China Sea.

The US also has a strong interest in the region, and is seeking to influence outcomes through its relationship with the Philippines. After skirmishes between the Philippines and China in 1995 over the Mischief Reef, in 1996 over the Campones Island, and in 1997 over Scarborough Shoal, Manila invoked its mutual defence treaty with the US.

As China becomes an ever-larger consumer of imported oil, more direct rivalry between China and the US is likely to break out in the region. The US has similar mutual defence treaties with Singapore and Thailand, while the UK has a similar agreement with its former colony Malaysia, and France with Vietnam. A dispute between nations in the region could therefore escalate into a wider conflict.

The South China Sea is also a highly important strategic region since half of the world's merchant fleet passes through a series of narrow channels every year. Three times as many oil tankers pass through the Straits of Malacca, which lead into the South China Sea, than through the Suez Canal. Almost two-thirds of these carry shipments of crude oil from the Persian Gulf, headed for China and Japan.

SIBERIA AND THE RUSSIAN FAR EAST

China and Japan are competing over access to Russian oil, and over the route the planned oil pipeline linking eastern Siberia with the Russian Far East will take. Russia recently announced that China would be the first recipient of the oil.

Initially, Japan appeared to have won the competition, when Russia announced in 2004 that it would build a 2,610-mile pipeline from Taishet near Lake Baikal to Nakhodka on the Sea of Japan coast. This was the route advocated by Japan. In early 2005, however, Russia announced that the pipeline would instead go from Taishet to Skovorodino near the Russian-China border, and that China would be the first recipient, with Japan and possibly South Korea receiving supplies at a later date.

Tokyo fears that the pipeline may never reach Japan, if, as a Russian energy official has speculated, oil reserves are less than predicted. The Japanese government has told Russia it may not provide financing for the $12 billion pipeline if there is little chance that the pipeline will reach the Sea of Japan.

In the long term there has been some speculation about a possible infiltration, or even annexation, of part of the Russian Far East by the Chinese.

Since 1991, around two million residents of Vladivostok, Khabarovsk and Far Eastern cities have emigrated to Moscow and western Russia, according to the 2002 census, while over three million Chinese have moved to Russia, most of them as traders. In some parts of the Amur, Kharbarovsk and Primorski regions, Chinese residents outnumber Russians. A rise in xenophobia and fears that the Chinese are attempting to take over the region have been reported.

Across the border in the Heilongjiang, Jilin and Liaoning provinces of China there are 130 million people, compared to only 7 million Russians and other Slavs in the Far East province. There has been no indication that Moscow is planning to provide incentives to attract more Russians back to the Far East.

There is a remote possibility that Beijing might decide to annex (or even buy) part of the Russian Far East, to provide more land for its large population and to gain access to the region's huge oil, mineral and water resources.

The Caspian

The Caspian region, and the oil-producing states of Central Asia and the Caucasus, have become extremely strategically important since the break-up of the USSR in 1991. The international oil companies are seeking concessions, while Russia and the US vie for influence with regional powers such as China, Iran, Pakistan and Turkey. The Caspian basin is one of the areas targeted for further exploitation in US plans to reduce dependence on the Middle East. Meanwhile, Russia is trying to reassert itself as the dominant power in the region, and China is competing for oil supplies. The Chinese national oil company CNPC has completed a pipeline to carry oil from Kazakhstan to western China.

Within the oil- and gas-rich states of the Caucasus and Central Asia, national leaders, many of whom have been in power since independence in 1991, are tightening their grip on their countries' natural wealth. Azerbaijan's former leader Gaidar Aliyev ensured that his son succeeded him as president when he died in late 2003, creating the former USSR's first dynastic succession. This could well be repeated in other countries such as Kazakhstan and Uzbekistan, where both leaders appear to be grooming their daughters for succession.

The recent revolutions in Georgia, the Ukraine and most recently Kyrgyzstan were watched with alarm by regional leaders, who have been stepping up security to prevent this happening again. Uzbek security forces shot dead an estimated 500 unarmed protestors in the eastern town of Andizhan in May 2005. Opposition leaders have compiled a list of 745 dead, while the Uzbek government puts the official figure at 169 but denies that any of these were civilians. (Nick Paton Walsh & Jalil Saparov, *The Guardian*, May 18th, 2005) Islam Karimov, the Uzbek leader, attributes the riot to Islamic fundamentalism, using this to justify further clampdowns. Torture in Uzbek prisons and imprisonment of opposition politicians and journalists is already widespread.

While Karimov's troops have put down the protests for now, the brutal way this was done will most probably lead to greater opposition in the future, and by taking such a strong stance against Islam he is sowing the seeds for a civil war or Islamic revolution.

While European leaders have widely condemned the killings, the reaction in Washington has been more ambiguous. A US State Department spokesman told journalists that the US was concerned over human rights in Uzbekistan, but also claimed that "members of a terrorist organization" had escaped from a prison in Andizhan.

For the US, Uzbekistan's main importance is strategic. Although it is the world's sixth biggest producer of natural gas, almost all of this is consumed domestically, and oil production is relatively modest. However, Karimov has been extremely useful to Washington through allowing the US to maintain military bases in the region. Since Operation Enduring Freedom began in 2001, the US has built a series of vast bases through the region: Bagram AB and Kandahar AB in Afghanistan, Karshi-Khanabad "K2" in Uzbekistan, and Ganci in Kyrgyzstan. US and coalition troops were deployed at several old Soviet bases in Uzbekistan, the largest being Karshi-Khanabad, where 1,000 troops remain at what has become an American city of air-conditioned tents in the Uzbek desert. The Ganci airbase (named after the chief of the New York city police, Peter J. Ganci, who died in the World Trade Center on September 11th) at Manas airport in Bishkek, Kyrgyzstan, has capacity for 3,200 troops and has also acquired semi-permanent status.

In Kazakhstan, President Nursultan Nazarbayev and various US oil companies are embroiled in the "Kazakhgate" scandal involving allegations of multimillion dollar bribes for access to the vast Tenghiz oilfield. Nazarbayev himself is alleged to have at least $1 billion secreted in a personal Swiss bank account. He could become another target for regime change if he remains in power or attempts to hand over the presidency to his eldest daughter Dariga Nazarbayeva. Former playboy Ilham Aliyev, who now rules Azerbaijan, is another leader whose rule could be challenged, as is Saparmurad Niyazov, the neo-Stalinist Turkmen dictator, who has used his country's gas revenues on palaces and prestige projects.

The Baku-Tiblisi-Ceyhan pipeline, opened in May 2005, is a potential target for terrorist attacks, despite being closely guarded along much of its route. It runs through the war-torn Ngorno-Karabakh region, and other areas where tensions between Azeris and Armenians are high. If the war in Chechnya was to escalate, there is a risk of a regional conflict, which would also drag in the US since Washington has committed itself to protecting the pipeline, which carries oil from Baku to the Turkish Mediterranean port of Ceyhan.

Moscow is also seeking to control routes along which oil is transported out of the Caspian. Part of the reason why Russia has been so determined to keep hold of Chechnya is that it is on the gateway between Russia and the Caucasus. Another sign of Russian determination to control oil shipments is the Russian oil transport monopoly Transneft's blockage of oil shipments to the Latvian port of Ventspils. Transneft, a company owned by the Russian government, was putting pressure on Latvia to sell the port to the company, effectively putting Latvia's largest port back under Russian control.

Russia and the four other states that border the Caspian Sea – Azerbaijan, Iran, Kazakhstan and Turkmenistan – are also engaged in negotiations over how to divide the sea between them, including its undersea oil and gas. Iran says it is opposed to the militarization of the sea, as well as to the building of undersea oil pipelines. Agreement has not yet been reached on how to divide the sea, and although by mid-2005 the five states appeared to be close to a compromise, this is an area with potential for conflict.

Latin America

Latin America is currently an oil-exporting region. However, over the next 35 years its population, growing at a rate of around 2 per cent per year, is set to double. Energy consumption is also set to rise, especially in Brazil's fast-growing economy. The main importer of Latin American oil is currently the US, though China – much to the US's consternation – has recently obtained new supply contacts with Venezuela. Latin America has in the past been an important source of oil for the US due to its proximity to US markets and its relative stability. In the future, however, exports of oil from Latin America are expected to fall as domestic consumption increases and oil production peaks and starts to decline.

Venezuela could also become a target for possible US-sponsored regime change. Relations between Washington and Caracas have worsened since the current Venezuelan President Hugo Chávez came to power in December 1998. Chávez, a socialist and Venezuelan nationalist, launched a process known as the "Bolivarian revolution" to redistribute wealth within Venezuela and to offer an alternative to US dominance in Latin America.

Chávez plans to extend the government's control over Venezuela's oil industry, which currently supplies around 15 per cent of US oil imports, and to use its increased revenues to reduce poverty.

Enforcement of a law passed in 2001 to increase the royalties payable by foreign corporations to the Venezuelan government for oil extraction started in November 2004. The following month, Venezuela signed an agreement with China, under which substantial amounts of Venezuelan oil would be sold to China. (This part of the agreement has not yet come into force, since Venezuela's oil has a high sulphur content, and China does not yet have facilities to process it.)

Both these steps alarmed the US, since they are strong indications that Venezuela is diversifying its energy markets and seeking to reduce its dependency on the US, which currently buys 60 per cent of its oil. Chávez himself has on occasion remarked about the way that Venezuelan oil is "subsidizing Mr Bush", a situation that he is seeking to change.

Since Condoleeza Rice took over from Colin Powell as US Secretary of State in January 2005, the US government and media have openly become more hostile towards Venezuela, and there are fears in Caracas that this is intended to pave the way for a possible US or US-backed invasion. Speaking to a US Senate foreign relations committee in January 2005, Rice said that the US government was very concerned "about a democratically elected leader who governs in an illiberal way." (Elise Labott & Juan Carlos Lopez, CNN, February 24th, 2005) CIA director Peter Goss has also highlighted Venezuela as the main Latin American nation that is of concern to the US, while playing down the violence and human rights abuses in Colombia. The US media has increasingly demonized Chávez, notably in a Fox News documentary titled "The Iron Fist of Hugo Chávez."

The US claims that Chávez is seeking to set himself up as a dictator and to use Venezuela's oil revenues to fund terrorists in Colombia and to destabilize Bolivia. Venezuela denies these allegations, and the US has not provided any concrete evidence to back them up.

Venezuela has struck back in the escalating war of words. In February 2005, the Venezuelan government accused the US of plotting to assassinate Chávez. Later that month, Venezuelan Navy

Commander Armando Laguna announced that a secret build-up of US Marines, military planes and amphibious vehicles had been detected on the island of Curacao (where US oil companies had built their offshore refinery). This gave rise to widespread panic within Venezuela about a US invasion, despite an assurance from the government of Curacao that it would not allow the island to be used to launch an invasion.

Chávez himself is convinced of the danger of a US attack on either himself or the country.

"If something happens to me, there is only one person responsible for it, and his name is George W. Bush," he said during a trip to India in March 2005. (Stuart Munckton, *Green Left Weekly*, March 16th, 2005)

In the event of a US or US-backed invasion, Chávez has threatened to stop all exports of oil to the US. "We want to supply oil to the United States. We are not going to avoid supplying of oil unless the US government gets a little bit crazy and tries to hurt us," he said, but added that: "if there is any aggression, there will be no oil." (Associated Press, March 4th, 2005)

Chávez has said several times that he believes Bush is planning to have him assassinated, and that criticisms of his regime are a ploy to allow the US to take control of Venezuela's oil.

"The United States government would very much like to keep all our oil for itself. But our oil reserve does not belong to Mr. Bush. The oil belongs to the Venezuelan people," he told the press during his visit to India. "We are just waiting for the United States to announce next that Venezuela has weapons of mass destruction." (Associated Press, March 8th, 2005)

Africa

Africa is becoming an increasingly important supplier of oil as the world's consuming nations – chiefly the US, France and China – compete for influence with the countries around the Gulf of Guinea. Africa has a very low rate of oil consumption compared to other parts of the world, and is therefore a promising source of imports. By 2015, 25 per cent of the US's oil imports are expected to come from Africa. While population increase and GDP growth are expected to drive up oil consumption, Africa is starting from a relatively low level of consumption.

In the last half-century, as seen in previous chapters, Africa has been the location of some of the world's most protracted and brutal oil-related wars, among them the Biafra War in Nigeria, the Angolan civil war and the ongoing civil war in the Sudan. If they are to avert further wars, African governments will need to find a way to spread the benefits of their oil exploitation to the entire population and to each ethnic group within the country. As yet, this is something very few oil-producing countries have achieved.

In many countries, from Venezuela to Congo Brazzaville to Kazakhstan, the sudden influx of oil riches has been too tempting for governments, and revenues have flowed into private bank accounts without bringing any benefits to the population as a whole. In the long term, the stark divide between rich and poor could lead to revolution or civil war. This is a particular problem for African oil producers since many African countries are artificial constructs created by the European colonizers, bringing together tens and sometimes hundreds of diverse groups with little in common and no loyalty to each other.

In Equatorial Guinea, where oil was discovered as recently as 1991, President Obiang and other top government officials were revealed to have already amassed a total of over $700 million in a private account with Riggs Bank in the US. (Justin Blum, *Washington Post*, September 9th, 2004) Much of this was brought to the bank in suitcases full of shrink-wrapped bundles of notes. The Securities and Exchange Committee (SEC) is investigating Riggs Bank for facilitating dubious transactions, including the payment of over $4 million in "scholarships" from oil multinationals to relatives of the president and his colleagues. Companies under scrutiny include ChevronTexaco, Exxon Mobil, Amerada Hess and Marathon Oil.

A failed coup attempt in late 2004 has led to a clampdown on political pluralism and civil society. Africa's "World War", essentially about dominance over the natural resources of the Democratic Republic of Congo (DRC), has ended in an uneasy peace, but the danger of regional conflict restarting is high. Another country with a strong risk of conflict is Chad, where large-scale oil production has just started following the opening of a pipeline to the Cameroon.

CENTRAL AFRICA

The Democratic Republic of Congo (DRC, formerly Zaire) was for almost a decade at the centre of a devastating war, as armies from seven countries fought for control of its enormous natural resources. Three million people died in the fighting itself or from disease or malnutrition. The first democratic elections since independence were scheduled for May 2005, but have been postponed due to violence in several Congolese towns and a lack of national infrastructure.

The DRC is one of the largest countries in Africa and is Africa's richest country in terms of mineral resources. As well as proven oil reserves of 1.5 billion barrels (and there is a high probability of more oil in unexplored areas), the DRC has 80 per cent of the world's cobalt, one-third of its diamonds, and the world's largest cadmium deposits, as well as considerable reserves of gold, manganese and uranium. The DRC also produces coltan (used in mobile telephones), timber, coffee, tin, zinc and palm oil.

Despite these natural riches, the DRC has a tragic history of poverty and brutal exploitation, first under its Belgian colonizers and then under the CIA-backed dictator Mobutu. The term "crimes against humanity" was first coined by George Washington Williams, an African American who visited the country when it was still the personal property of Belgian King Leopold II. Ten million people, half the country's population, were killed under Belgian rule, which lasted from 1886 to 1960. When colonial rule ended, the country was barely developed beyond the minimal infrastructure needed to extract and export its resources, and UN troops were sent in to restore order.

After independence, foreign interests continued to dominate the DRC, with the US taking over from Belgium as the main foreign power. But the US were not favourably disposed towards the country's first – and only – elected prime minister, Patrice Lumumba, because he was seeking greater economic and political independence from the US and other Western powers.

"[The UN] actually took a lot of trouble to protect him," Sir Brian Urquhart, a former United Nations under-secretary general who was present, said recently. "What we didn't know was that the CIA was planning to assassinate him and, in fact, sent two people down, one sharpshooter and one poisoner to do it. Both of whom, I am glad to say, were frustrated by the UN troops." (Garrick Utley, CNN, April 1997)

Despite the UN's efforts, Lumumba was assassinated a few months after he came to power.

The army chief Mobutu Sese Seko seized power in a military coup in 1965, allegedly with CIA backing. Mobutu was to rule the DRC (which he renamed Zaire) for 32 years, killing and torturing many of his own people. A staunch anti-Communist, Mobutu received over $1.5 billion in US economic and military aid between 1965 and 1991. The former US President George Bush (father of the current president) was a friend of the Zairean president, and had mining interests in the DRC.

Mobutu plundered the land, boasting that he had become one of the three richest men in the world, with a personal fortune of over $5 billion while, under his rule, one-third of the country's population died from malnutrition.

After the Cold War ended, Washington's interest in Mobutu as an anti-Communist disappeared, and his Western supporters became disillusioned with his greed. Mobutu clung onto power until October 1996, when the Rwandan army and Ugandan troops invaded the DRC. By May 1997, they had taken control of the country and installed Laurent Kabila, an exiled Congolese Marxist, as leader.

Many African observers assumed that the invasion had been masterminded in Washington; Rwanda and Uganda were the US's closest allies in the region. Rwanda was torn apart by genocide in 1994, when the government, led by the Hutus that make up 85 per cent of the population, launched a genocide against the Tutsi minority; 800,000 Tutsis and 50,000 Hutus were killed in under three months, before the Tutsi rebel force led by Paul Kagame invaded from Uganda and took power. A million Hutus fled to the DRC.

After Kabila was put in power, his relations with the Rwandan and Ugandan armies deteriorated, and in July 1998 he expelled the foreign troops from the DRC after the Rwandan army massacred many of the Hutu refugees. Rwanda and Uganda then invaded the DRC, starting Africa's "First World War". Angola, Namibia and Zimbabwe sent their armies in to support Kabila's forces, while Burundi joined the war on the side of Rwanda and Uganda.

The US has allegedly backed the involvement of its Central African allies, Rwanda and Uganda, in the war. The *Washington Post* reported that US soldiers had been seen in company with Rwandan soldiers in the Congo, although this has not been verified. Condoleeza Rice, then

National Security Adviser, said that foreign intervention was "unacceptable", but the US continued to supply economic and military support to both Rwanda and Uganda. As the US was such an important benefactor to both countries, it is assumed that had Washington urged them to withdraw their soldiers from the DRC they would have done.

Instead, the US put pressure on Kabila to sign the Lusaka Accord. Not only did the Accord incorrectly treat the conflict as a civil war, it also required a gradual rather than immediate withdrawal of foreign troops. Troops from Rwanda and Uganda remained in the eastern part of the DRC, ignoring the 180-day deadline for their departure. Kabila was assassinated on January 17th, 2001, the same day on which Lumumba had been killed 40 years before. He was succeeded by his son.

The UN documented the looting by foreign troops in the DRC during the war in a report released in April 2001. It describes mass looting and illegal extraction of mineral resources carried out by Rwanda, Uganda and Burundi in the eastern parts of the country. In 18 months, Rwanda made $250 million from coltan exports alone. Diamond exports from Rwanda and Uganda are reported to have soared since 1998, even though neither country has a diamond mine.

After the peace agreement, the DRC remains partitioned, and the government in Kinsala has no control over several large parts of the country. Although peace has lasted since the 2003 accord, tensions and the threat of renewed war remain high, especially in the east. The next test is the general election which has been postponed to the end of 2005.

CHAD

Chad became an oil exporter in July 2003, when the pipeline connecting its oilfields to the pumping stations on the Atlantic coast of neighbouring Cameroon started operation. It has become a test case for a new model of financial management; the World Bank has funded the pipeline project on the condition that Chad spends 95 per cent of its oil revenues on development projects.

The success or failure of this strategy, carried out in one of the world's poorest countries under one of the world's most corrupt governments, could set an important precedent for oil-dominated economies in Africa and elsewhere in the developing world. If it succeeds, it will reveal a way to exploit oil wealth to the benefit of an entire population. If it fails, Chad is most likely to plunge once again into the civil wars that have raged throughout most of its post-colonial existence.

War first broke out in 1965, precipitated by tensions between the Muslim north and mainly Christian south. Chad comprises more than 200 different ethnic groups. There have also been invasions from Libya in the north. The current president, Idris Deby, is a northern Muslim who seized power in 1990, and was then democratically elected in 2001.

Most of Chad's proven oil reserves are located in the southern Doba basin, near the border with the Central African Republic. A foreign consortium led by ExxonMobil, and also comprising the Malaysian company Petronas and ChevronTexaco, is in charge of developing the basin.

Construction of the 670-mile pipeline was part-funded by the World Bank, which offered a conditional loan based on oil-revenue spending restrictions. Chad was the first country to accept a loan with such conditions, under which 80 per cent of oil revenues must be spent on health, education and other development projects, 10 per cent will be allocated to an investment fund for future generations, and 5 per cent used for development projects in the Doba region.

If Chad adheres to the conditions set by the World Bank, it may avoid some of the pitfalls of other countries, where oil revenues have been squandered and exploitation has resulted in regional tensions and sometimes civil war.

However, the country is still relatively unstable and oil revenues could destabilize it further. Parts of the north are still in a state of war. Southern Chad, where the majority of the oil is located, is plagued by unrest and regular outbreaks of violence. In October 1997, security forces put down riots in the south, with the massacre of 80 unarmed civilians. Amnesty International reported that another 100 unarmed civilians had been killed in March 1998.

Whether the government in N'Djamena can keep the country under control and preserve a stable environment for oil exploitation remains to be seen. Its commitment to the agreement with the World Bank is already in question; in November 2000, the government used $4.5 million of a $25 million oil contract bonus from the

ExxonMobil-led consortium to buy weapons from Taiwan. Deby's government justified the purchase by saying: "Development needs to be protected."

EQUATORIAL GUINEA

A coup attempt against Equatorial Guinea's President Teodoro Obiang Nguema failed in March 2005. Details of the planned coup, which is alleged to have been led by a former SAS officer and financially backed by Mark Thatcher, son of the former UK prime minister, were apparently disclosed to British and US officials, who did not inform Obiang's government of the threat.

Equatorial Guinea is one of Africa's newest petro-states, where oil was only discovered in 1991. Previously, the country had been desperately poor, and although ExxonMobil is now exporting almost 300,000 barrels to the US every day, and President Obiang is said to have amassed some $700 million in a private US bank account, most people are still below the poverty line. Obiang's close advisers claim that $400 million is spent on health, housing and education each year, but there is no evidence of this.

Obiang has ruled the country for 25 years. Since the coup attempt, the country has been in a continuous state of alert, and the government has become increasingly paranoid and secretive. The reports that Mark Thatcher financed the coup, as well as the failure of British and American officials to warn Obiang of the danger to his regime – as required under UN conventions designed to protect incumbent heads of state – have increased the president's fears of an external coup effort backed by Western governments and oil companies. Further coups may be attempted as Obiang tries to tighten his grip on the country.

Conclusion

We now consume six barrels of oil for every barrel we discover. Meanwhile, the world's population is growing, becoming more affluent and consuming more oil than ever before. This is already precipitating a crisis in world energy supplies.

The last 150 years have been a period of expansion in the oil industry, with new oilfields being opened up and new countries explored. Reaching 'Peakoil' will spell the end of the cheap and plentiful oil that the world has come to expect. Although governments and the oil industry are playing down the idea that oil production will start to decline in the near future, Peakoil is approaching inexorably.

Estimates of when Peakoil will occur vary from three to five years, to decades. What can only be imagined at this stage is the turmoil into which it will plunge the world's oil importers. The wars in the Persian Gulf, Africa and Latin America described in this book are just a foretaste of the vicious struggle over diminishing oil resources that will ensue.

Competition for oil in West Africa, the Caspian and the South China Sea has already led to regional tensions and skirmishes. The fragile peace in several West African states, including Angola, Chad, Congo Brazzaville, the Democratic Republic of Congo and Nigeria, could be shattered at any time by the explosive mix of oil wealth and ethnic rivalries. The wars in Afghanistan and Chechnya might never have occurred except for their proximity to the oil-rich Caspian Basin. Both show signs of escalating, with neighbouring countries being dragged into a three-way standoff between Russia, the US and South West Asia. Meanwhile, an increasingly powerful China is seeking to exert its influence over the Spratly Islands and ultimately the whole South China Sea. It faces rivalry from Vietnam, Indonesia and other

South East Asian countries, with the possibility of Japan and the US becoming caught up in a regional war.

Can future oil wars be averted? Not without a dramatic cut in energy consumption or a conversion to alternative energy sources. The likelihood of either of these is not high.

Renewable fuel sources such as wind, water, biomass and solar power are being explored, with varying degrees of enthusiasm, in many countries, but no government has yet attempted to supply its country's entire fuel needs through renewable sources. In addition, the major oil companies have sought to block investment in nuclear and renewable energies.

Meanwhile, demand for oil is increasing every day. Within the next two decades, oil demand in the developing world is expected to increase by 91 per cent, led by the booming economies of China and India, and other highly populated countries such as Brazil, Indonesia, Pakistan and Nigeria. The developed world will see an increase of 33 per cent; despite energy conservation initiatives in some countries, our love for gas-guzzling SUVs and out-of-town retail developments shows no sign of abating.

Cutting oil consumption sufficiently to avoid future wars is something that no government wants to do. Any switch to alternative energy sources requires a sizeable investment in infrastructure, and the public backlash against any move to ration oil is likely to be explosive. Unless world leaders can find the conviction to take such steps, and consumers embrace self-sacrifice and restraint, the second half of the Oil Age will be even bloodier and more violent than the first.

Bibliography

Antonius, George, *The Arab Awakening: The Story of the Arab National Movement*, 1938, Simon Publications, 2001

Batatu, H., *The Old Social Classes and the Revolutionary Movements of Iraq*, Saki Books, 2004

Bealle, Morris A., *The House of Rockefeller*, All America House, 1959

Blair, John M., *The Control of Oil*, Random House, 1976

Blanche, Bruce & Jean, "Oil and Regional Stability in the South China Sea" in *Jane's Intelligence Review*, November, 1995

Chatterjee, Pratap, *Iraq, Inc.: A Profitable Occupation*, Seven Stories Press, 2004

Chernow, Ron, *Titan: the life of John D. Rockefeller, Sr.*, Random House, 1997

Clark, John G., *The Political Economy of World Energy: A Twentieth Century Perspective*, University of North Carolina Press, 1991

Cockburn, Patrick & Andrew, *Out of the Ashes: the Resurrection of Saddam Hussein*, HarperPerennial, 1999

Coll, Steve, *Ghost Wars: The Secret History of the CIA, Afghanistan, and Bin Laden, from the Soviet Invasion to September 10, 2001*, Penguin, 2004

Cordesman, Anthony & Abraham R. Wagner, *The Lessons of Modern War: Volume II, The Iran-Iraq War*, Westview Press, 1990

Cordesman, Anthony, *The Gulf and the West: Strategic Relations and Military Realities*, Westview Press, 1988

Croissant, Michael P. & Bülent Aras (eds), *Oil and Geopolitics in the Caspian Sea Region*, Westport, CT: Praeger, 1999

Curtis, M., *The Ambiguities of Power: British Foreign Policy since 1945*, Zed Books, 1995

Davenport, E.H. & Sidney R. Cooke, *The Oil Trusts and Anglo-American Relations*, Macmillan, 1924

Doxey, Margaret P., *Economic Sanctions and International Enforcement*, Macmillan, 1980

Engdahl, William, A., *Century of War: Anglo-American Oil Politics and the New World Order*, Pluto Press, 1992

L'Espagnol de la Tramerye, Pierre, *The World Struggle For Oil*, Alfred Knopf, 1924

Feffer, John (ed.), *Power Trip: US Unilateralism and Global Strategy after September 11*, Seven Stories Press, 2003

Gibb, George S. & Wall, Bennett H., *Teagle of Jersey Standard*, Tulane

University, 1974

Gilbert, Martin, *Winston S. Churchill*, Vol. 4, Part 1, Heinemann, 1976

Global Witness, *Time for Transparency: Coming clean on oil, mining and gas revenues*, 2004

Goralski, Robert & Russell Freeburg, *Oil & War: How the Deadly Struggle for Fuel in World War II Meant Victory or Defeat*, William Morrow, 1987

Hanighen, Frank, *The Secret War*, John Day Co., 1934

Heinberg, Richard, *The Party's Over: Oil, War and the Fate of Industrial Societies*, Clairview, 2003

Higham, Charles, *Trading with the Enemy: An Exposé of The Nazi-American Money-Plot 1933–1949*, Delacorte Press, 1983

Horne, Charles F. (ed.), *Source Records of the Great War*, Vol. 1, National Alumni, 1923

The International Petroleum Cartel, Staff Report to the Federal Trade Commission, released through Subcommittee on Monopoly of Select Committee on Small Business, US Senate, 83rd Cong., 2nd session, Washington DC, 1952

Klare, Michael, *Resource Wars: The New Landscape of Global Conflict*, New York: Henry Holt and Company, 2001

Klare, Michael, *Blood and Oil: How America's Thirst for Petrol is Killing Us*, Hamish Hamilton, 2004

Kleveman, Lutz, *The New Great Game: Blood and Oil in Central Asia*, Atlantic Books, 2003

Lapping, Brian, *End of Empire*, Paladin, London, 1989

Lawson, Thomas W., *Frenzied Finance, The Crime of Amalgamated*, Ridgway-Thayer Co, 1905 (reprinted New York: Greenwood Press Publishers, 1968)

Lieber, Robert J., *Oil and the Middle East War: Europe in the Energy Crisis*, Harvard Center for International Affairs, 1976

Louis, William R., *The British Empire in the Middle East, 1945–1951: Arab Nationalism, the United States, and Postwar Imperialism*, Clarendon Press, 1985

Lundberg, Ferdinand, *America's 60 Families*, Vanguard Press, 1937

Mansfield, Peter, *A History of the Middle East*, Viking, 1991

Marder, Arthur J. (ed.), *Fear God and Dread Nought: The Correspondence of Admiral of the Fleet Lord Fisher of Kilverstone*, Vol. 1, Jonathan Cape, 1952

McAuliffe, Dennis, *The Deaths of Sybil Bolton: An American History*, Crown, 1994

McAuliffe, Dennis, *Bloodland: A True Story of Oil, Greed and Murder on the Osage Reservation*, Council Oak Books, 1999

McNaugher, Thomas, *Arms and Oil: US Military Strategy and the Persian Gulf*, The Brookings Institution, 1985

Mejcher, Helmut, *Imperial Quest for Oil: Iraq, 1910–1928*, Ithaca Press, 1976

Meyer, Lorenzo, *Mexico and the United States in the Oil Controversy: 1917–1942*, 2nd edn., University of Texas Press, 1977

Mintz, Morton and Jerry S. Cohen, *Power, Inc.: Public and Private Rulers and How to Make Them Accountable*, Bantam Books, 1997

Mitrokhin, Vasili & Christopher Andrew, *The Mitrokhin Archive: The KGB in Europe and the West*, Penguin, 2000

Mowrer, Edgar A., *Germany Puts the Clock Back*, Penguin, 1937

Murillo, Mario A., *Colombia and the United States: War, Unrest and Destabilization*, Seven Stories Press, 2003

O'Connor, Harvey, *The Empire of Oil*, Monthly Review Press, 1955

Odell, Peter, *Oil and World Power*, Taplinger, 1971

Pees, Samuel T., *Oil History*, www.oilhistory.com

Pelletiere, Stephen, *America's Oil Wars*, Praeger, 2004

Pelletiere, Stephen, *Iraq and the International Oil System: Why America Went to War in the Gulf*, Maisonneuve Press, 2004

Philip, George, *Oil and Politics in Latin America: Nationalist Movements and State Companies*, Cambridge University Press, 1982

Ristuccia, Christiano A., *1935 Sanctions Against Italy: Would Coal And Crude Oil Have Made A Difference?*, Linacre College, Oxford, 1997

Sampson, Anthony, *The Seven Sisters: The Great Oil Companies and the world they made*, Hodder and Stoughton, 1975

Scott, Peter D., *Drugs, Oil and War: The United States in Afghanistan, Colombia, and Indochina*, Rowman & Littlefield, 2003

Shirer, William, *Rise and Fall of the Third Reich*, Fawcett, 1960

Sick, Gary & Lawrence Potter (eds), *The Persian Gulf at the Millennium*, St. Martin's Press, 1997

Staley, Eugene, *War and the Private Investor: A Study in the Relations of International Politics and International Private Investment*, Doubleday, Doran & Company, 1935; Chicago: University of Chicago Press, 1935

Tarbell, Ida M., *The History of the Standard Oil Company*, McClure, Phillips and Co., 1904

Valencia, Mark J., *China and the South China Sea Disputes* (Adelphi Paper No. 298), Oxford University Press and International Institute for Strategic Studies, 1995

Vidal, Gore, *Dreaming War: Blood for Oil and the Cheney-Bush Junta*, Clairview, 2003

Villari, Luigi, *Fire and Sword in the Caucasus*, T.F. Unwin, 1906

Yergin, Daniel, *The Prize: The Epic Quest for Oil, Money & Power*, Simon & Schuster, 1991

Index

Also available from Conspiracy Books:

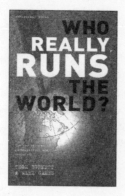